FIDEL

FIDEL

HOLLYWOOD'S FAVORITE TYRANT

HUMBERTO FONTOVA

Since 1947
REGNERY
PUBLISHING, INC.
An Eagle Publishing Company • Washington, DC

Cataloging-in-Publication Data on file with the Library of Congress.

ISBN 0-89526-043-3

Published in the United States by
Regnery Publishing, Inc.
One Massachusetts Avenue, NW
Washington, DC 20001
www.regnery.com
Distributed to the trade by
National Book Network
Lanham, MD 20706
Printed on acid-free paper
Manufactured in the United States of America

10 9 8 7 6 5 4 3 2 1

Books are available in quantity for promotional or premium use. Write to Director of Special Sales, Regnery Publishing, Inc., One Massachusetts Avenue NW, Washington, DC 20001, for information on discounts and terms or call (202) 216-0600.

To Cuba's greatest generation: the freedom fighters, living and dead, of Brigada 2506, the Escambray Rebellion, and all the rest who fought Communism; and to the parents who sacrificed all to bring us to America, most especially to my own parents, Humberto and Esther Maria.

CONTENTS

PREFACE

Cuba is only ninety miles away, but very few Americans know that a Communist tyranny that rivals North Korea's—and that had nuclear weapons decades before North Korea did—is just off the coast of Florida. The history of Castro's revolution is known to everyone *personally* in little Havana in Miami. But it is virtually unknown beyond there—or at least the truth about it is unknown. So liberals, and the liberal media and liberal Hollywood, get away with the most outrageous lies about Cuba and Cuban Americans. This book is meant to bust their myths with truth.

It's also a book to express gratitude to the thousands who put their lives on the line to fight Communism in Cuba—and to the United States that has given us, as exiles, the warmest welcome anyone has ever received. The process of becoming Americans wasn't easy for our parents, who came with no money, no prospects, and no English. They had to succumb to such barbarisms as forsaking siestas, dining before 10 p.m., and—*Dios mio!*—watching their children date without chaperones. But their children were spared the horrors, humiliations, and degradations— the firings squads and prison camps—of life under the Communists.

In America today, these Cuban parents number in the hundreds of thousands. You might call me and my Cuban American contemporaries "America's *luckiest* generation;" our freedom, prosperity, and happiness resulted from the sacrifices of two different (though always considered brother) nations' greatest generations: our parents and the Americans, the World War II generation, who welcomed us. This book is a small way of saying thanks.

Humberto Fontova
New Orleans, Louisiana, December 27, 2004

CHAPTER ONE

THE TERRORIST NEXT DOOR

On **Saturday morning,** November 17, 1962, FBI headquarters in Washington, D.C., took on "all the trappings of a military command post," according to historian William Breuer.[1] As well it might. The night before, an intelligence puzzle had finally come together and revealed a criminal plot that staggered the G-men. These were agents who had foiled Nazi plots to blow up American oil refineries in World War II. They had fought Soviet agents for two decades. They weren't easily impressed, but they were worried now.

They hadn't slept in thirty-six hours. They were haggard, red-eyed, seriously wired, and super tense. Time was nearing to swoop down on Fidel Castro's plotters. Raymond Wannall and Alan Belmont sat in an office just down the hall from that of FBI director J. Edgar Hoover. Belmont was Hoover's second in command. Wannall was head of the bureau's intelligence division. They had special agent John Malone, who ran the New York field office, on one phone line. On other lines they talked with FBI agents in Manhattan who were trying to keep surveillance on the ringleaders of a massive terrorist plot.

The intelligence was hair-raising. Agents of Fidel Castro had targeted Manhattan's busiest subway stations—including Grand Central Station—for rush hour explosions. This was no chump operation. Nor was it a military operation. It was something the United States didn't know much about in 1962: terrorism. The plotters planned the fiery death and maiming of thousands of New Yorkers. More evidence came in showing that the subway wasn't the only target: Gimbel's, Bloomingdale's, Macy's . . . twelve detonators . . . several major incendiaries . . . five hundred kilos of TNT. "Blasts are timed for *the Friday after Thanksgiving*," came the latest intel. Five hundred kilos of TNT primed to hit on the busiest shopping day of the year. A day when parents take their kids to meet Santa Claus.

"Keeping the Cuban suspects under physical surveillance all that night of the seventeenth without their knowing they were being watched put an enormous burden on those New York field agents," Raymond Wannall later reported to the *New York Times*. "But they managed it with great skill."[2] These were J. Edgar Hoover men—there were no acceptable excuses for any intelligence or security "breakdown" in those days. The old man simply wouldn't stand for it.

Notice the date again, November 1962. It was just weeks after the Cuban missile crisis, and the country was still badly rattled.

With the terrorist plot unfolding, J. Edgar Hoover's FBI realized we were looking down the barrel of a genuine threat from the same place—Cuba. As proof, there was none of the saber-rattling of the Cuban missile crisis. That's for bluff. And as Ernest Hemingway wrote in *Death in the Afternoon* about bulls that snort and paw the ground, an animal bluffs in order to *avoid* combat.

Khrushchev wanted peace; Castro didn't. True, in 1957 the redoubtable *New York Times* had passed along his heartfelt message, "You can be sure that we have no animosity toward the United States and the American people."[3]

But here's the same Fidel Castro confiding in a letter to a friend a month later: "War against the United States is *my true destiny*. When this war's over I'll start that much bigger and wider war."[4] (Please note: This was before any alleged "bullying" by the United States. In fact, Castro said this while the U.S. State Department and CIA were backing Castro's movement, and even helping to finance it.) After defecting in 1964, Castro's own sister brought an unmistakable message to Congress: "Fidel's feeling of hatred for this country cannot even be imagined by Americans." She testified to the House Committee on Un-American Activities: "His intention—his OBSESSION—is to destroy the U.S.!"[5]

"My dream is to drop three atomic bombs on New York," snarled Raul Castro, Fidel's brother, in 1960.[6] And don't forget, Raul Castro is almost assuredly Fidel Castro's successor.

Atomic bombs might have been a tad ambitious, but Fidel's 1962 bomb plot was serious enough. The March 2004 Madrid subway blasts, all ten of them, killed and maimed almost two thousand people. The al Qaeda–linked terrorists used a grand total of one hundred kilos of TNT, roughly ten kilos per blast. Rafael del Pino, who once headed Castro's air force and defected in 1987, has confirmed that Castro's 1962 bomb plot involved *five hundred kilos of TNT*, among other explosives and incendiaries.

The head Castroite terrorist of the 1962 plot was Roberto Santiesteban. He worked—surprise!—at the United Nations, where fellow conspirators José and Elsa Gómez were also to be found. Santiesteban had arrived in the U.S. on October 3, 1962, on a diplomatic passport and served as aide to Castro's UN ambassador, Carlos Lechuga. Two other conspirators were Marino Suero and José García, both Cuban immigrants, naturalized Americans, who lived in New York and ran a costume jewelry shop in Manhattan. Their shop was the plotters' headquarters and storage facility. Suero and García also belonged to the Fair Play for Cuba Committee. The FBI had already outed the Fair Play for Cuba Committee as a Castro-funded "front group." Its membership rolls would later include Lee Harvey Oswald, a name everyone would know in a year's time, as well as CBS correspondent Robert Taber (he became the Committee's executive secretary), leftist filmmaker Saul

Landau (now a professor in California and an "adviser" on several CBS and PBS "specials" on Castro), and *The Nation* magazine co-owner Alan Sagner (whom President Clinton appointed as head of the Corporation for Public Broadcasting in 1996).

The FBI knew that the Cuban plotters were to meet that night of November 17 in García's shop on West 27th Street, in the heart of Manhattan's garment district. "Hey, wait a minute!" you say. "How'd the FBI know this? How'd they have them pegged?" The answer is: moles. The FBI penetrated the Castroite group. Bureaucratic types call it "HUMINT" (human intelligence). Remember, this was J. Edgar Hoover's outfit. This was the FBI well before the Frank Church Committee and Jimmy Carter gelded it.

"Got Suero and García in sight," reported John Malone on the phone to Alan Belmont in Washington, D.C. "Can arrest them easily."

"Anything on Santiesteban?" asked Belmont.

"We have the area [around the UN] staked out but haven't spotted him yet," answered Malone.

"Then hold off," ordered Belmont.

The FBI wanted a clean sweep, the three ringleaders nabbed together. And Santiesteban seemed the likely leader. Nabbing his cohorts prematurely could send him underground in a flash. The plot obviously involved dozens more conspirators and might be reactivated. Another ten Cuban "diplomats" serving at the UN were suspected by the FBI of running a sabotage school training in the use of explosives and incendiary devices.

Two hours later, Malone relayed field agent reports that Suero and García were getting skittish.

"Hold off," ordered Belmont again. "Let's wait for Santiesteban."

"We discussed these decisions amongst each other," recalled Raymond Wannall. "And we all supported Al [Belmont] completely on his decision to hold off until Santiesteban was spotted. But we were sure happy we weren't the ones making this tough call. If it didn't turn out right—whoa, boy—Mr. Hoover would not have been very happy. We knew Al could feel Mr. Hoover's unseen pressure right over his shoulder that entire night and morning."[7]

Another hour went by, with the caffeine-addled field agents maintaining their increasingly precarious surveillance. They were watching Suero, who was in a parked car on Third Avenue and East 24th, whiling away his time necking passionately with an unknown woman. These weren't "suicide" bombers—not by a long shot. They looked forward to their rewards in Havana: stolen mansions, stolen limos, lobster and champagne, chauffeurs, free travel, nubile señoritas at their beck and call, the usual Communist perks.

García, meanwhile, was preparing for the meeting at his costume shop. At 10 a.m., Belmont got another call from Malone in New York. "We got Mr. Three in sight," said a tense Malone. "Roberto Santiesteban is walking along Riverside Drive, heading for a car with a diplomatic license plate."

"Grab them all," ordered Belmont. "Round them up."

The agents closed in, but Santiesteban looked behind him, sensed their intentions and—beep-beep!—took off like the Roadrunner. He was sprinting down the sidewalk and hurdling hedges like a true Olympian. As he ran, he was jamming paper in his mouth and chewing furiously.

But six FBI agents were after him. Their hats (mandatory, no Starsky and Hutch attire back then) immediately flew off when they sprang to the chase. Their leather shoes slapped the concrete and their ties flapped furiously over their shoulders as they sprinted and leaped in hot pursuit. Finally they surrounded the suspect. They stood there panting and glaring at him. Finally an agent pounced. Santiesteban dodged him. Another FBI man grabbed hold, but the slippery Castroite spun and broke his tackle. Santiesteban dodged and weaved frantically, but the FBI guys managed to gang-swarm him. Santiesteban fell, raging and cursing, flailing his arms and jabbing his elbows like a maniac. They grabbed his arm and bent it behind his back just as he was reaching for his pistol.

Suero was plucked from his car without incident. His lady friend was questioned and released. García was in his costume shop stacking grenades and detonators in a vault when he heard the door open. "So early, Roberto!"[8] he said without turning. His shop had been locked. Only Roberto Santiesteban had a key. The G-men nabbed García.

Another group of agents had the much easier task of arresting the Cuban missions switchboard operator, Elsa Gómez, and her husband, José, as they left their apartment on West 71st Street. They gave in without a struggle.

The FBI estimated that from twenty-five to fifty others might have been involved in the plot. They soon discovered from interrogation and captured documents that the target list was even bigger than they had guessed. It included Manhattan's main bus terminal, oil refineries on the New Jersey shore, and the Statue of Liberty.

Castro and his UN diplomats wailed about "police brutality" and "diplomatic immunity." But on November 21, Santiesteban, Suero, and García were indicted for sabotage, conspiracy, and acting as unauthorized agents of a foreign government. Five months later, all were safely back in Cuba. We exchanged them for CIA agents that Castro had held since the Bay of Pigs invasion.

Had the Castroite terrorists succeeded in their plot, September 11, 2001, would be remembered as the second-deadliest terrorist attack on U.S. soil. How did the FBI foil Castro's men? With very gauche tactics: no computers, satellites, or graduate degrees in "systems analysis." Instead, they used wiretaps, payoffs, and shady characters. They often resorted to shameless guile, rampant double-crossing, and malicious backstabbing. It was a lot like serving in Congress. And, of course, it was Congress that gleefully dismantled the old Hoover FBI and rendered it incapable of preventing September 11, 2001, the way it prevented November 23, 1962.

Castroite espionage continues against the United States. In June 2003, President Bush expelled fourteen Cuban "diplomats" for engaging in "unacceptable activities." Seven worked—surprise!—at the United Nations. On September 14, 1998, the FBI arrested fourteen Castro spies in Miami who were known as the "Wasp network."

According to the FBI's affidavit, these Castro agents were engaged in, among other things:

- Intelligence gathering against the Boca Chica Naval Air Station in Key West, the MacDill Air Force Base in Tampa, and the headquarters of the U.S. Southern Command in Homestead, Florida
- Sending letter bombs to Cuban Americans
- One Castro agent, Antonio Guerrero, had compiled the names and home addresses of the U.S. Southern Command's top officers, along with those of hundreds of officers stationed at Boca Chica.
- Two other spies, Joseph Santos and Amarylis Silverio, were charged with infiltrating the spanking new headquarters of the U.S. Southern Command.
- A third man, Luis Medina, was spying on MacDill Air Force Base, the U.S. Armed Forces' worldwide headquarters for fighting "low-intensity" conflicts.

At the bail hearings, assistant U.S. district attorney Caroline Heck Miller said the urgency to act on the case was because "the defendant has made allusions to the prospect of sabotage being visited on buildings and airplanes in the Southern District of Florida."

Interestingly, *Jane's Defense Weekly*, the preeminent journalistic authority on military matters, reported on March 6, 1996, that since the early 1990s Cuban commandos had been training in Vietnam for attacks on installations remarkably similar to the Boca Chica and MacDill bases, with the "political objective" of bringing "the reality of warfare to the American public." Apparently the FBI didn't see any linkage. The *Jane's* article came out two years before the FBI arrested the Wasp spies.

These spies had also infiltrated the Cuban exile group Brothers to the Rescue. From them, Castro got the exact flight plan that resulted in the shooting down in February 1996 of two of the group's unarmed planes, which were flying a humanitarian mission. The pilots routinely flew over the Florida straits to rescue Cubans fleeing the Communist regime. Given that an estimated 50,000 to 87,000 Cubans have died in the "cemetery without crosses," these pilots were risking their lives to save desperate *balseros* from joining that terrible tally. Castro, Ted Turner's fishing buddy (Ted calls him "one helluva guy"), couldn't stand for that. So his MiG jets shot the planes down, over international waters, without warning and without trying to turn them aside. It was simply murder. Even the United Nation's Security Council condemned the attack.

Of the fourteen Castro spies charged in the Wasp network case, four managed to escape to Cuba, five pleaded guilty, and five pleaded innocent. At their Miami trial, the five pleading innocent had some vociferous defense witnesses, as you might imagine. What you might not imagine is that these staunch defense witnesses were two retired U.S. Army generals. Apparently planning attacks on U.S. military bases and being accomplices in the murder of four U.S. citizens mattered little to Generals Charles Wilhelm and Edward Atkeson. They spoke eloquently, and apparently authoritatively, in defense of Castro's spies. Wilhelm himself was the former head of the U.S. Southern Command and Atkeson had been the Army's deputy chief of staff for intelligence. Both men had served under President Clinton and had apparently absorbed the Clinton administration's policy of downplaying the Cuban threat. I'd love to know how the FBI reacted to their courtroom adversaries—American generals trying to discredit the FBI for uncovering the biggest espionage cell since the Cold War.

Wilhelm testified that he had scoffed at the FBI's repeated warnings about the spies infiltrating his command. No one could *possibly* penetrate his command's foolproof security, he insisted. Well, the jury scoffed at Wilhelm and Atkeson. The jury—from which Cuban Americans were excluded—found all five Castro spies guilty as charged.

Right after the trial, Generals Wilhelm and Atkeson visited Havana for a chummy session with Maximum Leader Fidel and Maximum

Brother Raul. General Atkeson even wrote an article in *Army* magazine about the meetings: "The *Comandante en jefe* appeared in the doorway. The well-pressed, upscale, fatigue uniform set him off immediately from his bland escorts. There were smiles all around as the poignancy of the moment became clear."

Both U.S. generals belong to the Center for Defense Information, a think tank that declared, "Each year, a delegation of U.S. military experts organized by the Center for Defense Information meets with Cuban military and political officials in Havana to explore ways the two countries might cooperate on regional security concerns." Clinton's former drug czar, General Barry McCaffrey, is a founding member of this non-governmental body.

In 1999, heavily influenced by these Clintonista generals, the Pentagon issued an official intelligence assessment that declared, "Cuba is no longer a threat to the U.S."

"This as an objective report by serious people," proclaimed Fidel Castro from Havana. "Cuba can no longer project itself beyond the boundaries of Cuba," said General Wilhelm in praise of the Defense Department report. "No evidence exists that Cuba is trying to foment any instability in the Western Hemisphere."[9]

Tell it to the Venezuelans and Colombians, General Wilhelm. But the big shoe fell on these Clintonista generals two years later—two days after September 11, 2001, in fact—when the Defense Department's top Latin American expert, the agency's "Cuba specialist," Ana Belen Montes, was arrested by the FBI as a Castro spy. She had authored the "Cuba is no threat" intelligence report that the shrewd generals had so recently and officially blessed.[10]

Worse, "Montes passed some of the United States' most sensitive information about Cuba back to Havana," said John Bolton, undersecretary for arms control and international security at the State Department.[11]

Lieutenant Commander James E. Brooks, a spokesman for the Defense Intelligence Agency, gasped that "he and his colleagues were *'stunned'* at the news!" of this spying.[12]

Just as intelligence professionals four decades earlier were "stunned" to learn that Castro was a Communist, "stunned" to learn he was stacking up nuclear missiles, and "stunned" to learn that Cuba was a big training camp for terrorists (the IRA, Black Panthers, PLO, and Carlos the Jackal are all alumni). They were "stunned" when it was revealed that Castro was a major drug trafficker and stunned that he sent troops to fight in Africa. Castro is always stunning American intelligence officials who cannot believe that a major terrorist regime is just off the coast of Florida.

Castro still dreams of turning the cold war hot. In August 2001, Castro visited Teheran to chum it up with the Iranian mullahs. "America is weak!" Castro declared at Teheran University. "We see this weakness up front. But don't worry, the mighty King will fall! Together Iran and Cuba can bring America to her knees!"[13] The crowd went nuts, as you might expect—Castro had been jerking the Great Satan's chain from only ninety miles away for almost half a century—and getting away with it.

The year before, on September 18, 2000, in an exclusive interview with Al-Jazeera television, Castro raved: "We are not ready for reconciliation with the United States, and I will not reconcile with the imperialist system!"[14] As of 2003, Cuba jams our satellite broadcasts into Iran using technology from China, which acquired it from the Clinton administration.

"Given its high economic and industrial potentials, Iran is prepared to collaborate with Cuba in all domains," declared Iranian Majlis speaker Gholam-Ali Haddad Adel in a meeting with the visiting Cuban vice president and chairman of Cuba's Olympic committee, José Ramón Fernandez, on January 16, 2005. "The solidarity between our nations and governments is the key to overcoming the U.S. hegemonic pressures. Cuban president Fidel Castro is a symbol of resistance against the U.S. throughout the world," said Adel. For his part, Fernandez expressed his country's interest in bolstering ties with Iran: "The Cuban government and nation will stand against the U.S. pressures and stand beside the Iranian nation." Fernandez also expressed his country's support for the undeniable right of the Iranian nation to have access to nuclear technology.[15]

"The unilateral nature of U.S. policy in her international relations must stop," declared Iranian ambassador to Cuba Ahmad Edrissian. "The U.S. cannot continue violating international law and it should respect the national sovereignty of other nations. There is no doubt that Iran is strengthening her economic and political relations with Cuba, and there exist other areas of interest for cooperation." Cuba is constructing a biomedical plant in Iran for "vaccinations against hepatitis B and the manufacture of interferon," we're told.[16]

Given that American intelligence is so often stunned about Castro, it's probably not surprising that Hollywood and the liberal elite fawn over the guy. "Cuba's own Elvis!"—that's how Dan Rather once described his friend Fidel Castro.[17] Oliver Stone, another friend, describes Fidel as "very selfless and moral" and "one of the world's wisest men."[18] "A genius!" agreed Jack Nicholson. Naomi Campbell said meeting Castro was "a dream come true!"[19] According to Norman Mailer, Castro is "the first and greatest hero to appear in the world since the Second World War."[20] Jean-Paul Sartre said, "Castro is at the same time the island, the men, the cattle, and the earth. He is the whole island."[21] Not to be confused with the gallant Che Guevara, of course, whom Sartre pronounced, "the most complete human being of the twentieth century."[22]

Actress Gina Lollobrigida cooed, "Castro is an extraordinary man. He is warm and understanding and seems extremely humane."[23] Francis Ford Coppola simply noted, "Fidel, I love you. We both have the same initials. We both have beards. We both have power and want to use it for good purposes."[24] Harry Belafonte added: "If you believe in freedom, if you believe in justice, if you believe in democracy, you have no choice but to support Fidel Castro!"[25] All this for a dictator who plotted a bigger mass murder of Americans than Osama bin Laden carried out on September 11, 2001.

But liberals still love the Cuban tyrant. In November 1995, Castro made a triumphant visit to New York. He was the star speaker and main attraction at the United Nation's fiftieth anniversary bash—the guest of honor. "The Hottest Ticket in Manhattan!" read a *Newsweek* story that week. It hailed Castro as the "Toast of Manhattan!" *Time* magazine agreed. "Fidel Takes Manhattan!" it crowed.

"Fidel Castro got, by far, the loudest and warmest reception in the [United Nations] General Assembly" wrote *Time* magazine. (The United Nations has been sweet on Castro for a long time, and still is. During an April 2000 summit in Havana, Secretary-General Kofi Annan proclaimed, "Castro's regime has set an example we can all learn from.")[26]

Castro plunged into Manhattan's social swirl, hobnobbing with dozens of glitterati, pundits, and power brokers. First off, David Rockefeller invited him to a celebrity-studded dinner at his Westchester County estate.

For Fidel's convenience, the dinner was moved to the Council of Foreign Relations' Pratt House on East 68th Street in Manhattan. After holding court for a rapt Rockefeller, former secretary of defense Robert McNamara, Dwayne Andreas (chairman of the Archer Daniels Midland Company), and Random House's Harold Evans, Castro flashed over to media mogul Mort Zuckerman's Fifth Avenue pad, where a throng of talking heads, including a breathless Mike Wallace, Peter Jennings, Tina Brown, Bernard Shaw, and Barbara Walters all jostled to hear the Comandante's every comment, clamoring for autographs and photo-ops. Diane Sawyer was so overcome in the mass killer's presence that she rushed up, broke into that toothy smile of hers, wrapped her arms around Castro, and smooched him warmly on the cheek.[27]

And the mass murderer had barely scratched the surface of his fan club. According to the U.S.-Cuba Trade and Economic Council, on that visit, Castro received 250 dinner invitations from celebrities, power brokers, millionaires, pundits, and socialites. They could forgive the atheist Fidel for wanting to blow up New York Christmas shoppers in 1962 because most of them had probably never regarded him as a terrorist in the first place.

When Fidel planned his terrorist mass murder in New York, terrorism was virtually unknown to Americans. In 1962, the *New York Times* (and every other newspaper) called the Cuban terrorists "would-be saboteurs" or "revolutionists." In a way, this was progress, because just three years earlier the *New York Times* had hailed Fidel as "a humanist, a man of many ideals, including those of liberty, democracy, and social justice."

One of the few newspapers to peg Fidel from the beginning was the national newsweekly *Human Events*, which, like the *New York Times*, is still around. On August 17, 1957, *Human Events* published an article that included an interview with Spruille Braden, former U.S. ambassador to Cuba. Braden called the *New York Times* out by name. The famous Gray Lady, he claimed, was smitten with a dangerous Communist whose name was Fidel Castro.

"Fidel Castro was a ringleader in a bloody uprising in Bogotá, Colombia, in April 1948," started the *Human Events* article. "That uprising was engineered and staged *by Communists*. The Colombian government subsequently published documentary evidence of Fidel Castro's role as a leader. The appearance of this Cuban at the head of the uprising in his own country *stamps the insurrection as Communist*."

While liberals no doubt snickered at such "McCarthyism" (Joe McCarthy had died only two months before), it was *Human Events* that was the prophetic voice, not the reporting of Herbert Matthews in the *New York Times*. *Human Events* knew what was proved with the blood of the thousands of victims that Fidel Castro and Che Guevara sent to the firing-squad.

"The yells of '*VIVA CUBA LIBRE!...VIVA CRISTO REY!...ABAJO COMMUNISMO!*' would make the walls of the fortress tremble every night," wrote Armando Valladares, who listened from his cell in Havana's La Cabaña prison while waiting his turn at the blood-spattered stake.

Luckily, a volley from the firing squad (it varied from five to ten men, each man paid $15 a shot, by the way) never reached Valladares. He served twenty-two years in Castro's dungeons, fled to America, and wrote an international bestseller about his horrific prison ordeal, titled *Against All Hope*. The international Left tried to discredit Valladares and trash his book. But President Ronald Reagan—a longtime *Human Events* subscriber—read the book and promptly appointed him as the U.S. delegate to the UN's Human Rights Commission. Who better? Reagan reasoned. International leftists ripped their hair out in exasperation, but Valladares, working under America's UN ambassador Jeane Kirkpatrick, gave Castro hell at the United Nations.

In 1961, the year Valladares had been yanked from his home in a dawn raid and imprisoned on utterly bogus charges, Castro had his firing squads working triple shifts. "They usually started at 1 a.m.," says former political prisoner Gustavo Carmona. "And the volleys would echo through the prison till after dawn." Hundreds of Cuban patriots (and dozens of American citizens) crumpled every week. By 1965, so efficient were the firing squads that victims were bound to the stake wearing a white T-shirt with a nice eight-inch black circle on the center of the chest. No excuse for missing the vitals now, muchachos.

Not all these martyrs and heroes bound to the execution stake had the energy to bellow in defiance. Before being dragged to the *paredón* (the wall) and bound to the stake, many had been drained of most of the blood in their bodies. The blood was then sold on the world market. This is according to Dr. Juan Clark, a Bay of Pigs veteran, former Castro political prisoner, and nowadays professor of sociology at Miami-Dade Community College. Dr. Clark's research into Castro's blood market has included interviews with dozens of political prisoners and defectors who confirmed the practice. Dr. Clark has written extensively on the issue, in both articles and books.

Why would Castro market blood? Because it is one of his few economic successes. He managed to utterly destroy Cuba's sugar, tobacco, and cattle industries—all major Cuban exports in the pre-Castro years.

The man acclaimed by the *New York Times* as a "humanist, idealist, and Robin Hood" had rendered a nation that once had the eleventh highest living standard—not in the hemisphere, not among tropical countries, but in the world—utterly destitute, utterly bereft of foreign exchange. It is also, apparently, Communist practice. To this day the Red Chinese have a similar policy of recycling useful portions of their execution victims, marketing the bodily organs of prisoners who are shot in the back of the neck.

There are other sources for Castro's blood-marketing as well— namely, U.S. court records, including those filed by an American woman, Katy Fuller, in the Eleventh Circuit court of Miami-Dade County. Her father was killed by Castro's firing squads in 1960. Here is a portion of *The Estate of Robert Otis Fuller* v. *The Republic of Cuba*, filed May 5, 2002: "Agents of the Castro Government, acting under orders of the Castro Government, led Bobby Fuller to a firing squad where he was shot and killed after being tortured by having his blood drained from his body. Thereafter, his body was thrown into an unmarked mass grave in an unknown location."

Here's another lawsuit filed by an American family against Cuba's "president," as Peter Jennings invariably labels him.[28] "In one final session of torture, Castro's agents drained Howard Anderson's body of blood before sending him to his death at the firing squad."

Howard Anderson was a U.S. citizen but had been a resident of Cuba since World War II, when the Navy had stationed him there. Among his other friends was my uncle Carl Brumier, a fellow U.S. Navy fighter pilot. In April 1961, Castro's goons dragged Anderson from his home in a dawn raid. They always came at dawn.

When people wondered why so many Cuban Americans were emotional over the dawn raid to repatriate Elián González to Cuba—this was one big reason why. There were few Cuban American families that didn't have a family member, friend, or neighbor dragged off in a dawn raid. The tears in Little Havana over the raid ordered by President Clinton's attorney general, Janet Reno, were tied to terrifying flashbacks of friends who were seized in similar raids and never returned.

Howard Anderson was a successful businessman in Cuba, owning a chain of service stations and a Jeep dealership. He was a happy family man with four children, including a cherubic little blonde girl named Bonnie, then five years old. He was the president of the American Legion's Havana chapter, and he was beloved by his Cuban neighbors. Howard was everything that Castro's Communists hated: an athletic, popular American naval veteran living in Cuba; a successful businessman; a happy family man; and a friend to freedom-loving (anti-Communist) Cubans.

Enduring horrible tortures, this courageous man refused to rat out the Cuban freedom fighters. "Death to the American!" screamed Howard Anderson's Communist prosecutor at his farce of a trial on April 17, 1961. "The prosecutor was a madman," says a Swiss diplomat who witnessed the trial, "leaping on tables, shrieking, pointing. He called them rotten fruit and declared that the only thing they were good for was to fertilize the land with their carcasses."[29]

Anderson simply glared back.

Two days after his "trial," Howard Anderson's turn came. They say he refused a blindfold in order to glare at his executioners. He was probably in shock at the time from the blood draining.

"*Fuego!*" The bullets shattered Howard Anderson's body at dawn, and vultures swarmed in for the feast.

"Those firing squad volleys rang like a dinner bell to the birds," says Cuban freedom fighter Hiram Gonzalez, who was imprisoned in La Cabana at the time of Anderson's murder. "Those firing squads had been going off daily since January 7, 1959, the day Che Guevara entered Havana. It didn't take long for the birds to catch on. Flocks of them had learned to perch in the surrounding trees and atop the wall that surrounded La Cabana fortress. After the volley, they swooped down to peck at the bits of bone, blood, and flesh that littered the ground. Those birds sure grew fat." Feeding them as well were young men like Rogelio Gonzalez, Virgilio Companeria, and Alberto Tapia, Havana University students and members of Catholic Action, none over twenty-one years old. They refused blindfolds too, and perished yelling, "Long live Christ the King!" They were just three of fourteen thousand young men that Fidel sent to mass graves.

Howard Anderson's body was dumped in a mass grave, though his wife discovered the grave and snuck in to put a cross over it. Anderson's daughter Bonnie grew up to become a CNN reporter. In 1978, her journalistic duties took her to Havana, where Castro was due to release some political prisoners. At a reception, Castro approached Bonnie Anderson, smiled broadly, and asked whether she remembered him, and how was her mother.

Bonnie Anderson was disgusted by Castro—and also by her boss, Ted Turner, who cozied up to the dictator. In early 1997, CNN pledged itself to respectful reporting of the Castro regime. Exactly a week after CNN's pledge, CNN had the first Havana bureau ever granted to a U.S. network. Last year, by the way, the Andersons won their suit against Castro—and no, Bonnie Anderson no longer works for CNN.

Bonnie Anderson had a very personal reason to know about Castro. So do Cuban Americans. But in the next chapter, I'll provide a little refresher course about what the liberal apologists forget about the terrorist next door.

CHAPTER TWO

THE CUBAN FÜHRER

Journalists have always been suckers for Castro. "Castro is honest," reported *Newsweek* magazine on April 13, 1959. "And an honest government is something unique in Cuba.... Castro is not himself even remotely a Communist."

"We can thank our lucky stars Castro was no Communist," wrote William Attwood in *Look* magazine on March 3, 1959.

"The Cuba of Fidel Castro today is free from terror." That's blonde bombshell Dickey Chapelle in (surprisingly) *Reader's Digest*, April 1959.

Five hundred and sixty-two men had been riddled by firing squads without trial by this time. Habeas corpus had been abolished. And Cuban jails held five times the number of political prisoners as they had under Fulgencio Batista. For the first time in Cuba's history, many of the prisoners were women. Their crime? Having been wives, daughters, and mothers of the executed men. Most of these were of humble background, many black.

"Civil liberties have been restored in Cuba and corruption seems to be drying up. These are large steps forward, and they were made against fearful odds," continued Chapelle's story.

"Dickey Chapelle would always bring back the facts," said Bill Garrett, one of Chapelle's editors. "No matter how long it would take. Dickey would stick with a story."

I searched in vain for any updates from La Chapelle regarding Cuba. But a movie on the life of this pioneering feminist journalist is in the works, with Jennifer Aniston in the leading role and Brad Pitt as her love interest. I'll be sure to check it for "facts."

It's not just the media. Politicians have been suckers too. "I think that Fidel Castro is a good young man." That's former president Harry Truman, quoted in the *Washington Post* on July 31, 1959. "He seems to want to do the right thing for the Cuban people, and we ought to extend our sympathy and help him to do what is right for them." Give 'em Hell Harry was probably relying on the rosy media reports when he came to that conclusion. President Eisenhower himself seemed swayed. At a press conference, he said, "Now such things [branding Castro a Communist] are charged, but they are not easy to prove. The United States government has made no such charges."[1] But Eisenhower later wised up.

The trouble was that it was hard for anti-Castro voices to be heard through all the liberal praises of Castro. Have you ever heard of Guillermo Belt? Probably not. He was a retired Cuban diplomat who warned the United States in 1958, "If the Castros come into power, there will be a bloodbath in Cuba." Belt was desperate to undo the U.S. State Department's Castrophilia. "A social revolution will take place in Cuba," he continued. "The Communists will control the government of Cuba."[2]

The plain fact about Castro is that Castro was a terrorist before terrorism was cool. He started way back in April 1948, when he was part of the Communist-led riots that rocked Bogotá, Colombia. The Communist-led mobs went berserk, looting, burning, and killing more than five thousand people. That riot lit a ten-year-long civil war called "La Violencia." By 1958, 100,000 Colombians had been massacred. And Castro—still a student at the University of Havana in 1948—was there at the beginning, earning his revolutionary credentials.

Those credentials include an admiration of Hitler. Cuba's Líder Maximo has always shamelessly aped the German Führer. *Mein Kampf* was among Castro's favorite books in college. The very title of Castro's manifesto, *History Will Absolve Me*, comes almost word for word from Hitler's famous courtroom defense for his Rathaus Putsch in 1924. "You may pronounce us guilty," declared Hitler at his trial. "But the goddess of the eternal court of history will absolve us."

"Condemn me. It doesn't matter," declared Castro to the packed courtroom in 1953 during his own trial (for a putsch of sorts, his guerrilla attack on the Moncada barracks—a miserable military failure—that led to his arrest). "History will absolve me!"[3]

Heck, even Castro's official title, *Líder Maximo*, copies Hitler's Führer (leader). Except, typical for Castro, he had to one-up even Hitler. He had to throw in that "Maximum" bit, similar to Francisco Franco with his "Generalissimo" (the most general), to distinguish himself from mere chump generals like Alexander the Great, Hannibal, and Julius Caesar. Castro had to distinguish himself from chump "leaders" like Hitler too.

Another trait Hitler shared with his Cuban understudy was this: "Adolf Hitler never converses. He preaches and blusters, treating every utterance as revealed religion from on high. There's no getting a word in when he starts." That's historian John Toland quoting an early Hitler intimate. That description also suits Castro to a T. Ask anyone who's known him.

"When Fidel got going, Che Guevara himself would shrink up in a corner like a whimpering little puppy," says early revolutionary acquaintance Miguel Uría. "Especially when Fidel started insulting Che. It was embarrassing. You never heard such cursing, such savage abuse. I almost felt sorry for that Argentine assassin, jackass—and as became increasingly evident—wimp."

Early on in his career as a revolutionary and terrorist, Castro targeted Americans, even before his Cuban revolution stole $2 billion in U.S. property and riddled dozens of Americans with bullets from firing squads—after having tortured them, of course. In 1958, Castro's July 26 Movement kidnapped fifty Americans near America's Guantánamo naval base. Most were Marines and Navy men on leave. A few were civilian workers from a U.S. mining company headquartered nearby. They were on a bus, bound for a weekend's rest and relaxation, when Raul Castro and a band of his guerrillas hijacked them at gunpoint. Raul dictated that the American hostages be employed as human shields. The government of Cuban Presidente Fulgencio Batista was waging a desultory (half-assed) campaign against the Castroite guerrillas. Now, because it feared an errant bomb or bullet might hit an American, Batista ordered a complete cease-fire in the area, which of course helped the Castroites, who received more illicit arms shipments unhindered.

Events on the other side of the globe freed the American hostages. In Lebanon that summer there was a crisis. Militant Sunni Muslims (sound familiar?) threatened violence against the elected (but Christian and pro-Western) president of Lebanon, Camille Chamoun. President Eisenhower dispatched five thousand Marines and the crisis abated. The very week our Marines were splashing onshore in Lebanon, Castro released his American hostages—coincidence, no doubt.

The Castroites are old hands at another form of terrorism: hijackings. Three months after kidnapping Americans on leave, Castro's rebels hijacked a Cubana Airlines prop-jet bound for the United States and tried to force it down near Raul's guerrilla headquarters in Cuba's Oriente province. The terrorists were idiots who couldn't recognize that the landing strip was too short. The plane crashed, leaving few survivors. Keep in mind that in 1958 "plane hijacking" was unheard of. Once again, Castro was leading the way when it came to terrorism.

And of course, what would terrorism be without bombs? In November 1958, Castro's thugs set *one hundred* bombs to explode in Havana (*La noche de las 100 bombas*). These were small bombs, like the three in those hotels in 1997. Castro's point was to make noise, shake up Batista's position, provoke his undisciplined police to brutal reprisals. Much mayhem, much damage to property, and a few wounded and five or six dead. Castro was a "rebel" at the time and still playing the "good cop" to Batista's "bad cop." So his goal wasn't to mass-murder Cubans, like he wanted to mass-murder Americans later in Manhattan. Castro's rebel group, at the time, had nothing to gain from the mass-murder of Cuban civilians.

Castro was deeply involved in bomb plots before he planned to murder women and children doing their Christmas shopping in New York in 1962. And he was hoping to do worse. Declassified Soviet documents—and Nikita Khrushchev's own memoirs—show that Castro pleaded with Khrushchev to launch a preemptive nuclear strike against the U.S.

On October 27, Castro sent a coded telegram to Khrushchev. "We have solid intelligence that the U.S. attack is coming within twenty-four to seventy-two hours," he lied. "Strike first. It's an act of self-defense—there is no other solution."[4] But while Castro was calling for a massive nuclear strike against the United States and vowing to fight "the Yankee invaders to the last man!" the Soviet ambassador to Cuba during the missile crisis, Alexander Alexeyev, reports that a "fearful" Castro made reservations with him for a first-class seat in the Soviet embassy's bomb shelter.

Some think Castro's itchy trigger finger was a bigger factor in Khrushchev's decision to yank Russian missiles from Cuba than was Kennedy's so-called blockade.[5] Fifty-five ships breached the blockade. Exactly one ship was boarded—and it was a U.S.-built ship, Panamanian owned, with Lebanese registry, and under Soviet charter. JFK, micro-manager *par excellence*, selected the ship himself. He wanted to demonstrate "our resolve." It carried burlap bags.

When Khrushchev took away the missiles, Castro went crazy: kicking walls, smashing glasses, and breaking windows and mirrors. The reason for Castro's fit was revealed the following month by his sidekick and Burlington Industries' charming T-shirt icon, Che Guevara. "If the missiles had remained," the campus poster boy and vodka salesman told the *London Daily Worker* in November 1962, "we would have used them against the very heart of the U.S., including New York. We must never establish peaceful coexistence. In this struggle to the death between two systems we must gain the ultimate victory. We must walk the path of liberation even if it costs millions of atomic victims."[6] (Che iconography on T-shirts and posters remains very popular, especially among peace activists and anti-nuclear demonstrators.)

Instead of killing millions, Castro had managed to kill only one Yankee during the crisis. According to Carlos Franqui, a former member of Castro's inner circle, Castro pressed the button launching the missile that shot down our U-2, killing Major Rudolph Anderson.

We all know the Beltway and Hollywood version of those "thirteen days" of the Cuban missile crisis. "This was American leadership unsurpassed in the responsible management of power," writes Camelot court scribe Arthur Schlesinger, Jr. "A combination of toughness, nerve, and wisdom, so brilliantly controlled, so matchlessly calibrated that it dazzled the world."[7] "The most dangerous crisis the world has ever seen," gasped JFK's secretary of state, Dean Rusk.[8] "[JFK] combined deliberation with planning, toughness with flexibility and coercion."[9]

"President Kennedy acted majesterially during those critical thirteen days...and demonstrated a comprehension exceptionally rare in the presidency....The U.S. and her young president were considered by people who love liberty as defenders of the free world," gushed Hugh Sidey.[10]

JFK himself pronounced: "We cut their balls off."[11]

Fortunately for us (and for mankind), the Knights of Camelot had been in charge. Their memoirs and the accounts of their court scribes and media toadies leave absolutely no doubt. Camelot's brilliance, perspicacity, leadership, resolution, and *cojones* saved the day, easing us back from the precipice of doom. "We resolved mankind's biggest crisis," beamed JFK.

Complete bullshit, I'm afraid.

"We've been had!" yelled Navy chief of staff George Anderson on October 26, 1962. He'd just been informed that JFK had "solved" the missile crisis. Admiral Anderson was in charge of the naval "blockade" against Cuba.[12]

"The biggest defeat in our nation's history!" bellowed Air Force chief of staff Curtis Lemay, whacking his fist on his desk.[13]

"We missed the big boat," said General Maxwell Taylor after learning the details of the deal with Khrushchev.

"Kennedy first goofed an invasion, paid tribute to Castro...then gave the Soviets squatters' rights in our backyard," said Richard Nixon.[14]

"We locked Castro and Communism into Latin America and threw away the key to their removal," said a shocked Barry Goldwater at the time.[15]

Democratic elder statesman Dean Acheson concluded, "This nation lacks leadership." Acheson was present at all the tense and momentous meetings conducted by the Knights of Camelot. "The meetings were repetitive and without direction," Acheson said. "Most members of Kennedy's team had no military or diplomatic experience whatsoever. The Ex-Comm [National Security Council Executive Committee] sessions were a waste of time."[16]

Our nuclear superiority over the Soviets was so overwhelming at the time, five thousand nuclear warheads against the Soviets' three hundred, that General Maxwell Taylor, head of the Joint Chiefs of Staff at the time, admitted in 1982: "Never did I have even the *slightest* preoccupation that there existed even the *slightest* possibility that nuclear war could result from that confrontation."[17] (Emphasis mine.)

Even Arthur Schlesinger, Jr. confessed in 1982, "Looking back on it, it seems to me we greatly exaggerated the risk of war in October 1962." In 1987, JFK's national security adviser, McGeorge Bundy, agreed. "With proper retrospection, I don't think the pressure was as great as the president thought at the time."[18]

Nikita Khrushchev wrote: "It would have been *ridiculous* for us to go to war over Cuba—for a country eleven thousand miles away. For us, war was unthinkable. We ended up getting exactly what we'd wanted all along. Security for Fidel Castro's regime and American missiles removed from Turkey. Until today, the U.S. has complied with her promise to not interfere with Castro and *to not allow anyone else to interfere with Castro*. [Emphasis mine.] After Kennedy's death, his successor Lyndon Johnson assured us that he would keep the promise not to invade Cuba."[19]

Recently declassified Soviet documents also reveal this conversation between Robert F. Kennedy and Soviet ambassador Anatoly Dobrynin. Kennedy told Dobrynin, "We can't say anything public about this agreement.... It would be too much of a political embarrassment for us."[20]

"It's a public relations fable that Khrushchev quailed before Kennedy," wrote Alexander Haig years later. "The legend of the eyeball-to-eyeball confrontation invented by Kennedy's men paid a handsome political dividend. But so much that happened was obscured by stage-management designed to divert public attention from embarrassing facts.... The Kennedy-Khrushchev deal was a deplorable error resulting in political havoc and human suffering through the Americas."[21]

So much for Camelot's diplomatic triumph, about which Fidel Castro boasted, "Many concessions were made by the Americans about which not a word has been said.... Perhaps one day they'll be made public."[22] Not by the Camelot gang.

On the fortieth anniversary of the missile crisis (October 2002), former defense secretary Robert McNamara, Kennedy speechwriter Ted Sorensen, and an elderly contingent of more of the "Best and Brightest" went to Havana for a "workshop" that included Russian officials. Throughout the entire media gala, there was not a single word about Castro's lust to press the nuclear button against the United States.

Instead, we saw a smiling Robert McNamara hailing his charming host as a "great statesman" for his conduct during the crisis.

Kennedy's secret deal with Khrushchev forbade any liberation of Cuba, not just by the United States but by any group or nation in the Western Hemisphere. Indeed, it became the responsibility of the United States to *prevent* any such liberation attempts. The Best and Brightest not only pulled the rug out from under Cuba's freedom fighters, they also sanctioned the stationing of forty thousand Soviet troops and KGB goons in Cuba. The Soviets were already aiding Castro's butchery of these freedom fighters.

The United States Coast Guard and even the British Royal Navy (when Cuban freedom fighters moved to the Bahamas) shielded Castro from freedom fighters in exile. In the Florida Keys and the Bahamas, the Coast Guard and Royal Navy were arresting and disarming the very exiles the CIA had been training and arming the month before.

In other words, Fidel Castro, that "brave and plucky underdog" who, according to his liberal groupies, practices "Machismo-Leninismo," in fact has survived all these years by hiding behind the skirts of the three most powerful nations on earth: the United States, the Soviet Union, and the British Empire. So after October 28, 1962, Castro enjoyed a new status of Mutually Assured Protection. And Cuban exiles willing to fight for freedom were suddenly rounded up for "violating U.S. neutrality laws." Some of these bewildered men were jailed, others "quarantined" and prevented from leaving Dade County, Florida. The Florida Coast Guard got twelve new boats and seven new planes to make sure Castro remained unmolested.[23]

The Cuban freedom fighters were betrayed by the Kennedy administration. On Attorney General Robert Kennedy's direct orders, scores of Cuban exiles had been infiltrated back into Cuba as part of Operation Mongoose to gather intelligence on the Castro regime.

"I'm really disappointed with the CIA," Bobby Kennedy had yelled at Miami CIA station chief William Harvey just weeks before the

Cuban missile crisis. "We don't even know what's going on in Cuba. Let's get some men in there."[24] Hundreds of Cubans in exile immediately volunteered for the near-suicidal missions—despite having earlier been betrayed at the Bay of Pigs by this very same administration.

CIA officer Richard Helms was in on the meetings with Bobby Kennedy. "These Cuban boys are wondering what our goals are," Helms told the young attorney general. "They're perfectly willing to risk their lives on infiltration missions they consider sensible. And to them sensible means actions that will contribute to their homeland's liberation. But they're starting to wonder if we're serious about helping them free their homeland." Kennedy immediately changed the subject.[25]

"I told my men that, in my opinion, Kennedy's people had no serious plans to overthrow Castro." That's what the head of a major anti-Castro group working with the CIA at the time in south Florida said. "I didn't want to mislead those young men. I simply couldn't do that. They were brave, highly motivated, and risking their lives on these missions. I told them Kennedy's people were using us mainly for intelligence-gathering. If they felt comfortable with that, then fine."[26]

Many did. They were looking at certain torture and firing squads if they were captured. The casualty rates for their teams ran to 70 percent. But they continued infiltrating Cuba at Camelot's behest. Among the hair-raising intelligence they radioed or carried back was information—the first information America had—on the Soviet nuclear missiles that were being planted in Cuba. The Best and Brightest, however, scoffed at the reports delivered by these brave young men.

National security adviser McGeorge Bundy was particularly incensed and dismissive. On the ABC Sunday chat show *Issues and Answers* on October 14, 1962, he said the reports of Soviet missiles in Cuba were nothing but "refugee rumors." "Nothing in Cuba poses a threat to the U.S.... Nor is there any likelihood that the Soviets and Cubans would try to install a major offensive capability," stressed the disdainful Bundy.

JFK himself had an idea who was planting these silly rumors: "There's fifty-odd thousand Cuban refugees in this country, all living for the day when we will go to war with Cuba, and they're all putting out this kind of stuff."[27]

A week later, with the missiles plain as day in U-2 photos, JFK publicly announced that they were there—and the world held its breath.

What had happened? Why the shift? Well, CIA head John McCone (a Republican) had finally insisted on some U-2 flights over western Cuba—where the Cuban freedom fighters and infiltrators had reported seeing the missile sites.

A few weeks earlier, America's U-2 program had been shifted from the CIA to the Defense Department, so Defense Secretary Robert McNamara controlled the authorization of U-2 flights—and he repeatedly forbade any over *western* Cuba. But McCone finally won the argument, which was threatening to become a political issue.

Many of the Cuban exile infiltrators who had given the Kennedy administration the intelligence in the first place—at great risk to their own lives—found themselves stranded in a Cuba swarming with Soviet soldiers after the "resolution" of the crisis. Dozens of these young heroes huddled in mangrove swamps along Cuba's coast, dodging Castro patrols and waiting for their scheduled "exfiltration" by motorboats back to the United States.

Their wait was in vain. Their mission accomplished, their evidence about genuine weapons of mass destruction only ninety miles away from America's coast (and hosted by the most pathologically anti-American regime in history) delivered, these heroes promptly fell through the cracks of the Kennedy-Khrushchev deal. They were expendable.

"Let's take all the necessary precautions to stop these Cuban exiles with the commando attacks they launch in order to seek publicity from upsetting the agreement," were President Kennedy's words to his attorney general brother the night of October 28, 1962.[28] Remember, mere days earlier Robert Kennedy had been cracking the whip to the CIA to launch *more* commando raids!

So now the scheduled boat runs to the Cuban coast by the infiltrators' comrades were canceled. These irksome "Cuban refugees" now died in suicidal firefights against Castro's troops or were captured, tortured, and finally bound to the stake in front of the blood-, bone-, and brain-flecked *paredón*. "*Viva Cuba Libre!*" they yelled.

Many of these men had fought at the Bay of Pigs. They could not have imagined that the Kennedy administration would betray them *again*. In that earlier disaster, as Russian tanks and fifty-one thousand Communist troops were about to overwhelm commander Pepe San Roman's starved, thirst-crazed, ammo-less Brigada 2506, he sent this last message to his CIA handlers just offshore: "How can you people do this to us?" He said this in English, as he had been educated in the United States.

Cubans captured at the Bay of Pigs were tortured and put under a death sentence. Castro said he would revoke that death sentence if they signed a document denouncing the United States. To a man they refused. "We will die with dignity!" barked their commander, Erneido Oliva, at his Castroite torturers. These heroes knew that it wasn't the United States that had betrayed them, but the young Kennedy administration. A guilt-stricken JFK ransomed them back, only to return them to the fight and sell them down the river again. I must add something else. Almost half of the 1,200 Bay of Pigs survivors enlisted in the U.S. Army in 1963. They volunteered for the Vietnam War. These men had seen Communism point-blank and were willing to fight it anywhere.

Ask Gloria Estefan. Her dad was one of these heroes, wounded as a tank commander at the Bay of Pigs, then wounded again as a second lieutenant in the U.S. Army in Vietnam. He volunteered for two tours of duty in Vietnam. Wounded, he died a lingering death (Agent Orange was suspected as a cause).

As a young girl, Gloria Estefan nursed her father through his final illness. But unlike the Hollywood Left, she's never milked her father's death for sympathy or to bash America. "My whole family paid a heavy price for freedom," she said succinctly. "My father fought for those freedoms both at the Bay of Pigs and in Vietnam. I watched him die a slow death for fourteen years. I'm not about to let anyone stomp on his ideals. I always find that people have very little information about what happened in Cuba. Everyone always constantly talks about and buys into the idea that the U.S. is responsible for Cuba's plight. But the only embargo in Cuba *is Fidel's embargo against the Cuban people*. [Emphasis mine.] So when they ask me I tell them. How can I forget what Communists did to my country and my family?"[29]

Had Richard Nixon demanded a recount in 1960 and exposed the Democrats' voter fraud in Illinois and Texas, my kids would speak Spanish, Emmylou Harris (rather than Gloria Estefan) would be the toast of Miami, most of Cuba's freedom fighters would be alive, and Fidel Castro would merit less textbook space than Pancho Villa, less even than Augusto Sandino.

The Bay of Pigs operation had been planned during the Eisenhower-Nixon administration. Nixon advised Kennedy regarding Cuba: "Go in!" The *Miami Herald* quoted Nixon as saying, "We should assist the Cuban freedom fighters openly. It makes no sense to leash them." One of Eisenhower's last recommendations before handing the reins over to Kennedy was: "We cannot let the Castro regime last! Castro begins to look like a madman. . . . Do whatever it takes!"[30] Well, we all know the rest of the story.

In a 1960 campaign speech, Kennedy said, "The Republicans have allowed a Communist dictatorship to flourish eight jet minutes from our borders. We must support anti-Castro fighters. So far these freedom fighters have received no help from our government. . . . We must make clear our intention not to let the Soviet Union turn Cuba into its base in the Caribbean—and our intention to enforce the Monroe Doctrine."[31]

"We shall pay any price, bear any burden, meet any hardship, support any friend, oppose any foe, to assure the survival and the success of liberty," Kennedy said in his inaugural speech in January 1961.

"I will never abandon Cuba to Communism. I promise to deliver this flag to you in a free Havana."[32] That was what JFK told the survivors of Brigada 2506 at the Orange Bowl on Christmas Eve, 1962. But Castro knew it was a lie. Kennedy had abandoned Cuba to Castro's tender mercies.

CHAPTER THREE

THE COWARDLY LEÓN

On January 12, 1960, Castro worked himself into a fine froth on Cuban television. He raved at his *revolución*'s sinister enemies. He took a break from Yankee-bashing for a few seconds and ripped into Spain as fascists!...Monarchists!...The Spanish embassy is a nest for counter-revolutionaries! A foul hive for the CIA! etc.

The broadcast was at night, and it so happened that the Spanish ambassador, Juan Pablo Lojendio, was home in his pajamas watching television. He saw Castro, grew livid, and summoned his chauffeur while grabbing a coat. "To the TV studio—and fast!"

If only the United States had had an ambassador like that. Every day, for ten months, Castro insulted the United States. The staff at the United States embassy had had enough and wanted to strike back, but Ambassador Phil Bonsal, a northeastern liberal from central casting, had given stern instructions against any hint of criticism or protest at Castro's crimes, thievery, and gutter-mouth. Our forbearance and enlightenment were supposed to impress all of Latin America.

Ambassador Lojendio didn't give a flying flip about forbearance and enlightenment. Honor and respect were more important. (Remember, this was Spain *forty-five years* ago.) He jumped out of the car before it stopped. He stormed into the studio and demanded: "Where's the comandante? Where's the premier?" A startled producer pointed at a door.

Castro was still fulminating in front of the cameras when the enraged ambassador burst into the studio. The studio crew scampered in confusion, tripping over wires, dropping their clipboards. The cameras shifted from Castro to Lojendio, to a shrugging producer, then back to Castro—just as the ambassador confronted him.

"Lies!" yelled a red-faced Lojendio, his pajamas visibly poking out from under his sports coat. "I have been insulted! I have been insulted! I demand a chance to reply! You cannot insult my government, nor my government's ambassador without the right to reply!"[1]

Castro gaped. His eyes bulged. For once he was speechless. Wide-eyed, he backed off and threw his hands in front of him—not with clenched fists, but pleading not to have any trouble. As Castro cringed, his band of bodyguards burst in to restrain the Spanish ambassador. The cameras were promptly shifted. When they came back, Castro was seen reaching for his coffee cup (brandy, actually) with trembling hands, almost spilling it.

After that, Spain got more respect, but the United States learned nothing from Castro the Cowardly León on television.

"Those Americans," snickered then Brazilian president Janio Quadros at a Latin American summit meeting, "are just like women. They have a masochistic streak; the more you slap them around, the more you get out of them."

From Spain, Castro got a serious tongue-lashing. From us, he got nothing—or actually, he got plenty. After shrieking, "Let the Yankees invade! I'll produce 200,000 dead gringos!"[2] (January 15, 1959), after branding the United States "a vulture preying on humanity!" and "the enemy of all Latin nations!" and "the enemy of the progress of all peoples of the world!" (July 1959),[3] and after confiscating American property and businesses, including millions from United States cattle and agricultural companies in Cuba, Castro received about $200 million in U.S. foreign aid from the time he took over on January 1, 1959, until Eisenhower declared, "There is a limit to what the United States in self-respect can endure. That limit has now been reached," and broke diplomatic relations with Cuba. That date was January 3, 1961.[4] The $200 million figure is provided by CIA inspector general Lyman Kirkpatrick, and consisted of U.S. government purchases of Cuban sugar at prices much higher than the world sugar price at the time.[5]

Castro's big boodle came a little later, in the summer and fall of 1960, and amounted to $1.8 billion worth of stolen American property. That's the biggest heist of U.S. property in history—and more than all the "nationalizations" (thefts) of U.S. property by twentieth-century Communist and "nationalist" regimes combined. But Castro started snatching U.S. assets from the beginning, after barely two months in power. On March 3, 1959, he commenced the mass larceny by "nationalizing" the Cuban telephone company, an ITT subsidiary. Three months later his agrarian reform law snatched millions more from United Fruit and the Pingree and King ranches, among others. Not to mention the hundreds of Cuban-owned farms and ranches that were "intervened," as they called it.

Many Cuban Americans from the Camagüey region recall the "intervention" at one of the region's most productive cattle ranches. The Castroites arrived and declared, as usual, that the ranch now belonged to "*la revolución*." And they, being official *revolucionarios* themselves, were certainly entitled to eat lunch. In preparation, the head *barbudo* (bearded one) started walking over to a pen that held the ranch's prize breeding bull, worth $22,000 (in 1959 dollars).

"Not that one!" the rancher yelled as he bustled over. "That's a *breeding* bull, worth $22,000! Makes no sense to..."

But he was heavily outgunned at the moment (all *barbudos* traveled in heavily armed gangs). The Castroite looked back at his cohorts and snickered while unlimbering his carbine. "You can't be serious?" the rancher pleaded, looking around wide-eyed, as the imbecile took aim. "Your own blasted *revolución* has much more to gain with that bull alive!"

Blam! The bull collapsed from a shot to the head. The *barbudos* doubled over laughing as the rancher covered his face with his hands. The Reds then butchered the bull for an impromptu barbeque, all the while threatening the rancher with the firing squad for his impertinence. The bull's worth was irrelevant. And chances are, the Castroites weren't even hungry. What mattered was a point-blank demonstration of who was now giving the orders in Cuba—and the heavy price of disobedience.

True to their tradition of outstanding—indeed, Pulitzer Prize– winning—reporting on Russian agricultural "reform" (the Ukraine Famine of 1931–33) the *New York Times* heartily applauded Castro's "revolutionary" larceny, thuggery, and idiocy (Communist economics). "An agrarian reform was long overdue in Cuba," sniffed a learned *New York Times* editorial in July 1959.

What decent person could disagree? We envision diligent Peace Corps types placing land titles into the gnarled hands of *campesinos*, their clothes ragged, their arms streaked with sweat and dirt but their faces beaming. "Rejoice!" we say. "The cruel system that throttled Cuba's agricultural production has finally been discarded!" "Rejoice!" we say again. "The selfish, lazy, and villainous are finally getting their just desserts. The virtuous and industrious are finally getting a chance in life!"

"This promise of social justice brought a foretaste of human dignity for millions who had little knowledge of it in Cuba's former *near-feudal* economy," were the *New York Times*'s exact words. (Emphasis mine.)

The problem was, in the 1950s the average farm wage in "near-feudal" Cuba was *higher* than in France or Belgium. And the average Cuban farm was actually *smaller* than the average farm in the United States, 140 acres in Cuba and 195 acres in the United States. In 1958, Cuba, a nation of 6.2 million people, had 159,958 farms, 11,000 of them tobacco farms. Plus, only 34 percent of the Cuban population was rural.

This is according to a U.S. Department of Commerce document titled "Investment in Cuba" (a public document available to all the Jayson Blairs and Walter Durantys at the *New York Times* at the time, I might add.)

And according to the Geneva-based International Labour Organization, in 1958 the average daily wage for an agricultural worker in Cuba was $3. If that sounds "near-feudal," consider that the average daily wage in France at the time was $2.73. In Belgium it was $2.70, in Denmark $2.74, in West Germany $2.73, and in the United States $4.06. Let's not even get into the average wage in the rest of Latin America or Asia, much less Africa. Though, nowadays, Cuba's standard of living can indeed be compared to Haiti's.

"The general impression of the members of the mission," continues the U.S. Commerce Department Study, "from travels and observations *all over Cuba* is that the living levels of farmers, agricultural laborers, and industrial workers are higher all along the line than for corresponding groups in other tropical countries." (Emphasis mine.)

A UNESCO report from 1957 says: "One feature of the Cuban social structure is a *large middle class*. Cuban workers are more unionized (proportional to the population) than U.S. workers.... The average wage for an eight-hour day in Cuba 1957 is higher than for workers in Belgium, Denmark, France, Germany. Cuban labor receives 66.6 percent of gross national income. In the U.S. the figure is 68 percent. 44 percent of Cubans are covered by social legislation." That's a higher percentage than in the U.S. at the time.[6]

Liberals then and now like to think of pre-Castro Cuba as a veritable U.S. colony, a sordid playground of prostitution and casinos, horribly exploited by American corporations! JFK himself said this in an interview with French journalist Jean Daniel in 1963: "I think that there is not a country in the world, including all the regions of Africa and any other country under colonial domination, where the economic colonization, the humiliation, the exploitation have been worse than those which ravaged Cuba, the result, in part, of the policy of my country."

"Calumny...cheap demagoguery." That's what an exasperated Spruille Braden, former U.S. ambassador to Cuba, said after reading JFK's idiotic claims in that interview. "That abysmal ignorance in Washington concerning this whole Cuban situation endures."[7]

In fact, only 5 percent of *invested* capital in Cuba in 1958 was American, and less than one-third of Cuba's sugar output was by U.S. companies. Cuba had a grand total of nine gambling casinos in 1958. Gulfport-Biloxi, Mississippi, have double that number today. And chew on this one: In 1957, when it was touted as the "playground" for Americans, Cuba hosted a grand total of 272,265 U.S. tourists.[8] That year *more Cubans vacationed in the United States than Americans vacationed in Cuba*. We had a "playground" too.

College professors regularly trot out the brutal landowners/oppressed peasant myth. I heard this version myself from one of my college history professors. His name was Stephen Ambrose. You'd think Eisenhower's official biographer and America's bestselling historian might have known better. Not when it came to Cuba, where Castro's siren song lulled his critical faculties to slumber. College professors might not know it, but the rest of us now know that the landless got no land anyway. They became slave laborers for Communist *kolkhozes* (state farms). Soviet advisers from the Ukraine began advising Castro's National Institute for Land Reform in early spring 1959. Many professors and *New York Times* journalists used to think Communism worked, but it's kinda hard to argue that now (to be honest, it was kinda hard to argue it then too). The Bolshevik Maxim Litvinov said "food is a weapon," and Communists have always used it as a weapon. Castro wielded the weapon early, snatching farms and ranches and then issuing his infamous ration cards to his subjects.

In 1958, the Cuban people had the third highest protein consumption in the Western Hemisphere. If you think that's interesting, take a look at this chart, compiled by an intrepid Cuban exile living in Spain:

	Food Ration in 1842 for Slaves in Cuba	Castro Government Ration since 1962
Meat, chicken, fish	8 oz.	2 oz.
Rice	4 oz.	3 oz.
Starches	16 oz.	6.5 oz.
Beans	4 oz.	1 oz.[9]

Turns out, when we say Castro "enslaved" Cuba we actually miss half the story—we actually *downplay* the issue. Turns out, the half-starved slaves on the ship *Amistad* ate better than Elián González does now. Remember that when you hear Eleanor Clift say, "To be a poor child in Cuba may be better than being a poor child in the U.S."[10] Remember that when you hear, "Socialism works. I think Cuba might prove that," which is what Chevy Chase said on Earth Day 2000, after a guided tour of Castroland.[11] Remember that when you hear Danny Glover blame the (easily avoidable, just buy the goods from Mexico) "unjust, unfair, and cruel" U.S. "embargo" rather than the Communist system for the poverty of Cuba.[12] Remember that when you hear Jesse Jackson say, "Viva Fidel! Viva Che!" as if the Cuban people have anything to viva Fidel and Che for.[13] Remember that when you hear Steven Spielberg say, "Meeting Fidel Castro were the eight most important hours of my life."[14]

And my favorite Spielberg quote, "I personally feel that the Cuban embargo should be lifted. I do not see any reason for *accepting old grudges being played out in the twenty-first century.*"[15] (Emphasis mine.) This from a man who specializes in making movies about American slavery, Jim Crow, and the Holocaust.

Cuba's stellar achievements in the field of health and nutrition saw Havana host the "Second Inter-American Conference on Pharmacy and *Nutrition*" in June 2003. The Massachusetts College of Pharmacy and Allied Health Sciences sponsored this farce and its president gave one of Castro's apparatchiks "the highest decoration that the U.S. College gives to outstanding personalities and institutions in the field of pharmacy and *nutrition*." (Emphasis mine.)

Two months earlier, Castro's police had rounded up more than a hundred "dissidents," put them through sham trials, and shoved them into dungeons. Their combined sentences total 1,454 years. Cuban jails offer patients free electroshock treatment and a weight-loss nutritional regimen. Thirty-four of the prisoners were journalists and independent librarians. Their crimes ran the gamut from possessing George Orwell's *Animal Farm* to accessing the Internet. The following month UNESCO (the United Nations Educational, Scientific, and Cultural Organization) awarded Castro's Cuba its coveted International Literacy Award.

A few months after that, Pulitzer Prize–winning writer Alice Walker—"I simply love Cuba and its people, including Fidel. He's like a great redwood."[16]—visited Havana for the 2004 International Book Fair. She crowed, "There is a direct correlation between the U.S. civil rights movement and Fidel Castro's socialist revolution.... It's important to stand with people who are struggling, because in the end we will win!"[17]

She was referring, of course, to her hosts (the jailers), not the jailed. Walker's hosts hold the record for the longest and most brutal incarceration of a black political prisoner in the twentieth century. His name is Eusebio Peñalver, and he served longer in Castro's dungeons than Nelson Mandela served in South Africa's.

"Nigger!" taunted his all-white jailers between tortures. "Monkey! We pulled you down from the trees and cut off your tail!" snickered Castro's goons as they threw him into solitary confinement. Might the Congressional Black Caucus or NAACP have a cross word for this regime—a white regime where today 80 percent of the political prisoners are black? Jesse Jackson doesn't, of course. He calls Castro "the most honest and courageous politician I've ever met." On Castro's last visit to Harlem in 1996, amidst a delirious, deafening, foot-stomping chorus of "Viva Fidel!" and "Cuba si!" his host Charlie Rangel gave him a bear hug.

Eusebio Peñalver spent thirty years in Castro's dungeons and remained what Castroites call a *plantado*—a defiant one, an unbreakable one. "Stalin tortured," wrote Arthur Koestler, "not to force you to reveal a fact, but to force you to collude in a fiction." Solzhenitsyn noted that "The worst part of Communism is being forced to live a lie." Peñalver refused to lie. He scorned any "reeducation" by his jailers. He knew it was they who desperately needed to be reeducated. He refused to wear the uniform of a common criminal. He knew it was the Communists who were the criminals. Danny Glover, Congresswoman Maxine Waters, Kweisi Mfume (former president of the NAACP), Jesse Jackson, and Alice Walker have all toasted his torturer.

"For months I was naked in a six-by-four cell," Peñalver recalls. "That's four feet *high*, so you couldn't stand. But I felt a great freedom inside myself. I refused to commit spiritual suicide."

Peñalver lives in Miami today. On May 20, 2003, to celebrate Cuba's independence day, he met with President Bush in the White House. "Castro's apologists," Peñalver told me recently, "those who excuse or downplay his crimes—these people, be they ignorant, stupid, mendacious, whatever—they are *accomplices* in the bloody tyrant's crimes, accomplices in the most brutal and murderous regime in the hemisphere." Then Alice Walker, Jesse Jackson, Kweisi Mfume, Danny Glover, and Maxine Waters are accomplices in the bloody crimes of a regime where 82 percent of the prison population is black and exactly .08 percent of the ruling Communist Party is black.

Some American blacks, however, have learned the truth about Cuba. "Cuban Communism should be wiped out!" said Anthony Garnet Bryant in 1980. "Cuban Communism is humanity's vomit!"[18]

Bryant, you see, was forced to *live* in Castroland, not just visit the place. In 1968, he hijacked a plane to Cuba to escape U.S. justice for several crimes. In 1980, after years of trying, and knowing he faced lengthy jail terms in the United States, he came home. "I'm deliriously happy to be back!" he beamed to U.S. magistrate Charlene Sorrentino in a Miami district court. She'd just sentenced him to a maximum security prison in Florida. "I've never seen a man smile so much in my life," remarked Judge Sorrentino.[19]

Happens all the time when people leave Cuba, Judge Sorrentino; they smile constantly, deliriously. Recall little Elián González—before Janet Reno ordered the raid that returned him to Castroland. Recall the scenes from the Mariel Boatlift. Sure, Anthony Bryant was entering a jail. But he'd just left a much ghastlier jail, Castro's Cuba.

"I'm living like a dog in Cuba!" That's former Black Panther Garland Grant, who hijacked a plane to Cuba in 1971. "I just want to get back to the United States! Just open my cell door, and I'll walk in! Here in Cuba the guards beat the shit outta me in jail, bashed out one of my eyes! They killed my buddy, just smashed his head against a wall, nothing to it, no inquiry, no nothing. Hell, these Communists can't do anything more to me that they haven't already done, except put a bullet in my head!"[20]

An AP reporter secretly interviewed Grant in his Cuban cell in 1977. "There's more racism here in Communist Cuba than in the worst parts of Mississippi! . . . Cuba ain't what people think. I'd rather be in jail in the U.S. than free here!"[21]

Both these black gentlemen found themselves in Castro's jails shortly after entering Cuba. Seems they tried the same attitude and lingo with Castro's cops as they had with American cops. A big no-no, they learned in very short order.

Aside from using food as a weapon, the Communists don't mind using real weapons to kill, maim, and torture opponents of the regime, even if they are in exile. Just as Stalin sent his goons to murder Trotsky (an assassin finally succeeded in planting an ice axe in Trotsky's brain in Mexico City in 1940), so too have Castro's goons hunted down exiled Cubans. Castro's hit squads got Aldo Vera on his doorstep in Puerto Rico by machine-gunning him in the back. They got Rolando Masferrer by blowing him to shreds with a car bomb in his Hialeah garage. And they got José de la Torriente with a bullet through his heart as he slept on a recliner in his Miami living room. When physical assassination is problematic, though, Communists know they can turn to the Western press for cooperative character assassination. The liberal media loves leftist dictators, and Castro is no exception.

Incidentally, after serving his twenty-year sentence in Mexico, Trotsky's assassin, Ramón Mercader, moved to Cuba. Castro personally appointed Mercader as Cuba's inspector general of prisons. When Mercader died in Cuba, he was buried with honors for all the successes for which the prisons could take credit: 15,000 firing squad executions (five times as many as Pinochet, and mostly of workers and country folk) and 500,000 gulag inmates (mostly proletarians), in a county with no freedom of speech, no labor rights, political repression, and economic policies that have inflicted starvation and slavery on people who once enjoyed one of best standards of living in the Western Hemisphere. Yet how often does the liberal media condemn Castro, much less his sidekick Che, who proudly signed his name "Stalin II"? The Cowardly Léon of Havana has nothing to fear from the fawning Western press. The *New York Times* taught him that at the beginning.[22]

One day in May 1959, Castro's air force chief, Major Pedro Diaz Lanz, met with his lifelong friend and fellow pilot Eduardo Ferrer. "Eddy, sell your business. Tell your dad to sell his business. The Communists are taking Cuba over. The bastards will seize everything. I know it. I'm leaving for the U.S. soon. I've got to do *something*. I've got to tell the Americans and the world what's going on here and start the fight against these Communists. Everybody seems asleep. But I've seen these Reds working behind the scenes."[23]

A week later, Diaz Lanz resigned his post, declaring publicly that Castro's civilian government was a front for Soviet-trained Communists. Diaz Lanz bundled his wife and kids onto a small boat and escaped to Miami. Weeks later, Diaz Lanz appeared at a public hearing before the Senate Internal Security Subcommittee (SISS). The date was July 14, 1959.

Jay Sourwine [general counsel for the SISS]: Do you think Raul Castro is the strongest Communist in the Castro regime?

Diaz Lanz: It's Fidel himself. I am sure he's the one who gives the orders and who decides everything.

Sourwine: Is Castro friendly to the United States?

Diaz Lanz: No.

Sourwine: But Fidel Castro has said on many occasions that he is friendly to the United States. You are saying that this is not true?

Diaz Lanz: He is lying.

Sourwine: Have you yourself seen instances of anti-American propaganda in Cuba under the Castro regime?

Diaz Lanz: Yes, sir.

Sourwine: Give us an example.

Diaz Lanz: Fidel Castro himself calls you "Yankee imperialists." He's always telling us we are going to have to fight the Americans—the Marines—and harping all the time on this theme. *He wants war with the U.S.*

Sourwine: Have you seen any instances of anti-American propaganda in connection with the indoctrination schools?

Diaz Lanz: Yes, sir.

Sourwine: You know there are many who say that Fidel Castro is not himself a Communist, that he is simply a tool or a captive of the Communists.

Diaz Lanz: I am completely sure that Fidel is a Communist.

Sourwine: You are completely sure that Fidel Castro is what?

Diaz Lanz: That Fidel Castro is a *Communist*....Also, I'm prepared because the Communists have a well-known system of trying to destroy the reputations of anyone who disagrees with them.

The Havana correspondent for the *New York Times*, Herbert Matthews, leaped to his typewriter and immediately wrote a front-page story against Major Diaz Lanz. "This is not a Communist revolution in any sense of the word," he wrote. "In Cuba there are no Communists in positions of control." And for good measure: "The accusations of Major Pedro Diaz Lanz are rejected by everybody." Then the character assassination: "Sources tell me that Major Diaz Lanz was removed from his office for incompetence, extravagance, and nepotism."[24]

But the piece de resistance was this: "Fidel Castro is not only not a Communist," the *New York Times*'s star reporter continued, " he's decidedly anti-Communist."

Matthews had a long record of reporting favorably on Communists; he did it during the Spanish Civil War, playing up the Communists as "democrats," agrarian reformers, the whole bit. But once the *New York Times* sounds her bugle, the rest of the media pack rush in behind her, from CBS News to the major national newspapers. "It's an outrage that Congress should give a platform for a disaffected Cuban adventurer to denounce the Cuban revolution as Communist," barked Walter Lippmann a few days later in the *New York Herald Tribune*. "It would be an even greater mistake *even to intimate* that Castro's Cuba has any real prospect of becoming a Soviet satellite," Lippmann wrote a week later in the *Washington Post*. (Emphasis mine.) Lippmann's 1958 Pulitzer Prize had noted "his distinction as a farsighted and incisive analyst of foreign policy."

The *Atlanta Constitution* yapped next. "Major Diaz Lanz is a simply a disgruntled soldier-of-fortune," wrote its publisher and editor in chief, Ralph "Conscience of the South" McGill, who was in Havana schmoozing with Fidel and Raul. "Reliable sources tell me that Major Diaz Lanz has been involved in clandestine money-making activities.... Diaz left Cuba because he was involved in black marketing." Ralph McGill would be awarded the Pulitzer Prize this same year for his "courage" in denouncing southern "intolerance and hatred." In 1964, LBJ decorated McGill with the Presidential Medal of Freedom. "The desire for individual dignity and freedom is in the genes of all mankind," proclaimed McGill during the solemn ceremony. But apparently he didn't worry about Cubans in the kindly prison camp of Fidel Castro.

There was no "alternative" media back then to keep the liberal media honest, but that brave little national weekly *Human Events* tried. Back on August 17, 1957, *Human Events* carried a prophetic article that read:

> Many on The Hill are beginning to say now: "We ought to be worrying more about the Communist menace in Latin America, on our very doorstep, than about Communism in the faraway Middle East." What's really behind the revolt led by Fidel Castro against the Cuban government, billed by the *New York Times* and the liberal press as a simple rebellion against dictatorship, comes into clearer focus from the following statement, obtained exclusively by the staff of *Human Events* from former United States ambassador to Cuba Spruille Braden. This retired American diplomat has long qualified as an expert not only on Cuba but also on all Latin America; having served in other posts south of the border, he

has in recent years won recognition as a critical observer of the workings of the Communist apparatus in the Caribbean and South America.

Mr. Braden says of Fidel Castro, leader of the fledgling Cuban revolt, that according to official documents he has seen, he is a fellow traveler, if not an official member, of the Communist Party and has been for a long time. He was a ringleader in the bloody uprising in Bogotá, Colombia, in April 1948, which occurred (and obviously was planned by the Kremlin) just at the time when the Pan-American Conference was being held in that capital, with no less a person than Secretary of State George C. Marshall present. The uprising was engineered and staged by Communists and the Colombia government and press subsequently published documentary evidence of Fidel Castro's role as a leader in the rioting which virtually gutted the Colombian capital. The appearance of this Cuban at the head of the recent uprising in his own country stamps the insurrection as another part of the developing Communist pattern of such subversion throughout Latin America—although a number of thoroughly decent and patriotic Cubans have been misled into sympathizing with, and in some cases supporting, the Fidel Castro movement.

This passage also appeared in Earl T. Smith's book *The Fourth Floor*. Smith was the ambassador to Cuba from mid-1957 until Castro's takeover in January 1959. He wrote the book to tell the truth about Castro's assumption of power. Another American diplomat—and friend—had warned Smith before he went to Havana: "Be careful down there, Earl. You are assigned to Cuba to preside over the downfall of Batista. The decision has been made that Batista has to go."

The Caribbean desk was on the fourth floor of the State Department's office building, hence the book's title. The State Department bureaucrats fought conservative Republican Smith every step of the way, not just ignoring but scoffing at his warnings about Castro's Communism. "I feel I owe it to the American people to try to establish the fact that the Castro Communist revolution need never have occurred," Smith wrote in the preface to his book.[25] Smith wrote that Castro's terrorists plotted to assassinate him. He also noted that Castro's Communist ties dated back to the late 1940s and that Castro had a criminal record from his college days that included several gangster-style murders. He criticized the United States government for being naïve and slapping an embargo on the Batista government to help Fidel the Communist and his *revolución*. America's previous ambassador to Cuba, Arthur Gardner, agreed with Smith about the Castro regime.

But even more explosive was the revelation that the State Department's chief of Caribbean affairs—who pressed the embargo against the Batista government—had been a Cuban Communist Party member in the 1930s. His name was William Wieland, but in the 1930s he had used the name Guillermo Arturo Montenegro and had been active in the Cuban Communist Party.[26] He was also friends with—guess who?—Herbert Matthews of the *New York Times*.

Now, back to the smear job on Diaz Lanz. The perfect proof that he was innocent of black marketeering was that he *resigned* from Castro's government. As any serious student knows, in Cuba the best place for enriching yourself from black marketeering of everything from machine guns to cocaine is from *within* Castro's regime. But more on that in the next chapter.

CHAPTER FOUR

THE DOPE TRAFFICKER NEXT DOOR

For years, Cuba received a $5 billion annual subsidy from the Soviets. In total, the Soviets pumped some $110 billion into Cuba. That's a pretty nice chunk of change, more than *five* Marshall Plans, in fact—and pumped not into the war-ravaged continent of Europe, but into an island of seven million people. From Soviet handouts alone, Communist Cuba should be wealthy. Instead, its people have government ration cards and starvation portions that make them far worse off than Cuban slaves in 1842. How did that happen?

First off, forget about the corruption of the Batistas, Trujillos, and Somozas. If you want to see Latin American corruption at its best and highest, Fidel Castro is your man. Cuban military defectors Rafael del Pino, Osvaldo Prendes, Juan Antonio Rodriguez, and Norberto Fuentes, among others, have told the tales, but the mainstream media mostly yawns.

Sometimes, though, court cases get a little more reporting. One such case began in 1987 when the U.S. attorney in Miami won convictions against seventeen drug traffickers who had used Cuban air force bases and Cuban MiG escorts for their cocaine shipments into the United States. Remember, Raul Castro runs Cuba's military.

So in 1993, the U.S. attorney in Miami drafted an indictment charging Raul Castro as a leader of a ten-year conspiracy that sent Colombian cocaine through Cuba to the United States. The Cuban defense ministry was declared a "criminal organization."

One of these smugglers, Reuben Ruiz, recalled in a PBS documentary, "My Cuban contact told me, 'Nobody will hurt you. The Cuban air force is completely at your service tomorrow.'"[1]

In the words of Dr. Rachel Ehrenfeld, author of the books *Evil Money* and *NarcoTerrorism*, "The Cubans provided safe haven, fuel, passports, radar escorts [for Colombian cocaine shipments]. And for all that, they were paid. In addition, they were taking commissions from each shipment of drugs that went through Cuba....In return, the same smuggling boats brought arms to the insurgencies—the Communist insurgencies that the Cubans were supporting in Latin America, in this case specifically the M-19 in Colombia." As another example of Castro's support for Communist insurgencies, CNN, on January 1, 1999, quoted commander Tiro-Fijo (Sure Shot) of the Revolutionary Armed Forces of Colombia (FARC) as saying, "Thanks to Fidel Castro, we are now a powerful army, not a hit-and-run band."

Drugs are where the money is for Cuban Communists who have destroyed their own economy. Cuban intelligence defector Manuel de Beunza said in the same PBS documentary, "I took part in a meeting where Fidel Castro himself ordered the creation of companies to be involved in drug dealing and smuggling."

Here's Rafael del Pino, Castro's air chief until defecting in 1987: "In the western part of Cuba, we have nineteen SAM missile sites and we have hundreds of radars and we have a regiment of MiG-23 interceptors. And it is completely impossible that a small airplane could fly from Colombia to the United States without the knowledge and the permission of Raul or Fidel Castro." The Colombian planes flew almost daily.

In July 2001, Madrid's TV Channel 5 broadcast a show titled "Cuba and Drug Trafficking." Spanish journalists posed as drug dealers and filmed (with hidden cameras) their dealings with drug dealers in Cuba. As to security? One Cuba-based dealer snorted, "Forget it. I pay for the security right here in Cuba. I answer only to the [Cuban] government."

"The evidence against Castro is already greater than the evidence that led to the drug indictment of Manuel Noriega in 1988," a federal prosecutor told the *Miami Herald* in July 1996. A total of four grand juries revealed Cuba's involvement in drug trafficking.

Yet nothing came of it. The Clinton Justice Department—the same gang that returned Elián González to Cuba—refused to pursue an indictment. Actually, the Clinton administration did the reverse: It issued a proposal for a joint U.S.-Cuba program to interdict drug shipments in the Caribbean. This was the brainchild of General Barry McCaffrey, then acting as Clinton's drug czar. Under the proposed program, a joint U.S.–Cuban command would share intelligence and surveillance equipment. "Our current Cuba policy is mistaken," McCaffrey stressed later in a Georgetown University speech. "We need to engage them on this issue." In 1995 and 1996, U.S. generals, at the instruction of the Clinton State Department, made several trips to Cuba to meet with Raul Castro and lay the groundwork for McCaffrey's brilliant plan, though the plan didn't come off. McCaffrey regretfully blames "congressional pressure"—which grew after Cuba shot down the Brothers to the Rescue planes—for foiling his grand alliance with the Castro brothers.

Meanwhile, drug czar McCaffrey attempted a similar joint effort with Mexico in 1997. McCaffrey heartily applauded the appointment of General Jesús Gutiérrez as Mexico's drug czar. "A man of absolute and unquestioned integrity," gushed General McCaffrey while hosting the visiting Gutiérrez in Washington, D.C.[2]

McCaffrey ordered the Drug Enforcement Agency (DEA) to share U.S. intelligence and surveillance technology with Gutiérrez—who two weeks later was arrested by the Mexican government for being on the payroll of Amado Carrillo, also known as the "Lord of the Skies," also known as Mexico's drug kingpin. "Some DEA officials consider Carrillo the world's most powerful drug trafficker," declared a PBS *Frontline* program.

During Gutiérrez's trial, where he got a seventy-seven-year sentence, we learned that McCaffrey's "man of absolute and unquestioned integrity" intended to give our DEA and CIA intelligence—and even our sophisticated electronic equipment—to "the world's most powerful drug trafficker." Moreover, Carrillo had a long relationship with Castro and had been a frequent guest at Cuba's Cayo Largo resort.

"Cuba is an island of resistance to the drug threat," declared the same sage and cocksure General McCaffrey at a press conference a little later in Havana. "They are very keen on cooperating in the fight against drugs. . . . They are sincere. . . . I am convinced these people do not intend to be, and represent no national security threat to us."[3]

"Poor Cuba," lamented General McCaffrey in a speech at Georgetown University shortly afterward. "Location puts it in the path of international drug crime. But I do not see any serious evidence, current or in the last decade, of Cuban government complicity with drug crime." Undaunted, in 1999 McCaffrey placed a direct hotline from the U.S. Coast Guard in Key West to the Cuban coast guard.[4]

And with curious coordination, on August 28, 2001, Cuba's justice minister expressed his willingness to cooperate with the Bush administration on drug interdiction, while General McCaffrey gave a speech at Georgetown University in which he lectured the Bush administration on why it should create a joint Caribbean drug interdiction command that specifically included Cuba.

But when it comes to Cuban cooperation, let's remember Dr. Rachel Ehrenfeld, who writes: "Cuba also provided radar services and escorts of Cuban coast guard boats for drug shipments." And here's what drug smuggler Reuben Ruiz says: "You know the big U.S. Coast Guard boats, the ones that are equipped with all the radars and everything?

Well, Cuba has those too, and they would scan the whole area to make sure it was clear of U.S. Coast Guard boats for us. . . . And they'd tell us, okay, the coast is clear this way—go this way, go that way."

When Republican congressman Lincoln Diaz-Balart of Florida learned of General McCaffrey's proposal for a joint command in Key West with a U.S. Coast Guard admiral and a Cuban commander in the same office, he said, "Why not include a kingpin from the Medellin cartel too!"

And who can forget famous Clinton financial backer (to the tune of $20,000) Luis "El Gordito" Cabrera, or the pictures of him from the 1995 White House Christmas party, smiling with Hillary and back-slapping with Vice President Gore. After he was arrested for cocaine smuggling—exactly two weeks after that party—pictures turned up of Cabrera smiling and backslapping with Fidel Castro.

The affection was warranted. Castro had approved Cabrera routing his cocaine shipments through Cuba in return for a nice cut of the profits. The details turned up during Cabrera's trial. During the Clinton years, there were well-documented investigations of Clinton contributors with links to Red China. The investigations finally forced the Democratic National Committee to return nearly $3 million in contributions. (These investigations were also the subject of several well-documented books, including *Year of the Rat* and *Red Dragon Rising* by Edward Timperlake and William C. Triplett II, and *Absolute Power* by David Limbaugh.) Communist Cuba has always been jealous of Red China, and some think Cabrera was Castro's attempt to gain his own influence over the White House. During the Clinton years, China received permission to buy high-tech militarily relevant technology for its nuclear weapons program. If Castro didn't get access to our nuclear technology, he at least came tantalizingly close to getting DEA intelligence and technology.

During his trial, Cabrera was eager to sing about his drug-smuggling arrangements with Castro in exchange for a lighter sentence. But Cabrera's lawyer, Stephen Bronis, was shocked to discover that Janet Reno's

Justice Department didn't want to hear about it. "It was pure politics and it stinks," Bronis told the *Miami Herald*.[5]

According to Bronis, Castro had told Cabrera, "I know your friends from Cali [the Colombian drug cartel]. I've met them. I know they're here in Cuba. I like doing business with them." But we don't need to rely on Bronis's word. We know from official Justice Department documents that Castro was so close to the Colombian cocaine barons that in 1984 Manuel Noriega visited Cuba, where Castro offered to mediate a spat between the Colombian drug lords and the Panamanian dictator. This information is in the United States' indictment of Noriega.

"Cuba was a paradise for us." said Alejandro Bernal during a December 2001 interview. Bernal was Mexican drug kingpin Amado Carrillo's contact with the Colombians. Bernal was interviewed in his country club prison in Colombia by Miami's *El Nuevo Herald* while awaiting extradition to the United States. "We lived like kings in Cuba, *hombre*. And this goes way back. All of us knew it. You wanna go to place where nobody bothers you? Five million dollars for Fidel—it's that easy. He'll see to it that nobody touches you."

But according to Bernal, Carrillo paid Castro considerably more than $5 million. Bernal says Carrillo had houses and hotel suites in Cuba, which he used for drug deals and torrid sessions with his mistress. This confirmed what Mexican authorities reported during an investigation in 1997, when they also discovered that Carrillo laundered hundreds of millions in drug money in Castro's Cuba. This investigation came right after Carrillo's death (he died from complications from attempted plastic surgery).

Hollywood likes to continually to retell the myth of how Castro cleaned up the allegedly gangster-ridden Cuba of Fulgencio Batista. The more interesting truth is that Castro is the dope trafficker next door, running the Cuban leg of the Colombian drug cartel. Funny how you don't often hear about that.

CHAPTER FIVE

ROCK AGAINST FREEDOM!

Havana hotels are off-limits to most Cubans, especially black Cubans. Cuba practices segregation, but somehow all the liberals who condemned South African apartheid swarm to Cuba's segregated hotels open the drapes and say, "Ah, will ya look at that beach!" Then they order room service champagne, fire up a Cohiba, and toast the enforcer of tourist apartheid.

Liberals—and the United Nations—called for economic sanctions against South Africa. The UN General Assembly passed the resolution: "We demand a total and immediate economic break with South Africa." Yet the UN General Assembly yearly denounces the U.S. "embargo" of Cuba. And so do American liberals.

"The Cuban embargo is the stupidest law ever passed in the United States," said Jimmy Carter, who when he was in the White House (recall his "human rights" foreign policy) imposed embargoes against South Africa, Rhodesia, Paraguay, Uruguay, Argentina, Chile, and Nicaragua.[1] (And unlike these embargoed countries, Cuba trades with every country on earth, and in 2003 the United States was Cuba's sixth biggest trading partner, despite being "embargoed.")

Someone remind me: What terrible threat did Rhodesia—which fought on the Allied side in both world wars and offered to fight alongside us in Vietnam—ever present to the United States? Fidel Castro called the United States a "vulture preying on humanity"—but Rhodesian prime minister Ian Smith (who flew combat missions on our side in World War II) never did, nor did he provide a haven for terrorists; indeed, he fought terrorists and Communists.

Someone remind me: When did apartheid-era South African firing squads shoot down scores of U.S. citizens, or steal $1.8 billion from American citizens, or travel to Cu Loc prison camp outside Hanoi to join in torturing American POWs to death, the way Castro's Cuba did? In fact, South Africa tried to stem Cuba-supported Communism in Africa.

In Latin America, someone remind me: When did Uruguay, or Paraguay, or Augusto Pinochet's Chile, or Anastasio Somoza's Nicaragua point missiles at us?

Perhaps sanctions are to be applied to punish regimes for their *internal* wickedness? Fine, but neither Ian Smith's Rhodesia, nor apartheid South Africa, nor Pinochet's Chile had political incarceration rates anywhere near to Castro's, or execution rates, or rates of state-supervised theft of private property, or the total denial of human rights, or anything remotely like the internal repression of the Cuban police state. During the height of apartheid, black Africans immigrated into South Africa; no one starved in Rhodesia because of state-run farms and rationing (they had to wait for Robert Mugabe for that); and Chile under Pinochet enjoyed a famous free-market economic recovery. Latin Americans aren't banging on Cuba's door, hoping to get into that Communist paradise; no one swims to Cuba hoping to enjoy greater freedom and a higher standard of living.

Ponder this for second, friends: Before Castro, more Americans lived in Cuba than Cubans in the United States. Cuba went from being the Western Hemispheric nation with the *highest* per capita immigration rate,[2] (yes, higher than the United States, including the Ellis Island

years) to one where 20 percent of the population *fled*, and where probably 80 percent sought to flee. They fled in planes and ships, they
crammed into the steaming holds of merchant vessels, they squeezed
in the wheelholds of transatlantic jets, they leaped into the sea on rafts
and inner tubes, knowing that their chances were about one in three of
making landfall. Thus they vote with their feet against a place Jack
Nicholson declared "a paradise." Thus they flee the handiwork of the
man Colin Powell assures us "has done good things for Cuba."[3] Thus
is their desperation to escape from Bonnie Raitt's "happy little island."
And these were but a fraction of those clamoring to flee.

"We emphasize the importance of maintaining sanctions. Sanctions
were imposed to help us end the apartheid system. It is only logical that
we must continue to apply this form of pressure against the South
African government."[4]

That's Nelson Mandela addressing (and thanking) the Canadian parliament in June 1990 for imposing and championing economic sanctions against South Africa. Yet need I mention that for more than forty
years Canada has been Castro's most generous business partner? Need
I mention how Canada consistently bashes the United States for its
"counterproductive" policy of sanctions against Cuba?

"Sanctions which punish Cuba are anathema to the international
order to which we aspire." That's Nelson Mandela in September 1998
while decorating Fidel Castro with the "Order of Good Hope," South
Africa's highest civilian award. Yet probably no world figure is more
associated with economic sanctions than Nelson Mandela.

"For a long time our country stood alone on applying sanctions to
South Africa. Ultimately, we were on the right side of history." That's
Democratic senator Chris Dodd praising sanctions. "U.S. sanctions
against Cuba can only be thought of as bullying tactics by the world's
strongest superpower against a small nation." That's Senator Dodd
speaking at the National Press Club in September 2002.

"There is no acceptable justification for the trade embargo or the
diplomatic isolation of Cuba," writes former senator George McGovern.

"The economic boycott of Cuba is a failure." For thirty years he's been banging the drums against it. He includes, of course, the obligatory dismissal of those who fled Castro's tyranny: "I wouldn't let a handful of noisy Cuban exiles in south Florida dictate *our* Cuba policy."[5] (Emphasis mine.)

By the way, notice McGovern's use of "our." Call me overly sensitive, but he seems to imply that those "noisy Cuban exiles" (United States citizens like me) don't qualify as gen-you-wine Americans. Imagine the repercussions, the media and Democratic caterwauling, if, say, Trent Lott or Tom DeLay expressed similar sentiments about any other ethnic group in America.

George McGovern—a Presidential Medal of Freedom winner (awarded by Bill Clinton)—is a longtime fan of the great Fidel. McGovern says his frequent Cuban host is "very shy, sensitive, witty.... I frankly liked him."[6] The Cuban Maximum Leader first hosted his American admirer in 1975. In May 1977, the bedazzled McGovern wrote a travelogue of his visit in—where else?—the *New York Times*. Fidel took McGovern on an "impromptu" jeep ride into the countryside. Occasionally they stopped. "Everywhere we were surrounded by laughing children who obviously loved Fidel Castro!" wrote the rapt gentleman from South Dakota.[7]

Alas, McGovern's visit also had a practical and humanitarian purpose. "In my pocket," wrote McGovern, "I carried a letter from the Boston Red Sox pitcher Luis Tiant requesting that his parents be permitted to leave Havana to see him play in Boston.... Castro assured me this could be arranged," gushed McGovern.[8]

How touching. Some people might have asked themselves: What's wrong with this picture? Why should a "president" decide whether Luis Tiant's parents travel to see their son pitch in the United States? And why should I be praising one who does?

Today, McGovern tells us that economic sanctions are "unjustifiable" and "always fail." Fine, let's rewind to *your own* congressional voting record in the late 1970s, senator. Let's stop on your views regarding

Rhodesia, Chile, and Nicaragua. Very interesting indeed. Turns out, sir, that you thundered to impose sanctions against all three.

Liberal Democrats, it turns out are a lot like the Hollywood (and music industry) Left when it comes to double standards about Cuba.

Carole King sang her little heart out for John Kerry during campaign fund-raisers in 2004. Bonnie Raitt did too, after her first choice, Howard Dean, went screaming out of the primaries. Both Carole and Bonnie have also proudly played in Castro's Cuba. Carole went in February 2002 and serenaded the Maximum Leader with a heartfelt "You've Got a Friend." Bonnie Raitt visited in March 1999 and stopped hyperventilating just long enough to compose a song in Castro's honor, "Cuba Is Way Too Cool!" Among the lyrics: "It's just a happy little island!" and "Big bad wolf [that's us, folks, the United States] you look the fool!"[9]

With Woody Harrelson gyrating beside her, the rapidly oxidizing chanteuse—she of the big red hair and the famous gray roots—rasped out her ditty at Havana's Karl Marx Theater. The occasion was "Music Bridges Over Troubled Waters" back in March 1999.

"Rock Against Freedom" sounds much better to me. A beaming Jimmy Buffet came on after Bonnie. Then came Joan Osborne, REM's Peter Buck, and former Police-men Andy Summers and Stuart Copeland. In between crooning and strumming, these cheeky free spirits all dutifully recited their scripts against the "embargo." (How did Jackson Browne miss this?) Against South Africa a decade earlier, of course, their script called for an embargo. "I Ain't Gonna Play Sun City!" shouted Bonnie Raitt herself, alongside Bruce Springsteen, Bono, Darryl Hall, and scores of similar political imbeciles on the 1985 recording titled "Artists United Against Apartheid."

Frank Sinatra, Rod Stewart, and Julio Iglesias all caught hell from their industry peers for a gig at South Africa's Sun City resort in 1984. These entertainers' crime was daring to march out of step with the glitterati's buffooneries and hypocrisies. Because the fact is that their Sun City gig was at a privately owned and *unsegregated* resort. But that was different: South Africa wasn't Communist, and the glitterati prefer Communists.

Most of the five thousand clapping Cubans in the audience were Cuban Communist Party members and their families. And, of course, these pop stars will gladly play in Havana's Karl Marx Theater. They'll gladly entertain an audience dedicated to the most murderous ideology in human history. According to researcher Dr. Armando Lago, many in Bonnie Raitt's and Jimmy Buffet's *very audience* had a hand in 110,000 political murders of their own. Maybe these musical hipsters didn't know that, or know that Castro's Cuba has the highest emigration, incarceration, and suicide rates for young people on the face of the globe.

When Cuba's overall suicide rate reached twenty-four per thousand in 1986, it was *double* Latin America's average and *triple* Cuba's pre-Castro rate. Cuban women are now *the most suicidal in the world*, making death by suicide *the primary cause of death for Cubans aged fifteen to forty-eight*. The statistics got so embarrassing that the Cuban government ceased publishing them; they are now state secrets. But we also know that Cuba has the highest (or third highest; the sources differ) abortion rate in the world. The suicide and abortion rates smack of hopelessness and despair.[10]

And while Jimmy Buffet and Bonnie Raitt proudly sing to the Communist regime, I wonder if they know that owning a Beatles or Rolling Stones record in Cuba was a criminal offense or that effeminate behavior, or wearing blue jeans, or being a man with long hair meant the secret police could dump you in a concentration camp with WORK WILL MAKE MEN OUT OF YOU posted in bold letters above the gate and machine gunners posted on the watchtowers. The initials for these camps were UMAP, not GULAG.[11] But the conditions were identical. Like Margaritaville, there's a lot of "wasting away" in Cuba, but it happens behind barbed wire and from slave labor, disease, malnutrition, beatings, and torture.

After their performance for Castro's toadies, the rockers and hipsters were invited to a private reception to meet Fidel himself. Knees weakened, mouths gaped, hearts fluttered, skin tingled, mass incontinence threatened. "We completely lost our composure," squealed English songstress Ruth Merry. "As we lined up, an excited Andy Summers of the Police stood next to me with his copy of Castro's *History Will Absolve Me.* Andy was nervously contemplating asking Castro to sign it—but he finally did!...Here were all these huge stars, quaking with anticipation!...I lost any composure and degenerated into a heap of nervous giggling for the rest of the evening!"[12]

I'm losing my composure too, Ruthie dear.

"Castro was very gracious," said a Mr. Cripps of a group named Combo Bravo. "He was dressed in a suit and tie!" "Castro and Mr. Cripps spoke for a few minutes through a translator, and another man was present who knew just about everything there was to know about all of us. A detail of Cuban intelligence that Mr. Cripps found eerie," noted one of the news reports. "Eerie," Mr. Cripps? Let me assure you, sir, if you *lived* in Cuba this minor detail would provide more than a vicarious little jolt.

And you know how rockers and hipsters are always big on wearing red ribbons to show how much they care about AIDS? Well, Castro's Cuba cares too. His regime banishes AIDS patients to "sanatoriums" in the countryside, where they are basically left alone to die. "Left alone" is the key phrase here. Think about it, in the words of Kris Kristofferson himself, "Freedom's just another word for" *being left alone.*

Or so it seemed to some of Castro's subjects. Word got around. "You mean no secret police constantly snooping over my shoulder? You mean no waving a stupid little flag for hours in the plaza while the Maximum Gasbag spouts his idiocies? You mean, I can say what I want? Read what I want?" AIDS suddenly became a disease of choice in Cuba.

In a film titled *Cursed Be Your Name, Liberty,* Cuban exile Vladimir Ceballos exposes this grim and almost inconceivable episode. Back in the 1980s, young people in Cuba who listened (or tried to listen) to American rock music—to Bonnie Raitt, Carole King, and Jimmy Buffet—were called *roqueros* and were special targets of the police. They were constantly harassed, beaten, and jailed. Ceballos's film documents how more than one hundred of these *roqueros* deliberately injected themselves with the AIDS virus.

It sounds stupid, crazy, and horrible, I agree. But to these people, banishment to AIDS sanatoriums was a taste of freedom. One scene shows a *roquero* AIDS victim holding a small, crumpled American flag. With trembling hands, he scrubs it clean, then drapes it slowly across his emaciated chest. This man preferred death by inches, a lingering death of suppurating sores, constant pain, and eventual dementia to living under the rule of the man Carole King warmly serenaded with "You've Got a Friend." He gave himself AIDS because it bought him a few years of life in the equivalent of a U.S. federal prison. On Bonnie Raitt's "happy little island," he reckoned this as freedom.

Perhaps some of these *roqueros* are crazy, but are they all that different from the tens of thousands who risk death to paddle into the Florida straits on inner tubes, Styrofoam chunks, and rusty barrels? They know the odds: one in three of making landfall. Errant tides, storms, and tiger sharks await. And the kids who squeeze into the landing gear of transatlantic jets—they know where these planes fly, the altitude, the temperatures. But they see a 70 percent chance of death and a 30 percent chance of escape worth it.

Way too cool, indeed, Ms. Raitt. And Ms. King? You've got a helluva friend.

CHAPTER SIX

CASTRO'S MURDER, INCORPORATED

Rock stars, Democratic congressmen, the Hollywood Left, and the liberal media who tour Cuba usually miss some of the most famous revolutionary landmarks of their host Fidel. La Cabana fortress and its execution range aren't often on the itinerary, for instance. In January 1959, the gallant Che Guevara immediately identified the moat around La Cabana as a handy-dandy execution pit. Alas, it didn't serve very handily for burial purposes, and the job of dragging out the hundreds of bullet-shattered bodies soon proved troublesome and messy.

Not to worry! Again, Castroite ingenuity came to the fore. I defer to an eyewitness here. A prisoner in Castro's dungeons for fifteen years, Gustavo Carmona reported that "During the mid-1960s, when some prisoners were dragged out and bound to the wooden execution stake, a heavy nylon sack was brought up to their knees. Their shirts sported a black circle eight inches wide at the chest. After the volleys, the sack was pulled up over the prisoner's head and tied closed to contain the blood, brain, and bone fragments. Then it was dragged off. All very neat." Just like the recycling bags so favored by the environmental Left!

By mid-1961, the binding and blindfolding of Castro and Che's ene-mies wasn't enough. Castro's firing squads demanded that their victims be gagged too, because the shouts of the heroes they murdered badly spooked them. "Their yells, their defiance was a great inspiration. I'll never forget it," recalls Hiram Gonzalez, who banged his fists in help-less rage against the bars in his cell.[1]

While some prayed and others cursed, the executioners yanked the martyrs from their cells, bent their arms back, and bound their hands. Two more guards came into play. One grabbed the struggling victim's hair and jerked his head back, trying to steady him. The other taped his mouth shut.

In 1961 (the "year of the *paredón*," as the Castroites deemed it), a twenty-year-old boy named Tony Chao Flores took his place at the exe-cution stake, but he hobbled to it on crutches. Tony was a photogenic lad, a cover boy, in fact. In January 1959, his smiling face had been fea-tured on the cover of Cuba's *Bohemia* magazine (a sort of combination *Time-Newsweek-People*). In the photo, Tony's long blond hair dangled over his tanned face, almost to his green *gallego* eyes. His trademark smirk showed below. The señoritas all swooned over Tony.

Tony was actually a rebel at the time. He'd fought Batista too, but with a different rebel group from Castro. Still, he'd taken the rebels at their word. Let's face it; we're all idealists and a bit gullible at eighteen.

But within days of marching into Havana, Castro's deeds began to manifest something different from what the innocent idealists hoped for: mass jailings, mass robbery, firing squads. The Reds grabbed all newspapers, magazines, radio, and TV stations. They banned elections, strikes, private property, and free speech. Each dawn, from one end of the island to the other, Castro and Che's firing squads piled up the corpses of any who resisted, until fifteen thousand heroes were buried.

Tony Chao wasn't one to whimper. Soon he became a rebel against Castro, and a formidable one, employing the same M-1 carbine he had used against Batista. Sadly, the Reds had infiltrated Tony's group and captured some of his compadres in arms.

Employing interrogation techniques lovingly imparted by their East German Stasi and Russian KGB mentors, the security forces finally pinpointed Tony's hideout. Castro and Che's goons were closing in, and Tony sensed it. He knew they'd come in overwhelming numbers, heavily armed with Soviet weapons. "Those sons of bitches ain't never taking me alive!" Tony vowed to his freedom fighter brothers.

At dawn, Tony saw the Reds approaching his hideout and ran upstairs, the high ground, as it were. He grabbed his carbine and a pistol, piled up some ammo, and barricaded himself. The shooting started and turned into a furious firefight. Tony blasted away, casings piling around him, his gun barrel sizzling. He bagged two of Che's scumbags in the deafening fusillade. But he'd taken seventeen bullets from their Czech machine guns himself, mostly in his legs.

Reds have always been big on show trials, so they wanted Tony alive. They wanted to display him as a trophy, to humiliate him before the nation as an example of what happens to the enemies of Fidel. And alive they dragged him off. Tony was bleeding badly and contorted with pain, but he wouldn't shut up. Curses shot from his mouth like bullets from those machine guns. "Cowards!" he snarled at his Communist captors. "Fools!" he taunted. "Idiots! Traitors! Slaves! Eunuchs! Faggots! Sellouts!"

The Reds took Tony to a hospital and doctors patched him up—not completely, now, just enough to keep him alive until his trial. Then he was dumped in La Cabana's dungeons and fed just enough to keep him alive. A month later they went through the farce of a trial and the verdict—naturally—was death by firing squad.

On the way to the stake at the old Spanish fort-turned-prison-and-execution-ground, Tony was forced to hobble down some cobblestone stairs. Again, Tony pelted his captors with dreadful curses and stinging abuse. "Russian lackeys!" Tony yelled again as they dragged him off. "*Maricones!*"

Finally, a furious guard lost it. "*Cabrón!*" (You bastard.) He yanked Tony's crutch away while another gallant Commie kicked the crippled freedom fighter from behind. Tony tumbled down the long row of steps and finally lay on the cobblestones at the bottom, writhing and grimacing. One of Tony's bullet-riddled legs had been amputated at the hospital; the other was gangrened and covered in pus. The Castroite guards cackled as they moved in to gag Tony with their tape. Tony watched them approach while balling his good hand into a fist. Then as the first Red reached him—bash, a right across his eyes. The Castroite staggered back.

The other Castroite rushed towards Tony. Tony got a good grip on his crutch and smashed it into the Red scumbag's face. "*Cabrón!*"

"I'll never understand how Tony survived that beating," says eyewitness Hiram Gonzalez, who watched from his window on death row. The crippled Tony was almost killed in the kicking, punching, gun-bashing melee, but finally his captors stood off, panting, and rubbing their scrapes and bruises. They'd managed to tape the battered boy's mouth, but Tony pushed the guards away before they bound his hands. Their commander nodded, motioning for them to back off.

Now Tony crawled towards the splintered and blood-spattered execution stake about fifty yards away. He pushed and dragged himself with his hands. His stump of a leg left a trail of blood on the grass. As he neared the stake, he stopped and started pounding himself in the chest. His executioners were perplexed. The crippled boy was trying to say something.

Tony's blazing eyes and grimace said enough. But no one could understand the boy's mumblings. Tony shut his eyes tightly from the agony of the effort. His executioners shuffled nervously, raising and lowering their rifles. They looked toward their commander, who shrugged. Finally, Tony reached up to his face and ripped off the tape.

The twenty-year-old freedom fighter's voice boomed out. "Shoot me right here!" roared Tony at his gaping executioners. His voice thundered and his head bobbed with the effort. "Right in the chest!" Tony yelled. "Like a man!" Tony stopped and ripped open his shirt, pounding his chest and grimacing as his gallant executioners gaped and shuffled. "Right here!" he pounded.

On his last day alive, Tony had received a letter from his mother. "My dear son," she counseled. "How often I'd warned you not to get involved in these things. But I knew my pleas were vain. You always demanded your freedom, Tony, even as a little boy. So I knew you'd never stand for Communism. Well, Castro and Che finally caught you. Son, I love you with all my heart. My life is now shattered and will never be the same, but the only thing left now, Tony...is to die like a man."[2]

"*Fuego!*" Castro's lackey yelled the command and the bullets shattered Tony's crippled body, just as he'd reached the stake, lifted himself, and stared resolutely at his murderers. The legless Tony presented an awkward target, so some of the volleys went wild and missed the youngster. Time for the coup de grace.

Normally it's one .45 slug that shatters the skull. Eyewitnesses say Tony required three. Seems the executioners' hands were shaking pretty badly.

Compare Tony's death to the arch-swine, arch-weasel, and arch-coward Che Guevara's. "Don't shoot!" whimpered the arch-assassin to his captors. "I'm Che! I'm worth more to you alive than dead!"

Then ask yourselves: Whose face belongs on T-shirts worn by youth who fancy themselves rebellious, freedom-loving, and brave? Then fume and gag at the malignant stupidity of popular culture in our demented age.

Castro and Che were in their mid-thirties when they murdered Tony. Many (perhaps most) of those they had murdered were boys in their teens and early twenties. Carlos Machado and his twin brother, Ramón, were fifteen when they spat in the face of their Communist executioners. They died singing Cuba's old national anthem, cursing Che Guevara's Internationale. Their dad collapsed from the same volley alongside them.

Hiram Gonzalez was finally released from Castro's dungeons twenty years after the execution of Tony Chao Flores, and he could finally tell Tony's story. Enrique Encinosa's book *Unvanquished: Cuba's Resistance to Fidel Castro* gives a stirring roll call of the Cuban patriots murdered by the Castroites. When will liberals stopping fawning over the leader of Cuba's Murder, Incorporated? When will there be a concert—"Rock for Cuba Libre!"—where Tony Chao Flores's picture, rather than Che's or Fidel's, is the icon? When will Tony's story, or that of his fellow Cuban heroes, be made into a major Hollywood motion picture?

Instead, in January 2004, Robert Redford's film on Che Guevara, *The Motorcycle Diaries*, received much praise and a standing ovation at the Sundance Film Festival.[3] They say this was the only film so raptly received. I wonder how many of those applauding the film on Che Guevara oppose capital punishment, unlike Che himself, who used it against men like Tony Chao Flores? Are there any psychiatrists in the house?

CHAPTER SEVEN

FIDEL'S SIDEKICK: THE MOTORCYCLE DIARIST CHE GUEVARA

"No, no!" said the Queen. "Sentence first—verdict afterwards."
"Stuff and nonsense!" said Alice loudly. "The idea of having the sentence first!"
"Hold your tongue!" said the Queen, turning purple.
"I won't!" said Alice.
"Off with her head!" the Queen shouted at the top of her voice.[1]

They say Lewis Carroll was a serious dope fiend, his mind totally scrambled on opium, when he concocted Alice's Wonderland, a place where the sentence comes first and the verdict afterward. If only Carroll had lived long enough to visit Cuba in 1959.

"To send men to the firing squad, judicial proof is unnecessary," Carroll would have heard from the chief executioner, Che Guevara. "These procedures are an archaic bourgeois detail. This is a revolution. And a revolutionary must become a cold killing machine motivated by pure hate. We must create the pedagogy of the *paredón*!"[2]

"We don't need proof to execute a man—we only need proof that it's necessary to execute him. Our mission is not to provide judicial guarantees. Our mission is to make a revolution."[3]

For the first year of Castro's glorious revolution, the Argentine Ernesto "Che" Guevara was his main executioner, and he executed at a rate that would have done any rival Communist—or National Socialist—proud.

Nazi Germany became the modern standard for political evil even before World War II. Yet in 1938, according to both William Shirer and John Toland, the Nazi regime held no more than twenty thousand political prisoners. Political executions up to the time might have reached two thousand, and most of these were of renegade Nazis themselves who were killed during the "Night of the Long Knives." Another murderous episode, the *Kristallnacht*, which horrified civilized opinion worldwide, caused a grand total of ninety-one deaths. This in a nation of seventy million.

Cuba was a nation of 6.5 million people in 1959. Within three months in power, Castro and Che had shamed the Nazi prewar incarceration and murder rate. One defector claims that Che signed five hundred death warrants, another says more than six hundred. Cuban journalist Luis Ortega, who knew Che as early as 1954, writes in his book *Yo Soy El Che!* that Guevara sent 1,897 men to the firing squad. In his book *Che Guevara: A Biography*, Daniel James writes that Che himself admitted to ordering "several thousand" executions during the first few years of the Castro regime. For certain, the first three months of the Cuban revolution saw 568 firing squad executions—even the *New York Times* admits it—and the preceding "trials" shocked and nauseated all who witnessed them. They were shameless farces, sickening charades.

Vengeance—much less justice—was not the point behind Che's murderous method. Che's firing squads were a perfectly rational, cold-blooded exercise to decapitate—literally and figuratively—the first ranks of Cuba's Contras. Five years earlier, when he was a Communist hobo in Guatemala, Che had seen Guatemala's officer corps rise against the Red regime of Jacobo Arbenz, who fled to Czechoslovakia. Che didn't want to repeat that experience in Cuba. He wanted to cow and terrorize the Cuban people against resistance to the revolution. These were all public trials. And the executions, right down to the final shattering of the skull with a massive .45 slug fired at five paces, were public too. Guevara made it a policy for his men to parade the families and friends of the executed before the blood-, bone-, and brain-spattered *paredón*.

The Red Terror had come to Cuba. "We will make our hearts cruel, hard, and immovable. . . . We will not quiver at the sight of a sea of enemy blood. Without mercy, without sparing, we will kill our enemies in scores of thousands; let them drown themselves in their own blood! Let there be floods of the blood of the bourgeois—more blood, as much as possible." That was Felix Dzerzhinsky, the head of the Soviet Cheka in 1918.

This is from Che Guevara's *Motorcycle Diaries*, the very diaries just made into a heartwarming film by Robert Redford: "Crazy with fury I will stain my rifle red while slaughtering any enemy that falls in my hands! My nostrils dilate while savoring the acrid odor of gunpowder and blood. With the deaths of my enemies I prepare my being for the sacred fight and join the triumphant proletariat with a bestial howl." Seems that Redford omitted this inconvenient portion of Che's diaries from his touching film.

The "acrid odor of gunpowder and blood" never reached Guevara's nostrils from actual combat. It always came from the close-range murder of bound, gagged, and blindfolded men. He was a true Chekist. "Always interrogate your prisoners at night," Che commanded his prosecutorial goons. "A man is easier to cow at night; his mental resistance is always lower."

Che specialized in psychological torture. Many prisoners were yanked out of their cells, bound, blindfolded, and stood against the wall. The seconds ticked off. The condemned could hear the rifle bolts snapping, and finally, "*Fuego!*"

Blam! But the shots were blanks. In his book *Tocayo*, Cuban freedom fighter Tony Navarro describes how he watched a man returned to his cell after such an ordeal. He'd left bravely, grim-faced as he shook hands with his fellow condemned. He came back mentally shattered, curling up in a corner of the squalid cell for days.[4]

Che's judicial models were Lenin, Dzerzhinsky, and Stalin. As they had used terror and mass executions, so did he. As they conducted show trials, so did he.

But in actual combat, his imbecilities defy belief. Cuban American fighters who faced Che at the Bay of Pigs and later in the Congo still laugh. The Bay of Pigs invasion plan included a ruse in which a CIA squad dispatched three rowboats off the coast of western Cuba (350 miles from the true invasion site) loaded with time-release Roman candles, bottle rockets, mirrors, and a tape recording of battle sounds.

The wily Che immediately deciphered the imperialist scheme. That little feint three hundred miles away at the Bay of Pigs was a transparent ruse! The real invasion was coming here in Pinar del Rio! Che stormed over with several thousand troops, dug in, locked, loaded, and waited for the "Yankee/mercenary" attack. His men braced themselves as the sparklers, smoke bombs, and mirrors did their stuff just offshore.

Three days later the (literal) smoke and mirror show expended itself and Che's men marched back to Havana. Not surprisingly, the masterful warrior had managed to wound himself in this heated battle against a tape recorder. A bullet had pierced his chin and excited above his temple, just missing his brain. The scar is visible in all post–April 1961 pictures of the gallant Che (the picture we see on posters and T-shirts was shot a year earlier.)

Cuban novelist Guillermo Cabrera Infante, a Fidelista at the time, speculates the wound might have come from a botched suicide attempt.[5] No way! snort Che hagiographers John Lee Anderson, Carlos Castaneda, and Paco Taibo. They insist it was an accident, Che's own pistol going off just under his face. So it was either a suicide attempt or ineptitude.

Later, many Cuban American Bay of Pigs vets itched to get back into the fight against the Communists (but with ammo and air cover this time). The CIA obliged and sent them with ex-marine Rip Robertson to the Congo in 1965. There they linked up with the legendary mercenary "Mad Mike" Hoare and his "Wild Geese." Here's Mike Hoare's opinion—after watching them in battle—of the Cuban American CIA troops: "These Cuban-CIA men were as tough, dedicated and impetuous a group of soldiers as I've ever had the honor of commanding. Their leader [Rip Robertson] was the most extraordinary and dedicated soldier I've ever met."[6]

Together Mad Mike, Rip, and the freedom-loving Cubans made short work of the alternately Chinese- and Soviet-backed "Simbas" of Laurent Kabila, who were murdering, raping, and munching (many were cannibals) their way through the defenseless Europeans still left in the recently abandoned Belgian colony.

Castro, itching to be rid of Che, sent him (codenamed "Tatu") and a force of his rebel army "veterans" to help the Congolese cannibals and Communists. The masterful Tatu's first order of business was plotting an elaborate ambush on a garrison guarding a hydroelectric plant at Front Bendela on the Kimbi River in eastern Congo. The wily Tatu stealthily led his force into position when they heard shots. Whoops! Hey! What the . . . ! The garrison Tatu thought was guarding the plant ambushed the ambushers. Che lost half his men and barely escaped with his life.[7]

The brilliant Tatu and his comandantes got a second chance to fight the mad dogs of imperialism at a place called Fizi Baraka in the eastern Congo, where his men had mountainous high ground, perfect defensive positions, and a ten to one advantage in men. Mad Mike and his CIA allies sized the place up and attacked. Within one day, the mighty Che's entire force was scrambling away in panic, throwing away their arms, running and screaming like old ladies with rats running up their legs. Don't take my word for it, take Che's—and the BBC's: "Che Gue-vara's seven-month stay in the Fizi Baraka mountains was, as he admits himself, an 'unmitigated disaster.'"[8]

One of the most hilarious and enduring hoaxes of the twentieth cen-tury was the "war" fought by dauntless Che and the Castro rebels against Batista. But I hear it was a kick—a fun way for adolescents to harass adults, loot, rustle a few cows, and play army on weekends with real guns, maybe even getting off a few shots, usually into the air. What seventeen-or eighteen-year-old male could resist? Petty delinquency became not just altruism here, but downright heroism. How many punks get such a window of glory? Normally these stunts land you in reform school. In Cuba in 1958, it might get your picture in the *New York Times*.

Here's an insider account of one such "battle," from "Comandante" William Morgan, as recounted to Paul Bethel, who was the press attaché at the American embassy in Cuba in 1959. Bethel describes "Comandante" Morgan recalling the ruse with "great merriment." "It was all a tremendous propaganda play.... We broadcast fake battle commands [using a short-wave radio], directed fictitious troops here and there, and had a helluva time.... For background noises we used Browning automatics, rifles and pistols.... We yelled a lot too."[9]

Here's another insider account from Bethel's superb and meticu-lously researched book *The Losers: The Definitive Report, by an Eyewit-ness, of the Communist Conquest of Cuba and the Soviet Penetration in Latin America*. This one features Che and his invincible "column" on their long march through Las Villas province: "Guevara's column shuffled right into the U.S. agricultural experimental station in Camagüey. Gue-vara asked manager Joe McGuire to have a man take a package to Batista's military commander in the city. The package contained $100,000 with a note. Guevara's men moved through the province almost within sight of uninterested Batista troops."[10]

This was part of the famous "Battle of Santa Clara" where Che earned his eternal fame. The *New York Times* of January 4, 1959, cov-ered this same "battle" and reported: "One Thousand Killed in 5 Days of Fierce Street Fighting. . . . Commander Che Guevara appealed to Batista troops for a truce to clear the streets of casualties. . . . Guevara turned the tide in this bloody battle and whipped a Batista force of 3,000 men."

All baloney, by the way. Statistically speaking, a nocturnal stroll through Central Park offers more peril than Castro's rebels faced from the dreaded army of the beastly Fulgencio Batista. According to Bethel, the U.S. embassy was a little skeptical about all the reports of battle-field bloodshed and rebel heroics and investigated. They ran down every reliable lead and eyewitness account of what the *New York Times* called a "bloody civil war with thousands dead in single battles." The embassy report found that in the countryside, in those two years of "ferocious" battles, the total casualties on both sides actually ran to 182.[11] New Orleans has an annual murder rate double that.

But to give them credit, most of Castro's comandantes—if not the *New York Times*—knew their Batista war had been a gaudy clown show. After the glorious victory, they were content to run down and execute the few Batista men motivated enough to shoot back (most of these were of humble background), settle into the mansions stolen from Batistianos, and enjoy the rest of their booty.

But Che's pathological power of self-delusion wouldn't allow him to do this. And he paid the price. When Che tried his hand at a guer-rilla war not against unmotivated Batistaites, but in Africa, where peo-ple actually shot back and everything, he was run out with his tail between his legs within months. Then, in Bolivia, he and his merry band of bumblers were betrayed, encircled, and wiped out in short order.

Here's a "guerrilla hero" who in real life never fought in a guerrilla war. When he finally brushed up against one, he was routed. Here's a cold-blooded murderer who executed thousands without trial, who claimed that judicial evidence was an "unnecessary bourgeois detail," who stressed that "revolutionaries must become cold killing machines motivated by pure hate," who stayed up till dawn for months at a time signing death warrants for innocent and honorable men, whose office in La Cabana had a window where he could watch the executions—and today he is a hero to the Hollywood and college campus Left.

Here's Communist Cuba's first "minister of industries," whose main slogan in 1960 was "accelerated industrialization," whose dream was converting Cuba (and the Western Hemisphere, actually) into a huge bureaucratic-industrial ant farm—and he's the poster boy for greens and anarchists who rant against industrialization.

Here's a sniveling little suck-up, teacher's pet, and mama's boy (his parents were limousine Bolsheviks), who was a humorless teetotaler, a plodding paper-pusher, a notorious killjoy, and all-around fuddy-duddy. In 1961, Che established a special concentration camp at Guanacabibes in extreme western Cuba for "delinquents" whose "delinquency" involved drinking, vagrancy, disrespect for authorities, laziness, and playing loud music—and yet you see his T-shirt on MTV's Spring Break revelers.

The only thing Che excelled at was the mass murder of defenseless men. Just as in 1940, when Stalin's commissars rounded up captured Polish officers, herded them into the Katyn Forest, and slaughtered them to a man, so Che tried to track down former Cuban army officers—and anyone else whose loyalty was suspect—and slaughter them to a man. Che's true legacy is simply one of terror and murder. That dreaded midnight knock; wives and daughters screaming in fear and panic as Che's goons drag off their dads and husbands; desperate crowds of weeping daughters and shrieking mothers clubbed with rifle butts outside La Cabana as Che's firing squads murder their dads and sons inside; thousands of heroes yelling at the firing squads "*Viva Cuba Libre!*" and "*Viva Christo Rey!*"; mass burials, secret graves, and sometimes crude boxes with bullet-riddled corpses delivered to ashen-faced loved ones.

When the wheels of justice finally turned, and Che was captured in Bolivia, he was revealed as unworthy to carry his victims' slop buckets: "Don't shoot! I'm Che! I'm worth more to you alive than dead!"[12] He had learned nothing from the bravery of the Cuban patriots he'd murdered. The champagne corks popped in Cuban American households when we got the wonderful news of Che's death in October 1967. Yes, our own compatriots serving proudly in the U.S. Special Forces had helped track down the murderous, cowardly, and epically stupid little weasel named Che Guevara in Bolivia. Justice has never been better served.

The writings he left behind are turgid gibberish, only underlining that he went through life with a perpetual scowl. Food, drink, good cheer, bonhomie, roistering, fellowship—Guevara recoiled from these like Dracula from a cross. "I have no home, no woman, no parents, no children, no brothers. My friends are friends only so long as they think as I do politically."[13] As a professional duty, I tortured myself with Che Guevara's writings. I finished glassy-eyed, dazed, almost catatonic. Nothing written by a first-year philosophy major (or a Total Quality Management guru) could be more banal, jargon-ridden, depressing, or idiotic. A specimen: "The past makes itself felt not only in the individual consciousness—in which the residue of an education systematically oriented toward isolating the individual still weighs heavily—but also through the very character of this transition period in which commodity relations still persist, although this is still a subjective aspiration, not yet systematized.[14]

Slap yourself and let's continue: "To the extent that we achieve concrete successes on a theoretical plane—or, vice versa, to the extent that we draw theoretical conclusions of a broad character on the basis of our concrete research—we will have made a valuable contribution to Marxism-Leninism, and to the cause of humanity."

Splash some cold water on your face and stick with me for just a little more: "It is still necessary to deepen his conscious participation, individual and collective, in all the mechanisms of management and production, and to link this to the idea of the need for technical and ideological education, so that we see how closely interdependent these processes are and how their advancement is parallel. In this way he will reach total consciousness of his social being, which is equivalent to his full realization as a human creature, once the chains of alienation are broken."

Throughout his diaries Che whines about deserters from his "guerrilla" ranks (bored adolescents, petty crooks, and winos playing army on the weekend). Can you blame them? Imagine sharing a campfire with some yo-yo droning on and on about "subjective aspirations not yet systematized" and "closely interdependent processes and total consciousness of social being"—and who also reeked like a polecat (foremost among the bourgeois debouchments disdained by Che were baths).

These hapless "deserters" were hunted down like animals, trussed up, and brought back to a dispassionate Che, who put a pistol to their heads and blew their skulls apart without a second thought. After days spent listening to Che and smelling him, perhaps this meant relief.

Who can blame Fidel for ducking into the nearest closet when this yo-yo came calling? Call Fidel everything in the book (as I have) but don't call him stupid. Guevara's inane twaddle must have driven him nuts. The one place where I can't fault Fidel, the one place I actually empathize with him, is in his craving to rid himself of this insufferable Argentine jackass.

That Che's Bolivian mission was clearly suicidal was obvious to anyone with half a brain. Fidel and Raul weren't about to join him down there, but were happy to see him go. Two months later he was dead. Bingo! Fidel scored another bull's-eye. He rid himself of the Argentine nuisance and his glorious revolution had a handsome young martyr for the adulation of imbeciles worldwide. Nice work.

Che Guevara was monumentally vain and epically stupid. He was shallow, boorish, cruel, and cowardly. He was full of himself, a consummate fraud and an intellectual vacuum. He was intoxicated with a few vapid slogans, spoke in clichés, and was a glutton for publicity. But ah! He did come out nice in a couple of publicity photos, high cheekbones and all. And we wonder why he's a hit in Hollywood.

CHAPTER EIGHT

CUBA BEFORE CASTRO

In 1955, a murderer and terrorist was in a Cuban jail. I'll let the prisoner himself, Fidel Castro, describe a Batista-era jail: "I feel like I'm on vacation!" No one ever got the same impression from one of Castro's jails. It gets even better: "Tonight it's angel hair pasta with calamari in red sauce and some Italian chocolates for dinner followed by an excellent cigar. Tomorrow morning I'll be in the courtyard again lying in a lounge chair in my shorts feeling the sea breeze in my face. Sometimes I think I'm on vacation."[1]

Funny how the liberal media, which regularly ignores Castro's gulag of torture and executions, invented a Batista that Castro wouldn't recognize. "Batista murdered thousands," wrote the incomparable Herbert Matthews in the *New York Times* in 1957, "usually after torture."

The *Chicago Tribune*'s Jules Dubois was more prosaic: "The Cuban dictator [Batista] is an egomaniac, a man of greed, a sadist. He crushes everyone who is an obstacle in his path. He orders the persecution, torture, assassination, and exile of his obstructionists. He directs the thought control of the entire population and insists upon the deification of his person and his relatives. He instills fear and total subjugation among his subordinates. He purges the judiciary to destroy the independence of the courts. He operates a police state with censorship of all media and limitless spies."[2]

Then the sagacious Dubois caps it: "It was not until Fidel Castro came along that the people of Cuba found the leader to fight for their lost liberty." Actually, it was not until Fidel Castro that inner tubes (for rafts) and ping-pong paddles (for oars) became the hottest items on Cuba's black market—or that Cuba even needed a black market. It was not until Fidel Castro that Cuba experienced the highest rate of emigration, per capita, of any nation in the Western Hemisphere in the twentieth century. It was not until Fidel Castro that the police state painted by Dubois became a reality.

But from the *New York Times* to the *Los Angeles Times*, from CBS to CNN, from Harvard to Berkeley, liberal pundits and professors all assert that pre-Castro Cuba was a pesthole of grinding poverty, oppression, and hopelessness.

Colin Barraclough of Toronto's *Globe and Mail* epitomizes these scribbling donkeys. "Fulgencio Batista presided over one of the most blood-soaked and corrupt, yet frighteningly successful, regimes of the century. Supported by an army of thugs and torturers, and aided by American mobster Meyer Lansky, Batista built an island of fantasy dedicated to the seven deadly sins. Batista's thugs protected their patch with sadistic pleasure—the bodies of those who objected to the corruption or the opulence were often found hanging from lamp posts. By the late 1950s, an evening out could be a disturbing experience. Your driver could turn around at a stoplight and show you photos of bodies bloodied with bullets and young faces ripped apart by tortures so savage that the daiquiris, the sweet roast pork, the yummy yams, the fine Havanas, the hot sex, nothing tasted good any more." Barraclough wrote this in 2004. Not content with denouncing Batista's Cuba, the rest of the article promotes travel and trade to Castro's Cuba.

Just a reminder: Batista's Cuba had the second highest per capita income in Latin America (higher than Austria's or Japan's) as well as net immigration (in 1958, for example, the Cuban embassy in Rome had applications from twelve thousand Italians for immigrant visas).[3] Castro's Cuba, on the other hand, has the highest political incarceration rate on earth (as of 1995, 500,000 prisoners had passed through Castro's gulag, according to the human rights organization Freedom House.[4] Given Cuba's population, Castro incarcerated at a higher rate than Stalin and is shunned even by Haitian refugees. But the only shortcoming of Castro's Cuba, according to the *Globe and Mail*, is that "All car-rental companies are state owned and rates are exorbitant." And, of course, the *Globe and Mail* criticizes the American trade "embargo."

Leftists just love how Castro has transformed Cuba, no matter what it's done to the Cubans. Armando Valladares, who served twenty-two years in Castro's dungeons before President Ronald Reagan appointed him U.S. ambassador to the UN Human Rights Commission, wrote:

> What shocked me the most about United Nations politics during my time there was the double standard of many governments. One of the most glaring examples was the attitude of the Spanish government under the leadership of Socialist president Felipe González. While I was in Geneva, friends in Spain sent me a copy of a confidential report on the violation of human rights in Cuba, prepared in secret by the Spanish Chancery itself. This report documented systematic torture, crimes, and cruel, inhumane and degrading treatment of Cuban political prisoners, including religious persecutions. But the Spanish foreign ministry's official document concluded by stating: "But even so, we cannot condemn Castro because that would be proving the Americans right."

"A week before this report was leaked to the Spanish press," continues Valladares, "the Spanish Chancery issued a statement declaring that Spain did not believe that Cuba had human rights problems."[5]

Here you have it, friends. Castro gets away with his wholesale butcheries, lies, repression, and terrorism because for half a century now, his bearded and military-clad figure has symbolized anti-Americanism in its most virulent—hence appealing—form.

But a few facts: Back in the bad old Batista days, so many hundreds of thousands of Spaniards sought immigration to Cuba that flustered Cuban officials finally imposed *quotas* to stem this flood of Europeans wanting to live in Cuba. From 1910 to 1953, Cuba took in more than one million Spanish immigrants (along with 65,000 immigrants from the United States)—and Cuba's population in 1950 was only 5.8 million.[6] Here's another fact that explains all the immigration: In 1958, Cuba had almost double Spain's per capita income. Quite a contrast from Castro's paradise. And how about this: Today, Spain's two biggest retail chains are owned (and were started) by Cuban exiles.

Here's something else: When the right-wing Spanish dictator Francisco Franco died in 1975, Fidel announced a national holiday—in honor of Franco, not in enmity. Something that many leftists don't acknowledge is that Castro has stayed true to his fascist roots. Indeed, leftists like José "Pepe" Figueres of Costa Rica and Romulo Betancourt of Venezuela were Castro's first and bitterest enemies in Latin America. They were socialists, all right—but they were pro-American socialists, hence instant foes. Franco, a genuine fascist with the blood of tens of thousands of Communists on his hands, was an instant friend, because of Spanish anti-Americanism.

All of this is no apology for Batista. Cuba's prosperity (higher per capita income than Austria or Ireland, *double* Japan's), its civil institutions (including a completely independent judiciary), and its free, vibrant, and sassy press were in spite of having a political hoodlum at the helm. But Batistiano *political* rule was benevolent compared to Fidelista *everything* rule.

Cuban Americans hear Batista compared to Castro in practically every political conversation: "Hey, both were dictators, right? And Cuba was horribly poor and exploited back then, right? So what's the big deal? At least now the people have pride, free health care, free education..."

"At first I'd want to tear my hair out!" That's Manuel Márquez-Sterling. His father, Carlos, helped write Cuba's constitution in 1940 and was considered by many Cubans and by U.S. ambassador Earl Smith as the winner of Cuba's last presidential election, in November 1958. Then Batista's people got hold of the ballots and declared Batista the winner. The U.S. embassy conducted its own investigation and considered Carlos Márquez-Sterling the legitimate winner. So did Fidel Castro, who'd threatened to assassinate Carlos several times unless he withdrew his name from contention (he didn't).

Castro knew damn well Márquez-Sterling would win. And he knew damn well this would blow Castro's scheme of filling Cuba's political power vacuum as the only "viable alternative to Batista." (This Castroite fable is still nearly ubiquitous among Cuban "scholars.") Having failed to intimidate Márquez-Sterling and botching a couple of assassination attempts against him, Castro's armed goons simply rounded up all the ballots at gunpoint and burned them. So there, Márquez-Sterling, said the Castroites. See? We won anyway.

Márquez-Sterling was Batista's best known and most vociferous political enemy in Cuba. His son Manuel was himself roughed up by Batista's police. He bristles at the equation of Batista with Castro. "The comparison is ludicrous, preposterous, completely idiotic. It's not even a case of apples and oranges. It's grapes to watermelons. I'm a retired college professor. I dealt with some of America's best-educated people. And I'd hear this outrageous idiocy repeatedly.

"Look, I finally said to all my students, faculty, cohorts, and friends. You find me a country—and not just in Latin America, but anywhere— that in its first fifty years of independence climbed to the world's top 10 percent in almost every socioeconomic indicator, as Cuba did. Go ahead, show me one.

"In the late 1950s, Cuba had a *political* problem, not a socioeconomic one. Overall, Cuba was rich, her people healthy and well-educated.

The Cuban peso was always on par with the U.S. dollar. Cuba's gold reserves covered its monetary reserves to the last penny. But that's only half the story, because Cuban labor laws were among the most advanced in the world. Cuban labor got a higher percentage of the national GNP than in Switzerland at the time.

"And regarding that vaunted Castroite health care we hear and read about constantly, in 1957, Cuba's infant mortality rate was the *lowest* in Latin America and the thirteenth lowest *in the world*, for heaven's sake! Cuba ranked ahead of France, Belgium, West Germany, Israel, Japan, Austria, Italy, Spain, and Portugal in that department. Now (and using Castro's own inflated figures) it's *twenty-fourth in the world*. And this with 60.4 percent of Cuba's pregnancies ending in abortion (which skews infant mortality rates downward). In 1957, Cuba had twice as many physicians and teachers in relation to population as the U.S. It ranked first in Latin America in national income invested in education and its literacy rate was 80 percent. In 1958, Cuba even had more female college graduates (to scale) than the U.S.

"Before Fidel, Cubans were already among the healthiest and best-educated people in the world—and it didn't require Hitler-level political executions and Stalin-level gulags to achieve. Back in the mid-1960s, my father, a Cuban scholar and political figure of wide reputation, the man who would have been Cuba's president with honest elections, wrote a manuscript seeking to set the record straight about the Cuban revolution. In it, he stressed many of the things I've just catalogued. Well, no U.S. publisher would *touch* it.

"But the president of one of America's biggest, most prestigious publishing houses at the time (a man who had never been in Cuba, by the way), had the courtesy to respond to my father in a curt rejection letter. 'Mr. Márquez-Sterling,' he wrote, 'You certainly have peculiar notions about Cuba.'

"So here's an American who got all his information about Cuba from Herbert Matthews of the *New York Times*, Jules Dubois of the *Chicago Tribune*, and Jack Paar, responding this way to the man who had lived

in Cuba his entire life, whose family had been involved in Cuban politics for two centuries, who helped draft the Cuban constitution of 1940,
and who probably won her last elections!

"Like I said, given the wholesale ignorance—let's be polite and call
it that—on Cuban matters, given the enormous success of Castro's propaganda offensive on these matters—you want to pull your hair out
sometimes!"

Well put, Mr. Márquez-Sterling. I know *exactly* what you mean. It
reminds me of my old college history prof, Dr. Stephen Ambrose:
"Castro threw out an SOB and liberated Cuba." Liberated Cuba from
what? There were no ration cards or food shortages under Batista.

There was no totalitarian control of the media. I'll quote a U.S. State
Department document here: "It is no exaggeration to state that during
the 1950s, the Cuban people were among the most informed in the
world, living in an uncharacteristically large media market for such a
small country. Cubans had a choice of fifty-eight daily newspapers during the late 1950s, according to the UN statistical yearbook." It is true
that newspaper articles were occasionally subject to modifications at
Batista's behest. More seriously, as in the case of Manuel Márquez-
Sterling, some of Cuba's cheekier reporters were occasionally jailed or
manhandled by Batista goons. But Batista's censorship was an on-again,
off-again type of thing.

Batista didn't control what Cubans learned in school. He didn't
decide who they worshiped, what they earned, where they traveled or
emigrated. Recall Jeane Kirkpatrick's book *Dictatorships and Double
Standards*, in which she distinguishes authoritarian from totalitarian
rule: "Authoritarian regimes do not disturb the habitual rhythms of
work and leisure, habitual places of residence, habitual patterns of family and personal relations.... Totalitarian regimes claim that the state
has jurisdiction over the whole of society—that includes religion and
family, the economy. The real point is that totalitarian regimes have
claimed jurisdiction over the whole person, and the whole society, and
they don't at all believe that we should give unto Caesar that which is

Caesar's and unto God that which is God's. They believe that everything is Caesar's—the government should claim it and control it."

Well, Batista probably didn't even qualify as *authoritarian*. He was
certainly no Franco or Pinochet, or even a Stroessner or Peron. (Had he
been, had he extinguished Castro's rebels like a true dictator, Miami
jukeboxes today would feature more Tanya Tucker than Gloria Estefan.)

The first two presidents I mentioned above (Franco and Pinochet)
were professional military men. Batista, though a "general" (self-
appointed), is said to have disliked military trappings. He'd made it
legitimately to sergeant in Cuba's pre-1933 professional military. He
merited that. Chances are he'd have made colonel, perhaps even general, on genuine merit. But his heart wasn't in it.

Batista joined the military, like so many others of his humble social
stratum in Cuba, as a means to get ahead in life, to get an education,
and to have a job. But Batista's true calling was politics. "I think you'll
find him a likable individual despite what others may have told you,"
Eisenhower told Earl Smith upon his appointment to ambassador in
the summer of 1957.[7]

Batista's first coup in 1933, known as the "Sergeants' Revolt," dis-
banded and demoralized Cuba's professional military, replacing much
of the professional officer corps with a new crop of self-appointed
"colonels" and "generals." This bunch was much better versed in political guile, corruption, and the third degree for political enemies than
in any of the military basics and virtues. A professional military would
have come in handy in 1958, but Cuba didn't have one.

President Batista always went out of his way to be photographed in
civilian clothes in a family setting. He was scrupulous in keeping his
uncouth military and police operatives well behind the scenes, and was
rarely seen with them in public. "Batista never wanted to be a black soldier," wrote Cuban journalist Gastón Baquero, himself black and
employed by Cuba's oldest and most aristocratic newspaper, *El Diario
de la Marina*. "Instead, Batista always longed to be a white *caballero*
[gentleman]."

The mulatto sergeant-become-president Fulgencio Batista always studiously avoided the "caudillo" image. That was for President Trujillo in the neighboring Dominican Republic, for President Pérez Jiménez in Venezuela, for President Rojas Pinillas in Colombia, and all the rest. Cuba was different from the rest of Latin America. It was more North American culturally, commercially, and—as Batista was desperate to prove—politically. Batista wanted to put up a respectable, democratic image.

Batista was mostly self-educated. He read voraciously and was always boning up on his English. He kept a bust of Abraham Lincoln in his office and a home in Daytona Beach. When Ike refused him exile in the United States he was hurt, but—as a shrewd and seasoned politician himself—he "understood the reasoning." All who knew Fulgencio Batista say he genuinely yearned to be a popular, democratically elected leader, which he'd actually been from 1940 to 1944.

Batista, de facto head of Cuba after his coup in 1933, voluntarily relinquished his post in 1940 and presented himself as a candidate in Cuba's presidential election that year. He won handily in what American observers described as scrupulously clean elections.

Another interesting fact: In 1940, at a time when Cuba's population was almost 70 percent white, Cuba's people elected a *black* president, one who'd been born to former slaves in a palm-leaf shack with dirt floors. Cuba's aristocracy still scorned Batista. As president, he was denied entry into the exclusive Havana Yacht Club.

Race was a factor in Cuba's revolution. When Batista's soldiers captured some of Castro's men who tried to invade Cuba from Mexico in 1956, they exclaimed "*Son blancos!*" (Hey, they're whites!) "Get them!" Many or most of Batista's soldiers were black and practically all of Castro's rebels were white.

"You're from the Georgia? Good! I really like your treatment of blacks up there. Down here all blacks are *marijuaneros* [marijuana smokers, dope fiends] or Batistianos." This was a July 26 Movement's (Castro's group) operative talking. He was signing up an American volunteer named Neil McCauley for Castro's rebel force in 1958.

Castro's regime replaced a government where Cuban blacks served as president of the senate, minister of agriculture, chief of the army, and as head of state.[8] Nowadays Cuba's jail population is 80 percent black, its governmental hierarchy 100 percent white. Only 10 percent of the Communist Party's central committee is black (and Cuba's most prominent political prisoner, Oscar Biscet, is black). In April 2003, three black Cubans "hijacked" a ferry and tried to escape to Florida. They were captured, given a summary trial, and executed by firing squads. Castro responded to the outrage of Cuban exiles with, "What's all this fuss about me shooting three little negritos?"[9]

"I never saw a black face on my official three-day tour of Cuba," says talk-radio host and columnist Lowell Ponte. "And that was a Potemkin tour back in 1977. I was a visiting journalist for the *Los Angeles Times*. Surely you'd think they'd try to snow me—like they snow so many others? Problem was, they were showing me around only to high government officials—and the Communists simply couldn't find one who was black!

"But finally they dragged one out. He was a principal at a school, where the little kids, after their Communist indoctrination, all went to work in a battery factory where their hands and arms were all exposed repeatedly to acid. . . . Try this any place else in the world and we'd have Oprah, Katie, Eleanor Clift, Rosie, the whole bunch, up in arms about 'child labor, child slavery.' Castro, naturally, gets away with it."

The corruption and sporadic brutality of Batista's regime rankled Cuba's middle and upper classes. "We didn't care who overthrew Batista as long as somebody overthrew Batista," said pre-Castro Cuba's wealthiest man, Julio Lobo. "I'll take complete chaos over Batista's rule." Lobo owned fourteen sugar mills, several Cuban banks, and Havana's baseball team. He said this while being interviewed by British historian Hugh Thomas. In the late 1950s, Lobo bankrolled Castro's July 26 Movement (perhaps partly as protection money to keep Castro's "guerrillas" from burning his cane fields and blowing up his sugar mills). Three months after Batista's overthrow, Lobo presented Castro's government, in a public ceremony, with a check for $450,000 as a goodwill gesture (or perhaps as more protection money against the confiscation affecting many of his competitors).

Exactly one year after this gesture of revolutionary goodwill, Lobo received a request on government stationery from the new head of Cuba's national bank, the noted economist Che Guevara. The legendary revolutionary wanted a word with the legendary businessman. At the midnight meeting, Guevara offered Lobo a government post as minister of agriculture. As a perk, Lobo could keep *one* of his fourteen mills and even his house. See? Guevara smirked. So much for those rumors about me as some rigid Marxist ideologue!

Julio Lobo asked for a day to think it over. He scooted out of Cuba the following night, without even packing a toothbrush. Castro and Che's offers were often the kind you couldn't refuse.

"We know now that Castro was trained as a Communist in 1946 and 1947 in the Russian embassy in Cuba." This was Julio Lobo in exile, giving the commencement speech to LSU's graduating class in 1963 (he was an alumnus). "We now know that Castro was sent to Bogotá to disrupt the Conference of Prime Ministers in 1948, where he took a very sinister participation, killing with his own hands several people.... Books give so many details about Castro's Communist activities during that period that it is incredible that he was not only not prevented but actually aided and abetted in the process of taking over Cuba.

"It is noteworthy that the laborers and peasants whom Castro purported to save always maintained a stony indifference to Castro's summons for a general strike. It was the idealistic bourgeois and the intellectuals who were what Khrushchev called 'useful idiots' who assisted and helped unwittingly the Communist takeover."

Lobo's audience included several Cuban exile students perfectly familiar with his record. LSU always held a sizable contingent of Cuban students, who often attended LSU to study chemical engineering for careers in Cuba's sugar mills. One of these students in the audience was my cousin, who told me that he and his fellow exiles applauded politely, but they all knew Lobo was one of the "useful idiots."

Another useful idiot was José "Pepin" Bosch, owner of Bacardi, another huge Cuban company—until Castro snatched its properties and the Boschs fled and refounded Bacardi in Puerto Rico. Bosch had backed and financed Castro's movement throughout the late 1950s—possibly with even *more* lucre than the shrewd and crafty Julio Lobo.

Early in the Cuban "rebellion," the United States government sent a "fact-finding mission" headed by CIA officer (and liberal) Lyman Kirkpatrick to Oriente province. The U.S. ambassador to Cuba, Arthur Gardner, had reported that Castro had Communist leanings. The pro-Castro Boschs were eager to convince Kirkpatrick otherwise, so the Bacardi folks became the "fact-finders'" hosts and guides. They made sure Kirkpatrick's men met all the "right people." Among them was an elegant young lady who spoke flawless English, Vilma Espin. "We only want," she told the shrewd CIA fact-finders, "what you Americans have: clean politics and a clean police system."[10] Lyman Kirkpatrick seemed highly impressed with Espin's credentials as a Cuban democrat. Unfortunately, Vilma Espin was a rabid (but secret) Communist Party member. Two years later, she married Maximum Brother Raul Castro, a man even more swinish and bloodthirsty than his brother Fidel.

During Castro's first year in power, Bacardi's José "Pepin" Bosch was still so smitten with the glorious *revolución* that he begged a plane seat and accompanied Castro on his triumphal April 1959 tour of the United States. "Radical chic" didn't start with Tom Wolfe's witty revelation in 1970. Bored and ditzy debutantes threw themselves at Castro and his "rebels." Take the aforementioned Vilma Espin herself. She was a graduate of both Bryn Mawr College and the Massachusetts Institute of Technology. Her father was a high executive at Bacardi and her family was rolling in money. Cuba's old aristocracy loved Castro until they were stuck *living* under his system—that radical chic-ness disappeared in a flash, and most of them ended up in exile.

Living under Fidel is hard even for most leftists. Practically all of Salvador Allende's Marxist partisans who found refuge in Cuba after the Pinochet coup have since fled in desperation—some to the United States. My own family had a branch of old-line Cuban Communist Party members. They live in Miami today.

Life in Castroland is damn hard for socialist ideologues. It's a cinch, however, for terrorists and gangsters. Those are Castro's true friends and cronies.

The amazing thing is that after having been forced to flee from Castro, Cuban Americans in Miami are now condemned by liberals. Liberals typically pronounce the words "Miami Cubans" as if smelling curdled milk, and they inevitably denounce them as Batistianos. "Cuba policy has not been decided in Washington," harrumphs Bill Press. "It's been decided in Miami, by former Batista supporters, who lost the revolution to Castro in 1959 and still think they can reverse history."[11] Or as my late history professor Stephen Ambrose said, "Those rich Cubans fled to Miami and started agitating to go to war in order to reclaim all their ill-gotten property." Even in some liberal (artistic, intellectual) Cuban exile circles, especially in New York or Spain, digs against Miami's Cubans are de rigueur on grounds of class. To them, "Miami Cuban" represents what red-state America is to American liberals.

Before Castro, Cuba had a huge middle class—36 percent of Cuba's population in 1957, according to the United Nations. Most who fled Cuba from 1959 to 1966 were middle class white-collar professionals. The book *Miami: City of the Future* cites a University of Miami study that a majority of south Florida's Cuban Americans qualified as blue-collar back in the old country. Almost all these Cubans fled with only the clothes on their backs.

In his book *The Spirit of Enterprise*, George Gilder titled a chapter "The Cuban Miracle." He wrote: "No other immigrant group so inundated a city and transformed it so quickly and *successfully*, while achieving such multifarious business breakthroughs as the nearly 800,000 fugitives from Castro's regime who made Miami their home after

1960." According to the U.S. Census Bureau, in 1997 Cuban Americans owned 125,300 companies, with annual revenues of $26.5 billion. The 1998 census showed that second-generation Cuban Americans have higher educational and income levels than Americans in general. And of course they vote Republican. No wonder liberals hate them.

CHAPTER NINE

STUPID LIBERALS IN THE CIA

" **C**astro is not only not a Communist,** he's a strong anti-Communist fighter."[1] That's what the CIA's reigning expert on Latin American Communism, a genius named Gerry Drecher (who worked under the alias of Frank Bender) said after meeting with Fidel Castro in 1959. Frank Bender also approached Rufo López-Fresquet, Castro's first economics minister who accompanied Castro on that trip to the U.S., and offered to share his intelligence with Castro in the joint anti-Communist fight.[2]

"Me and my staff were all Fidelistas." That's Robert Reynolds, who was the CIA's "Caribbean desk" specialist on the Cuban revolution from 1957 to 1960.[3]

"They were all pro-Castro." That's another CIA operative in Cuba at the time, Robert Wiecha. "All—and so was everyone in State, except [Republican] Earl Smith."[4] The CIA is a government bureaucracy like any other, with the same liberal bias, as Cuban Americans know all too well. Many able and patriotic Cubans walked away from the CIA from 1960 to 1962, amazed, aghast, and disgusted that the CIA wanted to work only with Cuban socialists. Former Fidelistas were their favorites.

This wasn't new for the CIA. From the beginning of the Cold War, it made a pet of the Democratic Left.

"We want for Cuba what you want for the U.S.," exclaimed Rubio Padilla to Allen Dulles, director of Central Intelligence. "We want free enterprise, the rule of law—not socialism."[5] Padilla was a medical doctor, a prominent lay Catholic leader, and one of pre-Castro Cuba's most respected figures. He was untainted by any Batista connection. In fact, he loathed Batista and had worked against him his entire life. Padilla wanted to work with the CIA in the anti-Castro fight. But after seeing the leftist bigotry of the agency, he predicted its efforts would end in disaster and refused to be a part of it. He worked tirelessly for decades, helping destitute exiles and seeking his homeland's liberation. But he wanted nothing more to do with the CIA.

Unhappily, this antipathy was often mutual. "I've dealt with a fairly rich assortment of exiles in the past," wrote CIA honcho Desmond Fitzgerald. "But none can compare with the Cuban group for genuine stupidity and militant childishness. At times I feel sorry for Castro—a sculptor in silly putty."[6]

Desmond "Des" Fitzgerald was a Camelot CIA man, Harvard educated and a Kennedy family intimate. "Bobby Kennedy and Desmond Fitzgerald conducted most of their business together at Washington cocktail parties and receptions, rather than in their respective offices," wrote John Davis in his book *The Kennedys: Dynasty and Disaster*.

"Des Fitzgerald always called the attorney general 'Bobby,' not 'Mr. Attorney General,' and he was photographed so often at Georgetown cocktail parties that his CIA cover was probably blown," said a CIA colleague.[7]

When Desmond Fitzgerald talks about "genuine stupidity," you ought to know that he was the mastermind of many ingenious plots to assassinate Castro. One was to employ an exploding sea conch. Another involved infecting Fidel's scuba regulator with tuberculous bacilli. Yet another plan was to douse his wetsuit with deadly chemical agents. As we know, none of these panned out. Fitzgerald finally settled on an ink pen with a poison hypodermic tip so thin that Castro wouldn't feel it when the assassin "accidentally" brushed it against him.

Many of the allegedly stupid Cuban exiles—and many of the CIA's own lower-level operatives (who were generally on excellent terms with the Cuban exiles)—tried to dissuade Fitzgerald from his ingenious plans. What troubled them more even than the Austin Powers–level brilliance of the schemes was the man Fitzgerald was entrusting with Castro's assassination. He was immensely proud that he'd set up an "inside job," recruiting a Cuban official for the deadly deed. The Cuban exiles tried to tell Fitzgerald that man he'd recruited to assassinate Castro was a double agent.[8]

The double agent was a Castro intimate named Rolando Cubela. He'd meet Fitzgerald or his subordinates in Brazil or France and then fly back to Havana and report them to his boss, Fidel Castro.

"You think Castro's just gonna sit on his ass and not retaliate?" snorted Frank Sturgis.[9]

Sturgis knew Castro personally from flying arms to Castro during the anti-Batista days. The CIA employed Sturgis as part of its anti-Castro effort. Castro answered Sturgis's question on September 7, 1963, shrieking: "We are prepared to answer in kind! U.S. leaders who plan on eliminating Cuban leaders should not think that they are *themselves* safe!"[10] (Emphasis mine.)

Lyndon Johnson came to agree with Sturgis. "I'll tell you something that will rock you," he said in an off-the-record chat with Howard K. Smith after viewing classified documents. "Kennedy tried to get Castro—but Castro got Kennedy first. It will all come out one day."[11]

General Alexander Haig came to agree with Sturgis too. Haig served as a military aide in both the Kennedy and Johnson administrations. "As I read the secret report, I felt a sense of physical shock, a rising of the hair on the back of my neck," Haig wrote. He was reading a classified report one month after the Kennedy assassination. "I walked the report over to my superiors and watched their faces go ashen." He was told: "From this moment, Al, you will forget you ever read this piece of paper, or that it ever existed."[12]

The classified intelligence report that so rattled Haig detailed precisely how a few days before the Dallas assassination, Lee Harvey Oswald, accompanied by Castro intelligence agents, had been spotted in Havana. He'd traveled there from Mexico City.

Haig saw this well before the Warren Commission report was published. Among the few people who knew that Oswald had traveled to Mexico City and visited the Cuban embassy were Cuban exiles: Salvador Diaz-Verson knew it, Carlos Prio knew it, and Emilio Nunez Portuondo knew it. This last got the hair-raising datum from a friend who worked at the embassy. The day after the assassination, Portuondo's friend, a closet Castro hater, recognized Lee Harvey Oswald's picture.

"*Asesinos*!" screamed Elena Garro, a Mexican national with friends at the Cuban embassy in Mexico City. The day after the assassination she stood pointing at the embassy building. "*Asesinos*!" she yelled, convulsing in sobs. She recognized Lee Harvey Oswald too. She'd seen him hobnobbing with Cuban embassy people several days earlier. A friend of Garro's, a Mexican intelligence agent named Manuel Calvillo, told her to watch it, and even to get out of town for a while. She was in danger from the Communists. Calvillo himself took Elena Garro and her daughter into hiding.[13]

"Castro always had his best intelligence people in Mexico City," says a man who often went up against them, longtime Cuban freedom fighter Raphael "Chi-Chi" Quintero, who today lives in Miami.

The aforementioned Portuondo was well known in diplomatic circles, by the way. He'd been Cuba's ambassador to the United Nations in the mid-1950s. Portuondo had already made a notorious name for himself when he ripped into the Soviets for their butchery of Budapest in 1956, causing much gasping and coughing from the assembled delegates to the General Assembly.

Immediately after Kennedy's assassination, Portuondo told U.S. intelligence that Oswald had been at the Cuban embassy in Mexico

City, but he refused to divulge his source. Ironically, on the very day of the Kennedy assassination, Des Fitzgerald was meeting in Paris with double agent Rolando Cubela, giving him the poison ink pen to take back to Havana.

The Central Intelligence Agency was scrupulous about excluding from its anti-Castro fight anyone with experience fighting Castro. Rolando Masferrer's private army in Cuba, *los Tigres*, specialized in giving the Castroite "rebels" a taste of their own medicine during the rebellion. "Hey, somebody had to fight the Castroites," snorted Masferrer in an interview years later. "Batista's army sure wasn't."

The CIA wanted nothing to do with the exiled Masferrer. Indeed, Masferrer was jailed in Florida right before the Bay of Pigs invasion. Repeatedly rebuffed by the CIA, the enterprising Masferrer was forming another private army and was poised for an invasion himself.

Or take a Cuban gentleman named Raphael Diaz-Balart. His two sons, Lincoln and Mario, are among the most effective conservative Republicans in Congress today. In May 1955, Batista personally ordered the release of Fidel Castro as part of a general amnesty after Castro had served a measly seventeen months of his fifteen-year sentence. Senator Raphael Diaz-Balart thought Batista's general amnesty stupid. In a speech in the senate chamber, he said, "Fidel Castro and his group have repeatedly declared from their comfortable prison that they will leave prison only to continue plotting acts of violence and whatever it takes to achieve the total power they seek." The senator continued, "They have refused to take part in any type of peaceful settlement, threatening both the members of the government and members of the opposition who support electoral solutions to the country's problems.

"They do not want peace," Senator Diaz-Balart stressed. "They do not want a national solution. They do not want democracy, or elections, or fraternity. Fidel Castro and his group seek only one thing: power—and total power at that. And they want to achieve that power through violence so that their total power will enable them to destroy every vestige of law in Cuba, to institute the most cruel, most barbaric tyranny... a totalitarian regime, a corrupt and murderous regime that would be difficult to overthrow for at least twenty years." Diaz-Balart was an optimist. It's now been more than forty years that Castro has brutalized Cuba. But the senator was right about everything else.

He continued, "This is because Fidel Castro is personally nothing more than a psychopathic fascist.... I believe this amnesty—so imprudently adopted—will bring days, many days, of mourning, pain, bloodshed, and misery to the Cuban people. For Cuba's sake, I ask God that I be the one mistaken."[14]

Why was Castro in prison to begin with? He'd been jailed for planning and leading the murderous attack on Cuba's Moncada army barracks—an attack that killed more than a hundred people on July 26, 1953. Not that Castro *personally* had a hand in any of the shooting; he always studiously avoided combat where the enemy might shoot back. "Run!" one former colleague remembers Castro shrieking when Batista's soldiers unexpectedly defended themselves. "Every man for himself!"[15]

"Wait a minute!" said the colleague. "What about the girls? We can't just...?" (Castro's July 26 Movement was a progressive bunch, shoving women into combat.) "No time to rescue the girls—no time for that!"[16] Castro gasped as he streaked from the battle zone like a gazelle on steroids.

Sadly, many of the saps Fidel and Raul left behind faced death and torture by Batista's soldiers. These enraged and undisciplined troops handed Castro his fondest wish: the July 26 Movement now had martyr and victim status, thanks to Cuba's then-free press. Unfortunately for Cuba, Batista had banned capital punishment. And Cuba had a completely independent judiciary. So Fidel received a pretty light sentence for plotting, leading, and inciting armed violence that left more than a hundred people dead. Actually, the judges who sentenced Castro to fifteen years almost apologized for it. According to Georgie Anne Geyer, Nieto Pineiro-Osorio, the judge who did the sentencing, "was vastly sympathetic to the Castro insurgents." Some judges, like Manuel Urrutia, voted for acquittal.[17]

A completely fair trial was possible under Batista; indeed, it was the norm. This ended in a flash when the "Castro insurgents" took power. No sooner had Castro entered Havana and assembled his sap cabinet than they reinstated the death penalty, abolished habeas corpus, and made their new revolutionary laws apply *retroactively*. The "trials" of "Batista's war criminals" were shameless farces, sickening charades. The chief prosecutor, Che Guevara, said it best: "Evidence is an archaic bourgeois detail."

You might think that Senator Raphael Diaz-Balart had Castro's number in 1955. Well, in 1960, Diaz-Balart, living in the United States as an exile, testified before a U.S. Senate subcommittee. Its hearings were titled "Communist Threat to the United States through the Caribbean."

> "As a Cuban, I appreciate the hospitality extended to me by this great brother country and am happy to respond to the subpoena of this distinguished committee," Diaz-Balart began.
>
> **Senator Kenneth Keating:** Mr. Balart, you refer to Fidel Castro as the most prominent member of the Communist movement in the Western Hemisphere, but probably not a *card-carrying* member.
>
> **Diaz-Balart:** Yes, sir, that is correct. From 1945, when Castro started at the University of Havana, he was always very close to the known Communists there. He was a perfect front man for them—until he started killing fellow students.
>
> **Jay Sourwine [general counsel]:** Do you know who shot Leonel Gomez in 1947?
>
> **Diaz-Balart:** Fidel Castro shot Leonel Gomez, because he thought Gomez, being a friend of then Cuban president Grau, would be an obstacle to Castro's ambitions.

Sourwine: Who was Manolo Castro?

Diaz-Balart: He was the president of the Federation of University Students at Havana University in 1947.

Sourwine: Is he alive?

Diaz-Balart: No. Fidel Castro murdered him in 1947, shortly after he tried to murder, but only wounded, Gomez.

Sourwine: Did you know Fernandez Caral?

Diaz-Balart: Yes, he was a sergeant of the Havana University police.

Sourwine: Is he still alive?

Diaz-Balart: No. Fidel Castro murdered him because he was pressing the investigation of Manolo Castro's murder.

Sourwine: Do you know Raul Castro?

Diaz-Balart: Yes, sir. He's Fidel Castro's brother.

Sourwine: Do you know if he is a Communist?

Diaz-Balart: Raul Castro is a very well-trained Communist agent. As a young man he went to Prague for training.

Sourwine: Do you recall giving us the names of two Russians whom you said arrived in Cuba in May 1959 to start labor agitation in Latin America?

Diaz-Balart: One was Eremev Timofei and the other Ivan
Arapov.

And so on. Here is a Cuban who loves the United States, who was a distinguished pre-Castro senator, who was privy to vital information about Soviet penetration into Latin America, and who knew all about Castro—an absolutely ideal CIA asset, right?

Wrong. The CIA repeatedly rebuffed Diaz-Balart. He was banned from political planning for the Bay of Pigs. He was even prohibited from joining the invasion force as a private citizen. He was willing to do anything to be involved, but the CIA said no. Worse than that, the INS started harassing him about his ability to stay in the United States.

"You'll have fun working with these guys," chuckled a CIA officer to Howard Hunt, who was known as the only conservative in his CIA circles. "These Cuban guys are all way to the left, Howard, all socialists."[18]

Before the Bay of Pigs, Hunt was instructed to fashion Cuba's government-in-exile and write a new, socialist constitution for post-Castro Cuba. Hunt, who was on good terms with hundreds of Cuban exiles, knew that Cuba already had a perfectly good constitution—the 1940 constitution that Batista violated and Castro abolished. But, Hunt lamented, "All the Cubans I was given to work with had originally backed Castro. I considered most of them shallow thinkers."[19]

The socialist ex-Fidelistas were a very touchy matter with Cuban exiles. Only months before, in Cuba, Fidelistas posing as born-again *anti*-Fidelistas had infiltrated and betrayed the biggest anti-Castro conspiracy yet mounted, known as the Trinidad or Trujillo conspiracy. Dozens were shot. Thousands were jailed.

The traitors were Eloy Gutiérrez Menoyo (present-day leader of a "pro-engagement," "anti-embargo," and pro-Democrat group in Miami called Cambio Cubano) and an American rebel named William Morgan (who ran afoul of Fidel and was executed by Castro's firing squad a year and a half later). In 1959, Menoyo and Morgan were revolutionary "comandantes" who occupied stolen mansions, drove stolen cars, and used stolen servants.

Herbert Matthews profiled Morgan in the *New York Times*. According to the top Cuba expert at the world's top newspaper, the strapping thirty-two-year-old Ohioan now serving as a revolutionary "major" was a humanitarian hero *and* a hero from World War II, a former paratrooper who had fought in the Pacific theater's bloodiest battles. Morgan's hometown *Toledo Blade* also took up his cause. The *Blade* reported that "Major" Morgan's force numbered five thousand when the revolution began—yet the number of anti-Batista rebels o*n the entire island* never exceeded a few *hundred* until the very last week of the "war," when they quickly quintupled to about three thousand. Such was the ferocity of the anti-Batista war, according to the *Blade*, that "only three thousand of Morgan's men survived the bitter fighting." Of course, we know that there was a grand total of 182 dead during the two-year-long "war."

The press was wrong about another thing. William Morgan was an AWOL G.I. who had never served a single day in World War II and had never seen a minute of combat. He'd been stationed in Japan well after the war and had missed the Korean War because he'd been jugged in the stockade. Earlier, as a juvenile in his hometown of Toledo, Ohio, he'd been arrested for armed robbery. After his court-martial and dishonorable discharge for escaping from the brig and stealing a guard's pistol, Morgan served time for robbery in two U.S. federal prisons.[20]

He was also a bigamist, having married a Cuban girl while his wife, still living in Ohio, was on his tail for child support for the two children he'd abandoned. In 1957, Cuba looked like a nice place for a guy like Morgan to hole up, Castro's band was the ideal outfit to join, and the *New York Times* was the ideal agency to spread Morgan's bullshit.

At any rate, Morgan and Menoyo, claiming they'd recently turned on Castro, joined the Trujillo conspiracy. Castro himself ordered this in order to set a trap. The rebellion was so named because Dominican president Rafael Trujillo was helping the anti-Castro rebels with arms, and some of them were exiled in the Dominican Republic. The rebellion was to start with two planeloads of armed Cuban exiles flying from the Dominican Republic to the town of Trinidad on Cuba's southern coast.

Interestingly, the ever friendly, cooperative, (and liberal) U.S. ambassador to Cuba, Phil Bonsal, got wind of the impending anti-Castro rebellion and immediately alerted Castro's government.[21] (No U.S. ambassador ever alerted the Batista regime about anti-government conspiracies to which the embassy was privy; indeed, many anti-Batista conspirators were actually given refuge at Guantánamo Bay.) Ambassador Bonsal believed that Morgan *really* was an anti-Castroite. Bonsal feared that Castro might mistakenly implicate the American embassy in the plot because Morgan was an American.

As we'll see later, Morgan, perennial delinquent though he was, finally did turn on Castro and died bravely—even heroically—in front of a Communist firing squad. But because of Morgan and Menoyo's treachery, many anti-Castro Cubans at the time were leery of the *arrepentidos* (alleged ex-Castroites) the CIA seemed so eager to recruit.

For its *military* invasion of Cuba, the CIA at first excluded Cuban exiles with a *military* background because Batista had dominated the military. But eventually, officers like Erneido Oliva, Hugo Sueiro, and many others passed the cut after a thorough screening by the CIA and State Department. To a man, the Cuban officers performed stupendously in combat and honorably in captivity. Some are soldiers to this day. Oliva is a brigadier general in the U.S. Army. Sueiro is a highly decorated Vietnam vet.

After the Cuban exiles caught on, they coached people on how to pass the screenings. "The Cuban Junta," dictated John F. Kennedy's national security adviser, McGeorge Bundy, for the post–Bay of Pigs government being built by the Best and Brightest, "will have a strong leftist orientation."[22]

It's no wonder that Earl Smith says that CIA men were among the most obstinately and passionately Fidelista of his embassy's staff. He mentioned that both in his Senate testimony in 1960 and in his 1962 book *The Fourth Floor*. Almost thirty years later, Tad Szculc confirmed the CIA's early Castrophilia in his book *Fidel: A Critical Portrait*. Szulc, a Castro admirer himself and—yes—a *New York Times* reporter, shows that the CIA's support for Castro went beyond sympathy. According to Szulc, CIA agent Robert Wiecha handed $50,000 to a representative of Castro's July 26 Movement in 1958.[23]

Not everyone in the CIA was pro-Castro; it was the higher-ups, the suits, who were. The CIA's lower-level, hands-on military men—men like Grayston Lynch, Rip Robertson, Pete Ray, Riley Shamburger, Leo Baker, and Wade Gray are revered among Cuban Americans to this day. Some of them have their names emblazoned in a place of honor at the Bay of Pigs monument in Miami. Walk through Miami's Little Havana and you'll find streets named after them. Mention these coura-geous men's names at any Cuban American gathering and then cover your ears, because the *vivas* could shatter your eardrums. Cuban soil was consecrated in the blood of our two peoples.

Not to be outdone by the stupid liberals in the CIA, there were plenty of—surprise!—stupid liberals in the State Department too. In 1957, the U.S. ambassador to Cuba, Arthur Gardner (a Republican) made the mis-take of warning his State Department superiors: "I saw a manifesto that he (Castro) had printed in Mexico, which stated his principles, what he was going to do. He was going to take over the American industries, he was going to nationalize everything. That, to me, meant only one thing, that this man was a radical. Castro talked and acts like a Communist and should not be supported by the U.S. Fidel doesn't carry a Communist Party card, but his brother Raul is a Communist, everybody knows it. . . . Yes, they [*New York Times* articles] built him [Castro] up to being the Robin Hood or the savior of the country. It did have a great effect."[24]

Along with their State Department cronies, the *New York Times* clam-ored to have Arthur Gardner replaced in 1957. John Foster Dulles acqui-esced and replaced him with Republican Earl T. Smith, who made the same mistake. "Castro is a Marxist," he told his State Department superiors after a few months at his post. Indeed, during his first week on the job, Smith got word that Castro's people planned to murder him. "Castro gives indications of his Marxism in his writings and speeches. There's no question that Communists control his movement. If he takes over, it will not be in the best interests of Cuba or of the United States."[25]

Smith was axed exactly a week after Castro took power. Cuba's own liberal media had much to do with Smith's axing. "Shame on Ambassador Smith!" wrote Miguel Angel Quevedo in his *Bohemia* magazine in January 1959. "Ambassador Smith is disfiguring the realities of the tragedy in order to disorient the State Department. Now that we are victorious, he should go and never return." The cover of this January 1959 issue featured the young, bearded Castro himself with the caption, "Honor and Glory to the National Hero!" Ten months later, *Bohemia* magazine's entire operation was confiscated by the National Hero's thugs and Quevedo was scrambling into exile for his very life. His journalists had ranted at Batista for seven years. Now these wiseacres were scrambling too. Six years after his magazine was confiscated and turned into a Communist propaganda organ, Quevedo, living in exile in Caracas, Venezuela, put a revolver to his head and blew his brains all over his living room.

Despite Gardner and Smith's warnings, the State Department imposed an arms embargo on Batista's government (and refused to ship arms it had already bought and paid for). Then Smith was instructed to tell Batista, "You no longer enjoy the support of the U.S. government." Smith protested the order, but met with Batista and did his duty.

The State Department actually gave Castro's new government official recognition before Castro had even entered Havana. "We put Castro in power," a bitter Smith said in Senate testimony two years later.

CHAPTER TEN

"WE FOUGHT WITH THE FURY OF CORNERED BEASTS"

Castro's rebels skirmished for barely two years; his rebels in arms numbered only four hundred in late 1958; and only 182 people died in Castro's "war" (though thousands died afterwards to Castro's firing squads).

But for some reason, most people don't know about a much bigger war that lasted for six years (1960–66), which killed 6,000 government troops, and which Raul Castro himself estimated involved 179 different bands of *anti*-Communist guerrillas and rebels, mostly rural, mostly peasant. All this happened on our very doorstep, eight jet minutes away. Cubans know it as the Escambray Rebellion.

You see, friends, Fidel Castro and Che Guevara's few military victories came not *as* guerrillas but *against* guerrillas, in the most brutal, cowardly, and disgusting type of *anti*-insurgency war—or really massacres. Who knows that one of the most protracted and brutal guerrilla wars in the Western Hemisphere was actually fought *against* Castro and Che by poorly armed, landless peasants in Cuba's Escambray mountains? Collectivization was no more voluntary in Cuba than in the Ukraine—but Cuba's Kulaks had guns (a few at the beginning, anyway;

the Kennedy-Khrushchev deal cut them off from American aid) and a willingness to fight.

For the Escambray Rebellion, no Cuban reporters existed, only Castro government propagandists and eunuchs. (Norberto Fuentes comes to mind here.) And the foreign reporters who rushed to Castro's press hut never turned up for this war, though it took Castro six years; tens of thousands of troops; scores of Russian advisers; squadrons of Soviet tanks, helicopters, and flame-throwers; and a massive "relocation" campaign to finally crush these incredibly valiant and resourceful freedom fighters. "We fought with the fury of cornered beasts," says one veteran from Miami.

"Cuban militia units commanded by Russian officers employed flame-throwers to burn more than a hundred palm-thatched cottages on the edge of the Zapata swamps," writes Paul Bethel. "The Guajiro occupants of the cottages were accused by the regime of feeding and giving comfort to counter-revolutionaries."[1]

"I'll never forget it," recalls Acelia Pacheco, who was a young girl at the time and was among the "relocated." "The Communists would pull up and simply start yanking everyone out of the house at gunpoint, jamming them into trucks, into carts, even onto mules. I'll never forget the sight of the little children, even babies, completely bewildered, crying, bawling, the looks on their dirty, tear-streaked little faces. The mothers, sisters, aunts, grandmothers—some crying, some shouting horrible curses at the Communists—all of us were dumped in concentration camps hundreds of miles away from our ancestral homes, with no food for days at a time. Most of the men were taken elsewhere and never seen again.... I *lived* through all that!"[2]

"Twelve of us guerrillas might find ourselves surrounded by five thousand Communist troops," recalls freedom fighter Guillermo Calzada. "We fought violent battles each and every day against these odds, without food, without water, without sleep.... I went thirteen days without eating. I had eight men with me for one battle and ended up the only survivor. We were in constant motion ... Russian helicopters overhead strafing us. . . . Worst of all were our armaments. We didn't have much. By 1963, the Escambray guerrilla who had a handful of bullets to his name considered himself damn lucky. We made every bullet count too, shooting the Communists well after we saw the whites of their eyes."[3]

And why did these men (and boys) fight? "I was a poor country bumpkin," says Escambray hero Agapito Rivera from Miami today. "I didn't have much, but I had hopes. I had aspirations. And I'd be damned if I'd go work like a damned slave on one of Castro and Che's state farms. I planned on working hard—but on my own, for myself, getting my own land maybe. Then I saw Castro and the Communists stealing everything from everybody. They stole my hopes, my dreams . . . I had no choice."[4]

Agapito Rivera had two brothers and nine cousins who took up arms in the anti-Castro freedom fight. He was the only survivor.

"A bunch of wimps. That's right—wimps," oinks Michael Moore about these men in his book *Downsize This*. "These Cuban exiles, for all their chest-thumping and terrorism, are really just a bunch of wimps. . . . They grabbed their assets and headed to Florida. . . . They came here, expecting us to fight their fight for them . . . these Cuban crybabies."[5]

"I didn't have anything Castro could *possibly* steal from me," laughs Eusebio Peñalver from Miami today. "I was a country negro. No farm. No mansion, no sugar mill, no yacht, not even a car. None of that stuff—but goddammit, I had my *freedom*! My *self-respect*! Those Communist pigs wanted me to bow down before them like my great-grandparents who were slaves!"

Peñalver answered his would-be slavemasters with repeated blasts from an M-1 carbine. For almost two years he gave the Castro Communists holy hell with that carbine. "If the odds were only ten to one, we thought the battle a breeze," he snorts. "Those Castro idiots came at us in waves, guess that's how their Russian masters trained them. We Escambray rebels would shoot our way out of three or four encirclements by those imbeciles a week.... But we couldn't go on—not without supplies. Surely we thought we'd get some from the Americans.... And we *did*, very early in the freedom fight. But it dried up. *Hombre*, we weren't asking them to bleed and die for us.... But good grief, we *did* need arms and ammo. We had plenty of men who wanted to join the freedom fight with us. 'Got any weapons?' we'd ask. 'No? Well then, let's wait till we get some.'"

The wait was vain. The odds and strangulation of supplies finally took their toll and Peñalver was captured. He ended up serving longer in Castro's prisons than Nelson Mandela did in South Africa's. But have you ever seen Peñalver featured at a UN, NAACP, or Congressional Black Caucus function? Peñalver is *the longest serving black political prisoner of the twentieth century*, yet our Castro-slobbering liberal media has made sure you've never even heard of him.

About a year into the Escambray Rebellion, who shows up in the area commanding government troops but the mighty Che Guevara himself. "And it couldn't have come at a better time," recalls a rebel. "We desperately needed some rest, some respite from the constant battles, to reorganize, try to resupply."

With the mighty Che commanding their opponents, the rebels got exactly what they needed—and *then* some. "At first we couldn't believe it," recalls the rebel. "Che's men simply lined up elbow to elbow, right out in the open like that, then swept through an area they thought held some rebels!"

Andy Jackson's men never had such easy pickings against redcoats at the Battle of New Orleans. "We slaughtered them," recalls the rebel. "Even against those outrageous odds, we were prevailing for a while. And we all got new arms and ammo—by taking them from dead Communists. It was great."

But it was short-lived. "Guess even by Russian standards Che was hopeless, and soon he disappeared from the battle zone," says the rebel. "We'd always heard that Fidel couldn't stand Che. Castro was always sending Che off on little errands—to give one of his long, boring speeches at the United Nations, at some Conference of Non-Aligned Nations in Africa, to the Punta del Este Conference in South America, anywhere, just to get that imbecile out of his hair for a while. Che's personality grated on many Cubans. He was the typical haughty Argentine, but with nothing really to be haughty about. He was great at massacring defenseless men at La Cabana, but that's about it."

Here he laughs. "A couple of years ago, my grandson comes home with some book assigned to him in a college class, *Che Guevara on Guerrilla Warfare*. I could only laugh—and loudly! Years ago when I was younger, crazier, I might have stormed over to the school and given that professor a piece of my mind, maybe slapped the living shit out of him too. Nowadays I can only laugh—and at all those Che T-shirts and watches and movies. Just laugh, laugh, laugh. I guess it's better this way."

Many a peasant hut was torched, villages destroyed, and villagers summarily executed during the Escambray Rebellion. Might *Platoon*'s writer and director offer some insight into these butcheries? Why yes, actually. Oliver Stone has a long association with the butcher himself. "[Castro] is very warm and bright…a very driven man, a very moral man. He's very concerned about his country. He's selfless in that way."[6]

Margarito Lanza Flores was another poor black Cuban. He reacted to the reinstitution of slavery in Cuba much like his brother in arms Eusebio Peñalver had, by raking the Communist enslavers with a Thompson machine gun. Soon Margarito was commanding a band of Escambray rebels himself, known as Capitan "El Negro" Tondique. His rebel band would pop up, blasting away, decimating Communist columns, and then vanish into the landscape. "El Negro" Tondique drove the Communists absolutely nuts.

"The Castroites called us bandits," snorts Tondique's brother in arms Arcadio Peguero from Miami today. "In fact, we survived by relying on the support of thousands of small farmers in the Escambray."[8]

That famous Maoist quote about how a guerrilla is a fish that swims and hides in the sea which is the people, etc., actually described these anti-Communist guerrillas to a T.

And the Communists knew it damn well. That's what led to the massive and brutal relocation campaign, in which they ripped thousands of farmers from their ancestral homes and lands in the Escambray and shipped them to concentration camps hundreds of miles away.

This made things much easier for the gallant Reds. And one morning, after a ferocious firefight, Captain Tondique found himself completely surrounded by hundreds of Russian-armed troops in a sugarcane field. Naturally, the Castroites were too scared to go in after the legendary "El Negro." So they set the canefield on fire from every corner and sat back. Tondique saw the flames closing in and knew how many hundreds of Communists he was up against that day, so he started digging into the ground and covered himself up with the dirt as the roaring flames passed over him. He lived but was burned horribly. The Reds swarmed in after the fire, spotted the horribly wounded Tondique (his face was a mass of huge black blisters, his hair scorched and matted to his head), and yanked him out.

They dragged him under a nearby bridge, stood him up, and prepared a firing squad. "*Fuego!*" bellowed the Communist commander, and "El Negro" was instantly on the ground—but scurrying away! He'd managed to hit the deck at the *exact instant* of the volley and it went over him. Tondique threw himself into the surrounding bushes and started to escape. "Get him!" shrieked the rattled Communist commander, Victor Dreke. "Get him! Don't let him get away!" The Communists surrounded the grimacing, limping Tondique in the bushes and emptied several clips from their Czech machine guns into his charred and shattered body.[9]

Interesting postscript: On November 13, 2002, Tondique's gallant murderer, Victor Dreke—a black himself but one who hired on at the Communist plantation as a guard and overseer—visited the United States as the guest of honor of Florida International University. Dreke was on a book tour, you see. He'd just written one detailing—among his other gallant Communist exploits—his massacre of Escambray peasants.

Zoila Aguila was a famous female guerrilla in the Escambray Rebellion (her moniker was "*la Niña del Escambray*"). After her family's farm was stolen and several family members murdered, la Niña grabbed a tommy gun, rammed in a clip, and took to the hills. For a year she ran rings around the Reds. But trapped without supplies, she was finally run down. For decades, la Niña suffered horribly in Castro's dungeons, but she lives in Miami today. Seems to me that her tragic story makes ideal fodder for Oprah, for all those women's magazines, for all those butch professorettes of "womyn's studies," for a Susan Sarandon role, for a little whooping up by Gloria Steinem, Dianne Feinstein, and Hillary herself. But whoever heard of la Niña?

Instead of la Niña, we got Rigoberta Menchu, the Guatemalan feminist-Marxist who wrote the book *I, Rigoberta Menchu,* an autobiography chronicling the suffering of indigenous Guatemalans at the hands of Guatemala's U.S.-backed military. The rotund Menchu (who resembles a well-tanned version of Bella Abzug) was showered with honorary doctorates from countless colleges, nominated as a United Nations "goodwill ambassador," and awarded the Nobel Peace Prize. Her book became required reading in practically every college and high school in the land.

But the book turned out to be a massive pile of baloney. This was exposed by—of all newspapers—the *New York Times.* One investigator, seeking to verify the book's account of Menchu's young brother dying of malnutrition, instead found the brother. But nothing changed for Menchu, nary an award or honor was rescinded. The Nobel Peace Prize stuck.

Menchu was a fraud. But in the Escambray Rebellion, thousands of bona fide peasant guerrillas vanished into unmarked graves, thousands of peasant families were driven from their modest homes at gunpoint and into concentration camps, and hundreds of battle-scarred veterans live in Miami today. But not one of them has received any of the attention or awards showered on Rigoberta Menchu—or Fidel Castro.

Why? Because, as liberal British historian Hugh Thomas wrote, "In all essentials Castro's battle for Cuba was a public relations campaign, fought in New York and Washington." (And Castro won that war big time. The Associated Press dispatches about Castro's "war" against Batista were written by Castro's own agent in New York, Mario Llerena. He admits this in his book *The Unsuspected Revolution*. *National Review*'s famous cartoon in 1960 showing a beaming Castro saying, "I got my job through the *New York Times*!" nailed it.

The Escambray rebels fought a real war against a real enemy. They'd hang the corpses of Castro soldiers with a sign: "Two Communist Russian lackeys dead for every Cuban patriot murdered." When captured, they sneered and spit at the Castroites.

One brave *guajiro* (Cuban for redneck) named Blas Ortega, twenty-one years old at the time, captured a Castroite informer-murderer and strung the quivering little weasel up from a guava tree. Weeks later, after expending his last bullet, Ortega himself was captured by the Communists. He was given a typical Communist show trial. The judge asked him if it was true that he'd hanged a "comrade" with a rope.

Ortega responded with head bowed. "That happens to be true, your honor. But now, having had time to reflect upon it, I've decided on a different approach under different circumstances."

The corpulent Castroite judge leaned forward. "I see."

"You see, your honor," Ortega resumed. "If I'd managed to get my hands on you, your honor, I'd have used a cable. No rope would hold your fat ass!"[10]

Blas Ortega was still laughing when minutes later he faced a firing squad. With him was another young rebel named Maro Borges. The Reds asked Borges if he had any last words.

"Why yes," responded Borges. "Thanks so much for the opportunity to allow me to express myself at these last moments of my life, my dear *companeros*. I feel I must let my feelings be known about this sad fratricidal war that so horribly disfigures our noble nation. So here it is, *companeros*: I shit on your cowardly, thieving Communist revolution! And I use Fidel's face to wipe my ass!"

The flustered firing squad quickly took aim. "*Fuego!*" yelled the enraged Castroite commander. Both young freedom fighters perished laughing.

Carlos Machado was lined up by a firing squad in Las Villas during the rebellion. "Are you going to crack?" they giggled while tying his hands.

"Glass cracks!" barked Carlos. "Men die standing!"

"Very well—*fuego!*"

Carlos was fifteen years old. His twin brother and father were killed with him.

For me, "family night" means a discount at a restaurant. In the Escambray Rebellion it meant half your family murdered by Castro's death squads. The Milian family lost twelve men in the Cuban freedom fight. When Escambray hero Blas Tardio crumpled in front of a Castro firing squad in March 1965, he was the fifth of six brothers to die.[11]

Cuba was on fire that year, from tip to tip, and Castro's firing squads were working overtime. At one point in 1961, one of every nineteen Cubans was a political prisoner.[12] You probably didn't know that. But the media has always ignored Castro's atrocities, even when they had their press hut nearby.

The mass murders were there from the beginning. The place was a field outside the city of Santiago. The date was January 12, 1959. Castro had just entered Havana, and the United States had already blessed his regime with official diplomatic recognition.

Seventy-five men, their hands bound tightly behind them, stumbled through the field in the dark, prodded by bayonets. They could barely see each other—it was 3:30 a.m. with no moon. Most of the men cursed. Some prayed. After walking a hundred yards through the damp grass, they were poked and shoved into a rough line near a large vehicle.

Suddenly a line of army trucks snapped on their lights and the vehicle behind the men shone in the beams. It was a bulldozer. The beams also showed the ditch it had dug—fifty yards long and six feet deep, with a fresh mound of dirt behind it. Five men broke from the group and ran, but were quickly recaptured, bludgeoned with gun butts, and dragged back into line. Most of the men glared resolutely ahead.

A group of women near the trucks were convulsed in sobs, yelling, pleading, wiping tears with their skirts. Many clutched rosaries. Bearded soldiers taunted them and jabbed them with rifle butts, keeping them huddled together.

"Cuban mothers," Fidel Castro had spoken into a phalanx of microphones the day before, "let me assure you that I will solve all Cuba's problems without spilling a drop of blood. Cuban mothers, let me assure you, because of me, you will never have to cry."[13]

Five more bearded soldiers stood in front of the trucks, nervously fidgeting with their machine guns. Their drunken commander stood off to the left, swaying, his head turning from the bulldozer and line of captives back to his machine gunners, then back again. Finally he nodded and raised his arm.

"*Viva Cuba Libre!*" The yell came from near the bulldozer, from the bound men glaring into the lights. The women erupted in anguished screams. The startled commander jerked his head, snarled something, and stamped his feet.

"*Viva Cuba Libre!*" Others picked it up. A chorus was starting from the entire line, even from the women. "*Viva Cuba—*"

"*Fuego!*" The enraged Castroite drunkard dropped his arm and the machine guns opened up, drowning the yells from the condemned men. Seventy-five bodies jerked violently and tumbled into the ditch. With the bodies still heaving and twitching and the blood pooling at the bottom of the ditch, the bulldozer rumbled to a start, clanked into position, and started pushing the earth over them. Two of the women fainted. Others broke through the cordon of soldiers and ran hysterically toward the mangled bodies in the ditch, seeking a last glimpse before the dirt covered their husbands and sons forever. None of them had received a trial.

On that very day, the British newspaper *The Observer* reported: "Mr. Castro's bearded, youthful figure has become a symbol of Latin

America's rejection of brutality and lying. Every sign is that he will reject personal rule and violence."

By the time Castro was cheered at Harvard Law School in April 1959, Mr. Castro's firing squads had slaughtered 568 men and boys, some as young as fifteen.

By the time Norman Mailer (an opponent of capital punishment) was calling Castro "the greatest hero to appear in the Americas," Fidel's firing squads had piled up four thousand corpses.

By 1975, when George McGovern (another opponent of capital punishment) was saying, "[Castro] is very shy and sensitive, I frankly liked him," the bullet-riddled bodies of fourteen thousand Cubans lay in unmarked graves.[14]

Combine this bloodbath with the jailing of more political prisoners per capita than Stalin did (more, in fact, than any nation on earth), add the ghastly deaths of seventy-seven thousand desperate Cubans in the Florida straits, add forty-five years of totalitarian oppression, and what do you get?

You get the December 2003 edition of *The Nation*, where Arthur Miller (a longtime foe of capital punishment) describes Castro as "exciting, a person who could probably have had a career on the screen, and one who'd undoubtedly win an election in his country."

"Castro is the most honest and courageous politician I've ever met! Viva Fidel!" That's a beaming Jesse Jackson (who wrote an entire book against capital punishment), arm in arm with Castro on a visit to Havana in 1984.[15]

Early in the revolution, not everyone immediately got with Castro's program, even among the Castroite legal team. Take a properly bearded and rebel-uniform-clad judge named Felix Pena. He presided over a famous trial in March 1959 of Cuba's pre-revolutionary air force pilots. They were accused of "genocide" because of a few forays against Castro's rebels in the mountains. Pena, the poor sap, had taken Castro's prattle about his "humanist" and "democratic" revolution seriously.

So he applied the tenets of civilized jurisprudence and found the charge of "genocide" against the men absolutely preposterous. No evidence, no witnesses; none of these pilots had bombed civilians. Precious few had even bombed or strafed the *rebels*. And a third of those on trial were the planes' mechanics. The aviators were acquitted.

Castro went on TV and screeched for a new trail against the "war criminals" and assembled a new judicial team with a new judge. (Almost six hundred army officers had already been murdered by firing squads on farcical charges, thousands more Cuban soldiers were in prison; now it was time to deal with the air corps.) The new judge dutifully found forty-five of the aviators (and even the mechanics) guilty and sentenced most of them to thirty years at hard labor.

Judge Felix Pena, by the way, was found in his office with a bullet through his head a few days later. And a few months after that, the judge who had condemned the airmen to prison (rather than the firing squad, as recommended by Castro), was *himself* found dead.

Sound like justice? Well, in 1959, the very year this crime took place, Harvard Law School hosted Fidel, and the Harvardites were not disappointed. "Castro Visit Triumphant," headlined Harvard's *Law School Forum* for April 30, 1959. "The audience got what it wanted—the chance of seeing the Cuban hero in person." The adoring crowd gave him a tumultuous reception. Fidel Castro (a white Spanish millionaire's son and Havana law school graduate who overthrew a black cane-cutter) was hailed as a man of the people.

Alas, this humble man of the people had actually applied to Harvard Law School in 1948. This was brought to light by Harvard's dean at the time, McGeorge Bundy.

Caught up in the exuberance of the event, Bundy declared that Harvard was ready to make amends for its mistake in 1948. "I've decided to admit him!" he proclaimed.[16]

Bundy's quip brought the house down. He triumphantly hoisted the arm of a dictator whose chief prosecutor Che Guevara declared, "To execute a man we don't need proof of his guilt. We only need proof that it's necessary to execute him."

One wiseacre at the Harvard lovefest brought up Castro's record of executions and questionable legal procedures.

"Only the worst of the war criminals have been shot," Castro replied. "And don't forget, Cuba's is the only majority revolution in Latin America in recent years."

The same smartass asked about the "retrial" of the acquitted aviators.

"If the defendant has a right to appeal," retorted Castro, "then so do the people!"[17]

Castro, whose "courts" declared, "Proof is secondary. We execute from revolutionary conviction!" could barely keep up with the invitations from the world's most prestigious universities. He'd already been acclaimed at Yale and Princeton, where jubilant upperclassmen hoisted the mass-assassin and abolisher of habeas corpus on their shoulders. "A riotous welcome," crowed Princeton's student paper. "A festive, crazy atmosphere, bubbling with enthusiasm." He had received similar receptions at the National Press Club, at the Overseas Press Club, at the United Nations, and in Central Park.

Cuba's true freedom fighters never got that reception.

CHAPTER ELEVEN

OPERATION CUBAN FREEDOM—NOT!

"**F**reedom is our goal," roared Pepe San Roman to the men he com-manded. "Cuba is our cause. God is on our side. On to victory!"[1]

Fifteen hundred men crowded before San Roman at their Guatemalan training camps that day. The next day they'd embark for a port in Nicaragua, the following day for a landing site in Cuba called Bahia de Cochinos—the Bay of Pigs. Their outfit was known as Brigada 2506, and at their commander's address the men erupted in cheers.

Every man in Brigada 2506 was a volunteer. They included men from every social stratum and race in Cuba—from sugarcane planters to sugarcane cutters, from aristocrats to their chauffeurs, and every-thing in between; some were family men, some were teenagers. Only a hundred of these volunteers had military backgrounds, but their gung-ho attitude impressed their American trainers, who were veterans of Omaha Beach, Bastogne, Corregidor, Inchon, and Iwo Jima.

Only two days later, one of these men, air chief Reid Doster, learned that the Kennedy administration had canceled the scheduled airstrikes. "What? Are they nuts? There goes the whole f—ing war!"[2]

First off, the administration's Best and Brightest nixed the original landing site at Trinidad. This coastal town a hundred miles east of the Bay of Pigs was originally chosen by the CIA and military men because it was a hotbed of anti-Castro sentiment. Rebellions had started there three months after Castro's takeover in January 1959. Also, the nearby Escambray mountains crawled with anti-Communist guerrillas who would join the invaders, and the local militia were known to be disloyal to the Reds. A concentration camp holding six thousand anti-Communist prisoners was located right outside Trinidad. The planned invasion supplies included weapons for them. Just as important, only two major roads led to Trinidad from the north, so any Castro troops moving in would have been sitting ducks for the Brigada's air force.

But landing in a populated area like Trinidad was deemed "too noisy" by the New Frontiersmen. They had a fetish about hiding America's role in the invasion. So, back to the drawing board for the planners—who returned with a landing site at the Bay of Pigs, a desolate swamp. This was worse from a military standpoint but had a good chance of success—*given total air superiority and the complete obliteration of Castro's air force.* This was stressed by the military and CIA planners, just as it's stressed here by me.

JFK's civilian wizards further demanded that the invasion take place at night. (That way nobody would notice it, you see.) The military planners gaped. From Operation Torch in North Africa through Normandy through Saipan and Okinawa through Inchon—nothing like this had ever been attempted. All those took place at dawn.

No matter. The Knights of Camelot had spoken.

Amazingly, the initial landing went fairly well. The beachhead and an airstrip were secured in the first few hours. Castro's soldiers were falling back, others surrendering, many others switching sides. "So many were surrendering I was actually worried!" says my cousin Alberto "Pilo" Fontova. "Heck, man, there's five or six of us guarding five or six dozen Castro troops! I kept thinking, 'What if these guys decide to turn on us?'"

Fidel and Che got the news and panicked. Castro blabbed insane and contradictory orders to all and sundry. First he rushed to a sugar mill near the invasion site where his troops were massing and where his orders spread further confusion, and then he rushed three hundred miles east to Pinar del Rio, where, he assured everyone, the "real" invasion was coming. He could tell from a huge fleet massing just offshore. He wasn't falling for that little feint at the Bay of Pigs. So he ordered the masterful Che Guevara to dig in there with thousands of troops and brace for the Yankee attack.

"*Seguro, mi Comandante!*" Che saluted and spent three days there, three hundred miles from the battle, without firing a shot. Just offshore from him were a few rowboats packed with Roman candles, bottle rockets, mirrors, and tape recorders: the CIA ruse. Che and his soldiers lucked out. Almost fifty thousand of their comrades were falling like flies at Giron. The Red tank columns and massed infantry reeled and staggered from the tiny Brigada's massed firepower. The lethal fury of the Brigadista attack had the Reds thinking they faced twenty to thirty thousand "Yankee mercenaries."

Their foes were actually a band of mostly civilian volunteers they outnumbered almost forty to one, with the amazing Erneido Oliva as second in command. But no amount of heroism and pluck could offset those odds without air cover.

Soon some planes roared overhead. The Brigadistas on the beach waved and cheered, until they looked closer and then were rocked from a massive blast in the bay behind them. A huge mushroom cloud rose. "Holy shit!" one gasped. "Fidel's got the A-bomb too?" No, not yet, but he had jet rockets hitting a ship laden with ten days' worth of ammo. The Brigada had expected that their air support would obliterate Castro's air force. Instead, Castro's air force obliterated the Brigada's ammo ships and control center. Eighty percent of the pre-invasion sorties to be flown by the Brigada planes from Nicaragua were canceled at the last moment by JFK. These airstrikes were—you guessed it—"too noisy."

Now the Brigada's lumbering B-26s provided rollicking sport for Castro's T-33 jets, and its troops and supplies even more. Castro had total control of the skies, and it was a turkey shoot. Fifty thousand Communist troops were massing for the counterattack. Squadrons of Soviet tanks were revving their engines, under orders from a Soviet commander.

All these forces were aiming at the abandoned Brigadistas, 1,400 of them, who had no hope of reinforcement or air cover. CIA man Grayston Lynch knew about the canceled airstrikes by now and figured the men were doomed. "If things get really rough," he radioed Commander Pepe San Roman, "we can come in and evacuate you."

"We will not be evacuated!" San Roman roared back to Lynch. "We came here to fight! Let it end here!"

The Brigadistas dug in deeper, counted their meager ammo, and tried to treat their wounded comrades. Things looked grim. But stationed only thirty miles off the Cuban coast was the carrier *Essex*. Dozens of deadly Skyhawk jets were on deck and primed for action. Their pilots were banging their fists, kicking bulkheads, and screaming against the sellout of their Cuban freedom-fighting brothers on that heroic beachhead. They pilots knew they could clean up Castro's entire air force with a few cannon bursts, obliterate his troop columns with a few bombing and strafing runs, and be back on deck in time for breakfast.

If the Brigada's own air force was allowed to fly, it could follow up with sorties against Castro's infantry and tank columns blundering down the only three roads to the beachhead. These roads were elevated over the surrounding swamp and completely open. The Brigada's B-26s would slaughter anything on them—Castro's very own "Highway of Death."

From that mission the Brigada's planes would refuel, rearm, and move on to hammer any more troops coming down Cuba's central highway from Havana. More defeats, more defections. The tide would turn. Cuba would be free.

The pleas made it to Chief Admiral Arleigh Burke in Washington, D.C., who conveyed them in person to his commander in chief. John F.

Kennedy was in a white tux and tails that fateful night of April 18, 1961, having just emerged from an elegant Beltway ball. For the closing act of the glittering occasion, Jackie and her charming beau had spun around the dance floor to the claps and coos of the delighted guests. In the new president's honor, the band had struck up the Broadway smash "Mr. Wonderful."

"Two planes, Mr. President!" sputtered Admiral Burke. The fighting admiral was livid, pleading for permission to allow just *two* of his jets to blaze off the carrier deck and support the desperately embattled Brigada.

"Burke, we can't get involved in this," replied Mr. Wonderful.

"Goddammit, Mr. President! We *are* involved. There is no way we can hide it. We are involved!"[3]

Interesting match here: In one corner, the man who blasted half the Imperial Japanese fleet to fiery rubble and sent it to the bottom of the Pacific at the Battle of Leyte Gulf. In the other, the man who managed to get his PT boat karate-chopped in half by a Japanese destroyer, a feat of nautical ingenuity that still has naval men scratching their heads— and one that almost got him court-martialed. Only some heavy political pressure saved Mr. Wonderful in 1944. Politics prevailed again that night in April 1961. JFK refused to help the freedom fighters. The election was over, you see.

So all those jets with their rockets and cannons, those destroyers brimming with artillery, those ace Navy pilots champing at the bit for action—all this was hogtied by strict orders from the commander in chief.

By the second day, almost half of the suicidally brave Cuban exile pilots had met a fiery death from Castro's jets. This was too much for their enraged American trainers at the base in Nicaragua. "We were so closely associated with the Cuban aircrews that we felt a real sense of responsibility," said Lt. Colonel Joe Shannon. "We felt a strong dedication to their cause. Now was time to show our friends how strongly we felt."[4]

Four of these trainers, Thomas "Pete" Ray, Riley Shamburger, Leo Baker, and Wade Gray, suited up, gunned the engines, and joined the fight. These weren't pampered Ivy Leaguers. They were Alabama Air Guard officers, men with archaic notions of loyalty and honor. They knew the odds. They went anyway. All four died on that first mission. They now have streets named after them in Little Havana. The remains of one of them were recently returned from Cuba and given an honorable burial in Birmingham. None of the administration's Best and Brightest were on hand to comfort the surviving family members. Several Cuban American families were.

Amazingly, at the Bay of Pigs, JFK did permit some *Essex* planes over the beachhead, but only to "observe" the slaughter; every request to engage the enemy was denied. In Peter Wyden's book *Bay of Pigs*, he reports that these Navy pilots admit to sobbing openly in their cockpits. They were still choked up when they landed on the *Essex*; some slammed their helmets on the deck and broke down completely. Navy airman Mike Griffin landed his jet on the *Essex* and walked up to the bridge to make a report "with tears streaming down his cheeks. . . . He was so angry and upset that it took a few minutes before he could utter a word," reported his commander.[5]

"I wanted to resign from the Navy," said Captain Robert Crutchfield, the decorated naval officer who commanded the fleet off the beachhead. He'd had to relay Washington's replies to those pilots.[6]

So what on earth were they there for? To take pictures, it turned out. That's all JFK authorized. "And boy," recalls freedom fighter Juan Clark, who was in the thick of the fighting, "you shoulda seen the Communists respond when those jets flew over! They all *stopped shooting*! Even the artillery bombardment stopped—and boy, was *that* nice!"

When Cuban prison guards heard about the "Yankee invasion," they suddenly made nice with the political prisoners. But it was all temporary—and it was only the reaction of Cubans who didn't plan on scramming to the Soviet Union.

The political prisoners gaped as army trucks pulled up and unloaded crate after crate of dynamite and other explosives. Soon the Communists were digging under the prison buildings and wiring the explosives. "We had the impression of sleeping over a powder keg," recalls prisoner Chanes de Armas. "There were some men whose nerves couldn't stand the torture and were permanently damaged.... It was horrible to think that from one minute to the next we could be killed in an explosion."[7]

At the time, ten thousand prisoners were crammed into the Modelo prison at the Isle of Pines. Castro was planning to blow them all up should the tide of battle turn against him. Remember, Hitler ordered the same thing in Paris when the going got rough for him. It never came off, because General Dietrich von Choltitz refused to carry out the order.

Some say Castro *still* plans to go out with a bang (and mass murder.) "Castro plans a *götterdämmerung*." That's Colonel Alvaro Prendes, former vice chief of the Cuban air force, after defecting in 1994. "The doomsday plan is codenamed *Lucero* [Lucifer]. If his regime becomes seriously threatened by an invasion or internal upheaval, dissidents will be rounded up and herded into tunnels beneath Havana to be exterminated with poison gas."[8] No wonder Oliver Stone says, "Castro is a very moral man, very humane."

We call them "men," but Brigadista Felipe Rondon was sixteen years old when he grabbed his 57 mm cannon and ran to face one of Castro's Stalin tanks point-blank. At ten yards he fired at the clanking, lumbering beast and it exploded, but the momentum kept it going and it rolled over little Felipe.

Gilberto Hernandez was seventeen when a round from a Czech burp gun put out his eye. Castro's troops were swarming in, but he held his ground, firing furiously with his recoilless rifle for another hour until the Reds finally surrounded him and killed him with a shower of grenades.

By then the invaders sensed they'd been abandoned. Ammo was almost gone. Two days of shooting and reloading without sleep, food, or water were taking their toll. Many were hallucinating. That's when Castro's Soviet howitzers opened up, huge 122 mm ones, four batteries' worth. They pounded two thousand rounds into the Brigada's ranks over a four-hour period. "It sounded like the end of the world," one said later.

"Rommel's crack Afrika Korps broke and ran under a similar bombardment," wrote Haynes Johnson. By now the invaders were dazed, delirious with fatigue, thirst, and hunger, too deafened by the bombardment to even hear orders. So their commander had to scream.

"There is no retreat, *carajo*!" Erneido Oliva, second in command, stood and bellowed. "We stand and fight!" And so they did. Right after the deadly shower of Soviet shells, more Stalin tanks rumbled up. A boy named Barberito rushed up to the first one and blasted it repeatedly with his recoilless rifle. The tank was barely dented but its rattled occupants opened the hatch and surrendered. In fact, they insisted on shaking hands with their pubescent captor, who was felled an hour later by a machine gun burst to his valiant little heart.

On another front, CIA man Grayston Lynch was talking with commander Pepe San Roman from his command post offshore. Lynch urged, "Hold on, Pepe! We're coming in. If we have to, we can evacuate."

"We don't want evacuation!" San Roman bellowed. "We came here to fight! We want more ammo! We want planes! For us, this ends here!"

Castro had fifty thousand men around the beachhead now. Oliva had one tank manned by teenager Jorge Alvarez and another by José Fajardo, who had left a wife and four-year-old daughter in Miami to volunteer for the freedom fight. The little girl would later be known as Gloria Estefan. Alvarez and Fajardo had already knocked out several massive Russian Stalins and T-34s. They only had two rounds of ammo left. Gloria's dad aimed and knocked out another tank. Then his own tank was blasted.

"Dammit!" thought Erneido Oliva as he saw the explosion and flames. But Gloria's old man opened the hatch and somehow clambered out, with his clothes on fire. He looked around, saw his commander, saluted, and started rushing up for further orders. "José collapsed midway to me," recalls Oliva. "He was horribly wounded. His face and half his body were a mass of blood—but José *wanted to keep fighting*! That's the real untold story about the Bay of Pigs!" Oliva stresses. "The heroism of our men, the fanaticism and professionalism these—mostly civilian volunteers with less than a month's training—displayed in combat. I was a professional military man, they mostly weren't. And I'll tell you, my men's heroism left me speechless—does to this day."

Now, with squadrons of Stalin and T-34 tanks closing in, Oliva had one tank left, manned by little Jorge Alvarez. He quickly knocked out two of Castro's Stalins. But he couldn't stem the flood. More Stalins and T-34s kept coming. So Alvarez—outgunned, outnumbered, and out of ammo—had no choice. He gunned his tank to a horrendous clattering whine and charged.

Alvarez rammed his tank into the attacking Stalin tank. The Red driver was stunned, frantic. He couldn't get a half-second to aim his gun. So Alvarez rammed him again, again, and again, finally splitting the Stalin's barrel and forcing its surrender. These things went on for three days.

The Brigada's spent ammo inevitably forced a retreat. "Can't continue..." Lynch's radio crackled—it was San Roman again. "Thousands of Communists closing in. Have nothing left to fight them. No ammo. No food. No water. Nothing to treat the wounded men. No nothing... destroying my equipment...." The radio went dead.

"Tears flooded my eyes," writes Grayston Lynch. "For the first time in my thirty-seven years I was ashamed of my country." These weren't the tears of Bill Clinton at a photo-op, either. Lynch had landed on Omaha Beach. He had helped throw back Hitler's panzers at the Battle of the Bulge. He had fought off human wave attacks by Chi-Coms at Korea's Heartbreak Ridge. And almost to a man, the

American officers involved in the invasion admit to breaking down under the emotional ordeal, watching helplessly as the Cubans they'd trained and befriended were abandoned and then overwhelmed by Castro's forces.

When the smoke cleared, more than a hundred Brigadistas lay dead and hundreds more were wounded, their very mortars and machine gun barrels melted from their furious rates of fire. For three days, 1,400 Brigadistas—without naval artillery and air support—had squared off against 51,000 of Castro's troops, Castro's entire air force, and squadrons of Soviet tanks. According to defecting Castroites, the Red forces took casualties of twenty to one against Brigada 2506.

The battle was over, but the heroism and horrors weren't. Paratroop commander Alejandro del Valle, his ammo expired and Red troops combing the long-doomed beachhead, jumped on a rickety sailboat with twenty-two other Brigadistas and shoved off. The first day at sea, their fury made them forget their wounds, their thirst, and the scorching sun. They spent it raging and cursing their betrayal.

By the eighth day, five of the men had died from their wounds or from thirst and exposure. They received a burial at sea from their comrades. By the tenth day, three more had perished. By the time a freighter picked them up, on the eighteenth day, ten had died, including del Valle. Dehydrated, starved, horribly sunburned, and probably delirious, he had leaped overboard with a knife to battle a huge shark that had followed them for a day. He thought the raw flesh might feed his slowly starving men. The shark escaped and del Valle was hauled aboard, where he lay down in a hollow-eyed daze and said nothing as night closed in. Next morning, his comrades found him dead.

The same day that Alejandro del Valle tried to escape, a hundred of his captured comrades were jammed into a tractor-trailer for transport to prison in Havana. "*No mas!*" yelled the desperate men from inside the truck. They were struck with gun butts, jabbed with bayonets, spit on, and jammed in tighter. "Men are dying in here! They're being crushed!"

"Good!" snarled the Castro commander. "That'll save us the bullets to shoot you." And he emptied the magazine of a Czech machine gun just over their heads (the only shots this gallant commandante fired the entire battle).

More bayonets jabbed and fifty more captives were shoved in. It took twenty Castro soldiers huffing and puffing to finally jam the doors shut and muffle the screams. It was an eight-hour drive to Havana in the scorching tropical sun. We hear horror stories of prisoners hauled off in cattle cars. Well, these men dreamed of a cattle car. This was a rolling oven. Soon the yelling stopped and the gasping started. No vents in this trailer; only the bullet holes let little wisps of air into the sweltering death chamber.

The Brigadistas beat vainly on the walls. With their last reserves of strength, they rocked back and forth, trying to tip the truck over on the bumpy roads. Sweat and excrement sloshed at their boots. The stronger captives lifted their weaker or wounded comrades toward those bullet holes for a precious gasp.

Finally the only effort in the chamber was gasping. "Could Dante's inferno be worse?" asked a survivor years later. Eight agonizing hours later, the trailer's doors finally opened in front of the prison camp. When all had stumbled out, ten remained on the filthy floor. They were dead.

The commander who ordered this atrocity was Osmany Cienfuegos. He was recently Cuba's minister of tourism.

On a lighter note, Brigadista Fernando Marquet recalls his capture: "Couple days after the battle, the Communists had us all tightly bound and crammed into an old sugar mill in the area. One morning I'm lying there all trussed up and I hear a babble of strange voices—a strange language, actually. Turned out it was French. Then the doors to the mill open up and who walks in but Che Guevara himself, wearing his famous *boina* [beret] and at just the right angle, too." The battle had been over for days, so it was time for the gallant Che to finally show up. "Che was surrounded by these French journalists, it looked like. And as you might imagine, these visiting French journalists were fawning *all over* Che, especially as a couple were women.

"I can imagine how Che had been laying it on 'em, too: detailing his gallant fight against all these old, rich, white millionaires, sugar mill owners—Yankee lackeys all—who'd come back trying to reclaim their ill-gotten plantations, yachts, factories, and fortunes by landing at the Bay of Pigs.

"Well, I was closest to the door so I was one of the first prisoners the French reporters saw. But I'm part black and I was eighteen years old at the time. . . . Those French reporters sure looked confused—and Che noticed this quickly. '*Hay Caramba!*' you could hear him thinking. 'Here I've been telling these reporters about those old millionaire whites we'd fought—and the first thing they run into is an eighteen-year-old black kid!'

"So Che immediately walked up to me. First he asks me what I'm doing there, as if someone my age and background shouldn't be there. 'I don't like Communism,' I told him promptly. Then he starts into my father and uncle being rich Batistiano crooks and such because my uncle was a congressman and my father worked for Cuban customs before the revolution. 'They are *not* crooks and we are *not* rich!' I told him.

"'And how have we been treating you, young man!' he asks suddenly with a quick smile and one eye on the French reporters.

"'Well, Che,' I answered, 'These damn ropes are pretty tight.' I grimaced. 'Think they're cutting off the circulation in my hands and legs.'

"'Over here—and pronto!' Che quickly commanded some guards. 'Now please loosen this man's binds!'

"Che probably didn't take his reporter guests to meet the Communists' biggest trophy: the captured Brigada's very commander, the very man who trained and led all those supposed white millionaire invaders, the very man who gave the Castro Communist forces such a ferocious and embarrassing stomping, who, when captured, snarled at the Castro general José Fernandez (who was born in Spain), 'The only reason you captured us, Fernandez, is because we ran out of ammo!' That's General Erneido Oliva—who is black too!"

The gallant Che also visited another group of prisoners, mainly wounded ones, including one named Enrique Ruiz Williams. No French reporters accompanied the gallant Che this time. He walked in, looked around, and snorted, "We're gonna shoot every last one of you." Then he turned on his heel and walked back out.

Two days after the battle, Castro had the tables finally turned on him. He was displaying some of his Bay of Pigs prisoners in front of his TV cameras, much like one might display a trophy buck. He was interrogating, wisecracking, and baiting them as though he were a Communist talk-show host.

The prisoners were thoroughly interrogated beforehand (the KGB had been coaching Castro's secret police for almost two years by now) to see who'd crack, who'd play along. Only these would get to go in front of the cameras. The goal was to get the Bay of Pigs prisoners to admit they were mercenaries in the pay of the U.S. government.

One of the prisoners was a black Cuban (later a U.S. citizen and Army officer) named Tomas Cruz. He and Felipe Rivero, Waldo Castroverde, Carlos de Varona, and many others gave every impression of having broken down. They said they'd be willing to go on camera and denounce the United States.

The Stalinist stage was set at Havana's sports arena and the cameras rolled. Castro's eunuch vice president, Carlos R. Rodriguez, was the opening act. He put the microphone to Felipe Rivero. "Nobody paid us to do a damn thing!" Rivero suddenly blurted. A rumble went through the crowd.

"We came here to fight Communism!" Rivero continued. "Men from every class and race in Cuba volunteered to come here and fight you!"

Rodriguez's lips trembled. The cameras didn't know where to focus.

"And another thing!" Felipe Rivero shouted. "We outfought you!"

Rodriguez's voice trembled as he started with the usual Commie mumbo-jumbo about "the masses" and "the people."

"Okay, fine!" Carlos de Varona jumped in. "You say you have the people with you? Then hold an election! That'll really tell us, won't it?"

Complete pandemonium. Even the diehard Commies in the crowd couldn't restrain themselves. Che Guevara himself had to snicker. A rumble of laughter, a rustle of claps, and hoots erupted from all corners. This was on Cuban national TV, remember. And Cuba—that impoverished, squalid little Third World country—had more TVs per capita than Canada or Germany.

Rodriguez was frantic. Finally the Maximum Leader himself pranced onto the stage. Only he could straighten things out. He had it all figured out, with an ace up his sleeve. So he approached the black parachutist prisoner Tomas Cruz. "We opened the beaches for you blacks," he sneered. "So what on earth are you doing with these Yankee mercenaries?"

Cruz didn't flinch. He looked Castro straight in the eye. "I didn't come here to swim. I came here to fight Communism! I came here with my brothers of every race to free my homeland from you and your Russian friends!"

After this, Castro decided to hold his show trials behind closed doors.

During their "trial," Cruz, Rivero, Castroverde, de Varona, and their comrades figured they were signing their own death warrants. Yet they faced down the most murderous psychopath this hemisphere has ever spawned. They mowed down his troops. They blew up his tanks. And then they spat in his eye.

A year later, Rivero was ransomed by a guilt-stricken JFK. But Castro almost had the last laugh. In 1967, Felipe Rivero found himself in a U.S. federal prison. His crime? Trying to overthrow Castro! Laugh or cry? You decide.

Rivero and the captured Brigadistas spent eighteen months in Castro's dungeons, where none of them broke under torture. When they were ransomed back to the United States, they gathered at Miami's Orange Bowl on December 29, 1962. Jackie Kennedy, with little John-John at her side, addressed the men.

"My son is still too young to realize what has happened here," Jackie said in flawless Spanish. "But I will make it my business to tell him the story of your courage as he grows up. It is my hope that he'll grow into a man at least half as brave as the members of Brigade 2506."[9]

But these men's bravery would not be just forgotten by liberals other than Jackie Kennedy. It would be deliberately trashed and slandered, just as it was betrayed by Jackie Kennedy's husband.

During a campaign speech in 1960, John Kennedy said: "The Republicans have allowed a Communist dictatorship to flourish eight jet minutes from our borders. We must support anti-Castro fighters. So far, these freedom fighters have received no help from our government."[10]

Two weeks before this, Kennedy had been briefed by the CIA (on Ike's orders) about Cuban invasion plans (what would later be known as the Bay of Pigs invasion). So Kennedy knew the Republican administration was helping the Cuban freedom fighters. But since the plans were secret, Kennedy knew Nixon couldn't rebut him. Four months later, 1,500 of those very Cuban freedom fighters whom "we must support" were abandoned by JFK.

"It was Nixon's gung-ho spirit that initiated the idea of invading Cuba," writes Gus Russo.[11] Nixon became, in his own words, "the strongest and most persistent advocate for setting up and supporting action to end Castro's regime." The U.S "should move vigorously to eradicate this cancer on our hemisphere and to prevent further Soviet penetration," he wrote later in *Reader's Digest*.[12] According to Howard Hunt, Richard Nixon was the Cuba project's "action officer" within the White House. National Security aide Colonel Philip Corso said, "Nixon was the hard-liner. He wanted to get rid of Castro. He wanted to hit him hard. He was a rough customer."[13]

"Nixon was the one in the White House applying the pressure," says Marine colonel Robert Cushman, who was Eisenhower's senior military aid in 1960.[14]

"Help the Cubans to the utmost," Ike berated JFK when handing over the reins. "We cannot let that government go on."[15] "We should take more chances and be more aggressive. The U.S cannot take being kicked around."[16] "Castro looks like a madman. If the Organization of American States won't help remove him, we should go it alone."[17]

Eisenhower said he was prepared to defend U.S. action against Cuba in front of anyone. He referred to Castro as an "incubus" and said helping Cubans rid themselves of him would be well worth the price.[18]

After the Bay of Pigs disgrace, Ike took JFK to the woodshed—though not publicly. He called the administration's handling of the Bay of Pigs "a dreary account of mismanagement, timidity, and indecision."[19] When JFK told Ike he worried how Latin America would react to American involvement in the Bay of Pigs, Eisenhower shot back:

"How on earth could you expect the world to believe we had nothing to do with it? Where did they get those ships, the weapons? How could you possibly have kept from the world any knowledge that the U.S. had been assisting the invasion? ... There's only one thing to do when you go into this kind of thing—it must be a success. ... This failure at the Bay of Pigs will embolden the Soviets."[20]

It seems that JFK brooded seriously over Ike and Nixon's advice. His security adviser Walter Rostow noticed this and advised him, "If you're in a fight and get knocked down, the worst thing to do is to come up swinging."[21] Now they could pause and think. "There will be plenty of times and places to show the Russians that we were not paper tigers. Berlin, *Southeast Asia*." (Emphasis mine.) So instead of knocking out a Soviet beachhead ninety miles away, Kennedy decided to intervene half a world away in an Asian jungle, where in the end the Democratic Congress decided to let the Communists win anyway—over the protests of President Richard Nixon—by refusing to aid the South Vietnamese army.

If this logic strikes you as odd, well, then, you're obviously not among the Best and Brightest that extend from the administration of John F. Kennedy to Senator John F. Kerry. The most striking thing

about these Best and Brightest is their overweening, almost pathological, arrogance. "Those bearded Commies can't do this to *you*," snarled
Robert Kennedy to his brother right after the Bay of Pigs. This reaction inspired Operation Mongoose (the psychological warfare programs aimed at destabilizing Fidel) and the Castro assassination
attempts. But notice, this was only because the Kennedys took it *personally*. To them it wasn't so much a matter of national security, much
less a matter of freedom for Cubans, but of getting even, of settling
scores. "Pride goes before destruction, a haughty spirit before a fall."[22]

JFK played politics with the Cuban exiles through his entire administration. One source, then CIA director John McCone, in documents
declassified in 1996, claimed that Castro had agreed to return the Bay
of Pigs prisoners seven months earlier than they were released.[23] But
the Kennedy brothers (both president and attorney general) feared the
Bay of Pigs issue coming up in the November 1962 congressional races.
So the prisoners were conveniently released Christmas Eve of 1962. A
few died in prison during those intervening seven months.

"I will never abandon Cuba to Communism!" That was JFK
addressing the recently ransomed Brigada and their families in Miami's
Orange Bowl on December 29, 1962. "I promise to deliver this Brigade
banner to you in a free Havana!"

"Hands up! You're under arrest!" That was the U.S. Coast Guard
(under orders of the Kennedy administration) to Cuban freedom fighters assembling in Key Largo for a landing in Cuba the following month.

"Hands up! You're under arrest, blokes!" That was the British navy
(after a tip-off by the Kennedy administration) to Cuban freedom fighters assembling in the Bahamas.

"You throw those Cuban exiles out and you close down their camps,
or we cut off your foreign aid!" That was the Kennedy and Johnson
administrations to the Dominican Republic and Costa Rica after Cuban
freedom fighters sought bases in those countries.

And in the swindle that ended the Cuban missile crisis, the Kennedy
administration promised no invasion of Cuba by anybody in the

hemisphere, including the Cuban exiles. Here's the most nauseating part: The pact with Khrushchev was made barely a month before JFK made his liberation promises in the Orange Bowl. Yet he addressed those men, their families, and his compatriots with a straight face. As Grayston Lynch writes, "That was the first time it snowed in the Orange Bowl."

The Brigada got more respect from its enemies than from JFK: Nine of the ten Castroite pilots who flew missions against the Brigada eventually fled Castroland.[24] They knew more about Castro than Kennedy did.

CHAPTER TWELVE

FIDEL AS BUSINESS PARTNER

Politicians who hail the business prospects of trading with Castroite Cuba forget that Fidel didn't just defraud U.S. stockholders, and he didn't just steal millions of dollars in American assets. He stole *billions* of dollars from American businesses: $1.8 billion from a total of 5,911 different companies, to be precise. Fidel pulled off the biggest such heist in *history*. He didn't obfuscate the matter, either. He crowed about it gleefully, then boasted that he'd never repay it—and hasn't, not a penny.

Castro doesn't pay debts, either. In 2001, the United States International Trade Commission Report said, "Cuba stopped payment on all its foreign commercial and bilateral debt with non-socialist countries in 1986." Reuters reported in June 2001, "Debt talks between Cuba and the Paris Club of European creditor nations are on hold.... On the table was $3.8 billion of official debt to Paris Club members, part of a much larger debt Cuba ran up through the 1980s, until it began to default on payments and then stopped talking with creditors."

And remember, back then Cuba was getting $5 billion a year from the Soviet sugar daddy. So what happened to *that* debt, you ask? Well, Fidel repudiated it, too, about $50 billion worth. "Soviet Union?" he frowns.

"What Soviet Union? Where is this Soviet Union?" No country by that name anymore, right? So how can he owe it any money? *No problema.*

Nelson Mandela's South Africa stepped in to offer comradely assistance to Fidel, and here are the results of that shrewd move: "Cuba's efforts to attract more investment from South Africa are being frustrated by the island nation's failure to pay a $13 million debt. South African Trade and Industry Ministry is wary of exposing itself to the Cuban risk until the debt is settled."[1] Mexico got bit too. Last year, Mexico's Bancomex, trying to recoup its ghastly losses from financing trade with Cuba, froze Cuban assets in three countries.

But some people never learn. The *Houston Business Chronicle* calls Castro's Cuba "a great new marketplace." I recently read a report from the head of Mississippi's recent trade delegation to Cuba. He gushed that they'd "had a chance to meet Cuba's business community." Problem is, Cuba has no business community—it's been the government since Castro took over. In fact, in recent years, the small number of private enterprises has actually *shrunk*. According to Moody's Investors Service, July 2002: "Recent Cuban government actions indicate that official attitudes toward economic reform may have soured.... Increased obstacles to private sector activities and restrictions to foreign direct investments reveal heightened concerns about the loss of political control inherent in the economic reform process."

But still they come. So many American businessmen come knocking and displaying their wares that Castro finally threw them a party. In July 2002, Cuba's Communist Party put on a rollicking Fourth of July bash at Havana's Karl Marx Theater. The festivities were "in honor of the noble American people on the anniversary of their independence," proclaimed Cuba's Communist Party newspaper, *Granma*. Fidel himself declared, "The cultural, spiritual, and moral legacy of the American people is also the heritage of Cuba and of the Cuban people!" And a choral group sang "Old Man River."

Wow. What happened to the United States as "a vulture preying on humanity" (circa 1960), or the United States as "the cancer of humanity" (circa 1968), or "We will bring America to her knees" (in Iran in 2001), or "worse than Hitler's Germany" (a Castroite staple for forty years). What a difference a few years—and going bankrupt—make. The sugar daddy Soviet Union is gone and Cuba's credit rating is now rated below Somalia by Moody's and below Haiti by Dun & Bradstreet. Another sign of Cuba's desperation is that Havana recently topped Bangkok as "child-sex capital of the world."

Today Castro has to pay cash for American products. But he and American companies are hoping to cozy up so he can get credit— guaranteed by American taxpayers through the Export-Import Bank. No risk to Castro and American businesses, only to you and me.

In the meantime, trade delegations visit Havana to chum it up with the murderers of Americans. Thousands of businessmen attended the U.S. Food & Agribusiness Exhibition at Havana's Palacio de las Convenciones on September 26–30, 2002. Among the dignitaries they might have met was Cuba's "minister of education," Fernando Vecino Alegret.

The book *Honor Bound: American Prisoners of War in Southeast Asia 1961–1973* provides some interesting biographical details on Alegret. During the Vietnam War, the Communists ran a "Cuba Project" at the Cu Loc POW camp (also known as "The Zoo") on the southwestern edge of Hanoi. The "Cuba Project" was a Josef Mengele–type experiment run by Castroite Cubans to determine how much physical and psychological agony a human can endure before cracking. The North Vietnamese never asked the Castroites for advice on combat, only on torture.

For their experiment, the Cubans chose twenty American POWs— mostly Navy fliers. One died: Lt. Colonel Earl Cobeil, a Navy F-105 pilot. His death came slowly, in agonizing stages, under torture. His torturer, nicknamed "Fidel," was identified in congressional hearings (and in the *Miami Herald* in 1999) with great probability as Cuba's minister of education, Fernando Vecino Alegret.

"The difference between the Vietnamese and 'Fidel,'" testified fellow POW Captain Ray Vohden, "was that more or less, once the Vietnamese got what they wanted, they let up, at least for a while. Not so with 'Fidel.'...'I'll show him,' 'Fidel' said to me. 'I'll make him [Cobeil] so happy to bow down when I finish with him, he'll come crying to me on his knees begging me to let him surrender.'" Vohden continued, "When I saw 'Fidel' with the fan belt I was surprised, because up to that time I had never heard of anyone getting hit like that. Slaps, punches, straps, manacles, ropes, yes. But 'Fidel' was going to show the Vietnamese a new trick.... Earl Cobeil had resisted 'Fidel' to the maximum. Now I could hear the thud of the belt falling on Cobeil's body again and again, as 'Fidel' screamed, 'You son of a beech, you fooker, you are cheating me. I will show you. I will show you.' I could hear the thud of the belt falling on Earl Cobeil's body again and again. I almost threw up each time I heard the belt hit Earl's body. I didn't think any human could endure such a thing. The guards all stood around laughing and yelling in Vietnamese. It had been far easier for me to endure the straps myself than to have to go through this.

"They [the North Vietnamese] tortured to obtain military information or a political statement, they punished us for breaking their rules...but rarely tortured indefinitely just for the sake of torture. Eventually, they always let up....However, 'Fidel' unmercifully beat a mentally defenseless, sick man to death."[2]

"Earl Cobeil was a complete physical disaster when we saw him," testified another fellow POW, Colonel Jack Bomar. "He had been tortured for days and days and days. I went down to clean him up. When 'Fidel' dragged us down there, he said, 'Clean him up, and if anything happens to this man, you, Bomar, are responsible.' Then he hit Cobeil right in the face, knocked him down again. His hands were almost severed from the manacles. He had bamboo in his shins. All kinds of welts up and down all over; his face was bloody. He was a complete mess. They brought him into the room and as far as we could tell, Captain Cobeil was totally mentally out of it. He did not know where he was. I don't think he knew where he had been or where he was going. He was just there. Then 'Fidel' began to beat him with a fan belt....

When he lost his temper, he was a complete madman. He would get red in the face; he just exploded with rage. So if you refused to bow to him like Cobeil refused to do…his temper just went out of control."

"Fidel's" monthlong beatings of another U.S. POW named Jim Kasler were "among the worst sieges of torture any American withstood in Hanoi," according to *Honor Bound*. "Fidel" flogged Kasler "until his buttocks, lower back, and legs hung in shreds, and at the end he was in a semi-coma."[3]

That bowing down—not just murdering Americans, but humiliating them in the process—is a Castroite hang-up.

"Kneel and beg for your life!" they taunted William Morgan as this American citizen was bound in front of a Castro firing squad on March 11, 1961. Both Fidel and Raul were in attendance. Morgan simply glowered back. An eyewitness, John Martino, says Morgan had walked to the execution stake singing "As the Caissons Go Marching."

"I kneel for no man!" Morgan finally shouted back.

"Very well, Meester Weel-yam Morgan." His executioners were aiming low, on purpose. "*Fuego!*"

The first volley shattered Morgan's knees. "See, Meester Morgan? We made you kneel, didn't we?"

Four more bullets slammed into Morgan, all very carefully aimed to miss vitals. They slammed into his shoulders. They slammed into his legs. He winced with every blast. Long minutes passed. Finally one of Fidel's executioners walked up and emptied a tommy gun clip into Morgan's back.[4]

These are the sort of people America's businessmen want to do business with.

Jimmy Carter tried the "be nice to Castro and he'll be nice back" approach by lifting the travel ban to Cuba in March 1977. Castro reciprocated by sending thousands of Cuban troops to Africa (where they used poison gas, sarin to be precise). He also sent thousands of psychopaths, killers, and perverts to America in the Mariel Boatlift. Thanks, Fidel!

Even earlier, in 1975, Gerald Ford (under Kissinger's influence) had relaxed the embargo. He allowed foreign branches and subsidiaries of U.S. companies to trade freely with Cuba and persuaded the Organization of American States to lift its sanctions. Castro reciprocated by starting his African invasion and by trying to assassinate Ford.

You read right. On March 19, 1976, the *Los Angles Times* ran the headline "Cuban Link to Death Plot Probed." Both Republican candidates of the day, President Ford and Ronald Reagan, were to be taken out during the Republican National Convention in San Francisco. The Emiliano Zapata Unit, a radical Bay Area terrorist group, would make the hits. When nabbed, one of the would-be assassins, Gregg Daniel Adornetto, sang about the Cuban connection. Their Cuban intelligence officer was Andres Gomez. Adornetto had met him years earlier when he'd traveled to Cuba for training and funding as a member of the Weather Underground.

Even President Ronald Reagan explored a deal with Castro, early in his first term. Alexander Haig met personally with Cuba's vice president, Carlos R. Rodriguez, in Mexico City. Then diplomatic wiz General Vernon Walters went to Havana for a meeting with the Maximum Leader himself. The thing came to nothing, because Walters had Castro's number. He reported that Castro was hell-bent on exporting revolution to Grenada and Central America. Reagan reimposed the travel ban, and within a year he booted Castro's troops out of Grenada. Reagan's support for anti-Communists in El Salvador and Nicaragua rolled back Castro's Marxist allies.

But during the Clinton administration it was time to play nice again. In 1993, Mobile, Alabama, became a "sister city" with Havana. Representatives of the two cities found ways to spend all sorts of American tax dollars on "get to know you" bashes. But the Cuban official who had so charmed Mobile during these years of "engagement" was unavailable to attend the ten-year celebratory bash for the sister cities. What happened?

Well, Oscar Redondo is his name, and he'd been fingered by the FBI and deported for espionage.[5] Even better, Castro defector Juan Vives tells us that Cuba's intelligence agency makes a point of taping the nighttime cavortings of "friends" who visit Cuba on such cultural exchanges. Vives says Gabriel García Márquez, Naomi Campbell, Kate Moss, and Jack Nicholson are among those recorded.[6] All you visiting trade delegations should be sure to smile at those chandeliers and sprinkler heads in your posh Havana hotel rooms.

The idea that American tourists will show Cuba's poor huddled masses what capitalism provides; what they're being denied; the idea that American "engagement," travel, and trade will undermine Castro's regime—all that is humbug.

Don't you think Cubans know perfectly well that they're poor and oppressed? Tens of thousands of them talk and visit with their American relatives weekly; when they brave storms and tiger sharks on floating chunks of Styrofoam, they don't do it for a thrill, like the yuppies in *Outside* magazine—seventy-seven thousand Cubans have died making the attempt.[7] Some 1.3 million tourists from free countries visited Cuba in 2002. Millions have been visiting for decades. Has it made a dime's bit of difference in any Castroite policy? Has it improved the lot of ordinary Cubans?

Like the European and Canadian tourists (and the roughly two hundred thousand Americans who went in 2003), any new flood of American tourists will stay in fancy hotels, dine in fancy restaurants, and rarely meet an ordinary Cuban. Every dollar they spend will be with a business owned and run by Castro's military.

It can't be said often enough: Castro's cold war is not over. "The much bigger war against America is my destiny." Castro wrote that in 1958, right before his "rebels" kidnapped fifty U.S. military personnel from Guantánamo.

In November 2003, the UPI reported on Castro's star pupil and current lifeline, Venezuela's Hugo Chávez. Chavez was caught providing funds and false passports to al Qaeda operatives. A week later, FOX News quoted North Korea's highest-ranking defector on the presence of North Korean weapons in Cuba.[8]

Liberals accuse Cuban Americans of being "blinded by emotion," of being "unable to see reason" with regard to Castro. But our posture is the empirical one—the one based on firsthand experience with the *Lider Maximo* and on the evidence. Our approach is based on what José Ortega y Gasset called "the Science of Man"—history.

"Private trade, self-employment, private industry, or anything like it will have NO future in this country!" That's what Castro shrieked into the microphones twenty years ago.[9]

"We will not change Cuba's political system or Cuba's economic system! We will accept no conditions for trade with the U.S.!" That's Castro in 2002.[10]

Castroland has the highest incarceration rate and the lowest press and economic freedom indexes on Earth, right alongside its ally North Korea. The Castroites are very vigilant against the slightest crack in the system. Castro himself warned Mikhail Gorbachev that his dabbling with glasnost and perestroika was a folly that would doom both social-ism and Gorbachev. He warned Daniel Ortega that allowing elections in Nicaragua would doom him. He was precisely right on both counts.

Liberals love to point at Cuban dissident and embargo opponent Osvaldo Paya. But they never point to the many Cuban dissidents who *support* the embargo—who in fact want it tightened. These dissidents (like Oscar Biscet and Marta Beatriz Roque) find themselves rotting in Castro's dungeons. Denounce the embargo from Cuba (like Paya) and your utterings will find themselves splashed throughout the Western press. You'll even be allowed to travel abroad to receive awards and kudos. Support the embargo, and you face the Castroite billy clubs.

Alcibiades Hidalgo was Cuban defense minister Raul Castro's chief of staff for over a decade. In 2001, he defected to the United States. "Lifting the travel ban would be a gift for Fidel and Raul," he told the *Washington Post* in an interview.

Castro doesn't deserve any gifts from us.

CHAPTER THIRTEEN

FIDEL'S USEFUL IDIOTS

The idiocies and gaffes by Western elites about Castro and Cuba would defy belief if they weren't by now predictable. Take Vanessa Redgrave. A few years ago, she remarked in an interview that Fidel was "good friends" with legendary Cuban patriot and poet José Martí. Only problem was that Martí died in a battle against the Spanish in 1895.

Take director Sydney Pollack and actor Robert Redford. In their movie *Havana*, they cast Fulgencio Batista as looking like an America businessman, with hair and eyes the same hue as Redford's. Cuban exile, novelist, and Cervantes Prize winner Guillermo Cabrera Infante later bumped into the famous Hollywood director, who turned red-faced with shock and embarrassment when a laughing Cabrera had to inform him that Batista was black.[1]

Both Pollack and Francis Ford Coppola (*Godfather II*) spent millions to achieve a realistic, historically accurate portrayal of the Havana of New Year's 1958, when Batista fled and Castro's rebels entered. To show the tumult and frenzied mobs, the crowds looting, the utter mayhem, they hired more extras than Mel Gibson in *Braveheart* or Ridley Scott in *Gladiator*. However, Havana was *deathly quiet* that night, the streets *empty*. Not one reviewer or major media source pointed out these astounding gaffes.

Part of the trouble is the "furious ignorance," as Guillermo Cabrera Infante calls it, about a nation that's been in the headlines for more than forty years. And part of it is double standards—like when the Spanish government honored Fidel Castro with honorary citizenship the *very week* it served indictment papers for murder against Augusto Pinochet.

Why not serve indictment papers to Fidel? Fidel has plotted cowardly murders his entire life. Even in high school Fidel got into an argument over a debt (he was always a deadbeat) with a schoolmate named Ramon Mestre, who pounded him like a gong. Fidel cried uncle and slunk away, whimpering that he'd go fetch the money he owed Mestre. Instead he came back with a cocked pistol, hoping to surprise and murder the unarmed Mestre, who'd already gone home. A bit later Fidel was fingered for two murders while attending the University of Havana. Both involved ambushes where the victim was shot in the back. Shortly after Fidel got to Havana, on January 6, 1959, he ordered his goons to arrest Ramon Mestre, whom he hadn't seen or heard from in fifteen years. Mestre ended up serving twenty years in horrible dungeons.[2]

Find old pictures of Fidel as a "guerrilla" in the Sierra Maestre and you'll notice his favorite weapon was a scoped rifle. He never had to get *anywhere near* a Batista soldier. Indeed, he'd start every "battle" (puerile little skirmishes) by firing off a shot in the distance. Then he'd let his "guerrillas" do the actual "fighting" (usually murdering unsuspecting soldiers in their bunks, terrorizing unarmed peasants, and rustling cows). While his men engaged in their murder and banditry, Fidel would scurry back to camp to talk to reporters.

One former guerrilla comrade, Huber Matos, (who later served twenty-five years in Castro's dungeons for the crime of having taken Castro's "democratic" and "humanistic" blather seriously) remembered what Fidel was like in "combat." "Fidel and I were on a hill in the Sierra and a Batista plane suddenly appeared—but way off, looked like a speck. Well, it dove and started shooting, strafing something below it. The plane was so far off and doing so little shooting I thought nothing of it," recalls Matos. "So I continued talking while watching the plane. Well, I'd been talking for quite a while and hadn't heard a word from Fidel—which is extremely strange. So I look around.... Where in the hell?

"Fidel was nowhere to be found. So I went back to the cave that served as our little encampment at the time—and there he was, huddled at the far side, trying to drink coffee with his hands shaking like castanets."[3]

That's the real Castro, but the useful idiots keep lining up to praise him. Take Norman Mailer's breathless ode to Fidel: "You are the first and greatest hero to appear in the world since the Second World War. It's as if the ghost of Cortez had appeared in our century riding Zapata's white horse."[4]

Take the perfumed love letter that Frank Mankiewicz, George McGovern's campaign manager, wrote about the Maximum Leader: "One of the most charming men I've ever met! Castro is personally overpowering. It's much more than charisma. Castro remains one of the few truly electric personalities in a world where his peers seem dull."[5]

Take leftist professor Saul Landau: "As Fidel spoke, I could feel a peculiar sensation in his presence. It's as if I am meeting with a new force of nature. Here is a man so filled with energy he is almost a different species. Power radiates from him."[6]

Castro the cowardly murderer—the real Castro—gives that spirit to the Castroite military. When it was sent to Angola, it emulated Che Guevara in *desastre* (disaster) and *fracaso* (complete failure) in its fight against the Unita (pro-Western) Angolan rebels and the South Africans (mostly black troops, by the way). Castro sent fifty thousand troops to Angola and got routed by the South Africans, who never had more than four thousand. According to Castro air force defector Rafael del Pino, Cuban MiGs actually had orders to *avoid* dogfights—to skedaddle at top speed—at the mere *sighting* of a South African Mirage. The MiGs' strict role was ground support, which is to say, strafing and bombing defenseless villages. In any other role they were blown from the skies like skeet.[7]

One story in Cuban defector Juan Benemelis's book *Castro: Terror and Subversion in Africa* was a gem. A few weeks after getting to Angola, the swaggering Cuban general Raul Diaz Arguelles snapped on his holster, affected a Pattonesque scowl, and mounted an armored vehicle with some fellow officers. They were off to the front. They'd arrived to kick enemy butt. They'd show Unita's Jonas Savimbi and those South Africans the tactical brilliance of Castroite officers. Within hours a South African patrol ambushed him. With a well-aimed bazooka blast they sent the mighty Arguelles and his toadies spinning through the air like those human cannonballs you see at the circus, which is fitting. Castroite commanders have always been more clowns than soldiers. They make Groucho Marx in *Duck Soup* look like Hannibal.

The few Castroite victories in Angola came from saturation barrages of Soviet rockets and artillery against poorly armed villagers, and in some cases, the Castroites used poison gas. As reported by *Evans & Novak* in 1988, quoting Dr. Aubin Heyndrickx, senior United Nations consultant on chemical warfare, "There is no doubt of it: Cubans used nerve gases against the troops of Mr. Jonas Savimbi in Angola."

In 1936, Benito Mussolini used gas against Ethiopians and caught hell from the League of Nations. Castro does the same—Angolan civilian casualties ran to half a million—and the League's successor appoints him to its Human Rights Commission!

Outside of the United Nations, the media, and liberal bastions, the Castroites always lose. In Nicaragua, a handful of Contras with a trickle of American aid sent the Castroites scurrying home. In Grenada, U.S. Marines and Rangers swept the floor with them. And the list of routs goes on. Three thousand Castro troops served with the Syrians in the Yom Kippur War, five hundred of them manning T-55 tanks along the Golan Heights. Yet within a week of its lightning surprise attack on Israel to storm its capital, the Syrian government was scrambling to evacuate from its own capital, Damascus. The Israeli forces (a tiny fraction of the Syrian/Cuban forces' size) counterattacked, blasted Castro's tanks into a smoldering scrap pile, and rolled over them like a speed bump.

What accounts for such unconquerable imbecility? How does one explain so incessant a string of blunders by such an endless parade of donkeys as those who infest Castro's military, you ask? Can't a *few* competent commanders emerge? Wouldn't the law of averages allow for it?

First off, Castro's troops are hapless draftees who probably detest the regime as much as anyone in Miami. They have no stake in its wars. But mainly, it's the rampant megalomania and paranoia of their commander in chief that accounts for the Cuban military's astounding stupidities and failures. Communist armies in general and Castroite armies in particular promote officers not on battlefield merit but strictly on political reliability, which is to say on lackeyism and cowardice.

Some say there was an exception in Arnaldo Ochoa. He was supposedly a "brilliant" commander in Angola, but in the Castroite military "brilliant" actually means "not quite a complete moron." Call him a Cuban McClellan. There were hints that he possessed courage and could think for himself. In 1989, Castro got wind of these alarming rumors and sprang to action. He slapped Ochoa with bogus charges of smuggling and murdered him in front of a firing squad.

This Communist promotion policy acts as a foolproof filter against courage, brains, intrepidness—the very things valued by the armies of free nations. Saddam Hussein's army did the same.

But Fidel has taught the world that reality doesn't matter. Murder, impoverish, tyrannize a country's people at your peril, but proclaim yourself a Communist, and the international liberal jet set will just love you.

And so will America's self-proclaimed "black leadership," which somehow knows more about Cuba than all those neighboring Haitians who pile aboard floating junk heaps hoping to make it to Florida, where, if they survive the journey, might make a living scrubbing congealed grease and burnt macaroni off pots for minimum wage. Don't these Haitians realize that Shangri-La lies a scant sixty miles to their west?

Haven't they heard Jesse Jackson singing the praises of the Maximum Leader? These Haitians must be oblivious to TransAfrica's Randall Robinson: "Cuba has universal health care and education and an infant mortality rate half that of Washington, D.C."[8] They probably missed Robinson proclaiming: "Whatever kind of race problem still exists in Cuba is dwarfed by the race problem that we have to contend with in the United States."

Didn't they hear pastor Calvin Butts welcome Fidel to Harlem's Abyssinian Baptist Church, saying: "It is in our tradition to welcome all who are visionaries, revolutionaries, and who seek the liberation of all people. God bless you, Fidel!"

Regarding the Harlem church lovefest, I'll quote directly from the *People's Weekly World*: "The mainly African American audience, which included New York Democratic representatives Charles Rangel and Nydia Velasquez, enthusiastically greeted the Communist leader with a ten-minute standing ovation. Chants of *'Cuba, si! Embargo, no!'* resounded from the rafters and sent a strong message of protest to New York mayor Rudolph Giuliani."

Then the walls shook with shrieks of "Fidel! Viva Fidel!" You see, Elombe Brath, head of the Patrice Lumumba Coalition and chair for the meeting, asked the audience, "Who would you rather come to Harlem? Fidel or Giuliani?"

"Fidel!" they erupted. "Fidel! Viva Fidel!"

(Funny how, judging by emigration, poor black Haitians seem to prefer Giuliani.)

Maxine Waters and Charlie Rangel might be useful idiots for Fidel, but back in 1959, Harlem's representative in Congress, Adam Clayton Powell Jr., knew better. He counseled the U.S. State Department: "If I were an American businessman I would pull out as fast I could.... Those who think Che Guevara is just a nice guy are badly mistaken. He's a definite Communist.... And he and Castro are already cooking up invasions of neighboring countries like the Dominican Republic."[9] Congressman Powell had just returned from a visit to Cuba and was reporting his concerns to the State Department.

The facts about Cuba's dictator stack up, but so do the liberal waffles. Starting in 2002, with the "lift the embargo" campaign under full steam, American "fact-finding" missions started popping up in Havana almost weekly. Governor Jesse Ventura, Senator Chris Dodd, former president Jimmy Carter, and many others gathered valuable info and insights, had eye-opening encounters, and concluded that lifting the embargo would work inexorably toward Castro's doom.

In summer 2002, the Center for International Policy organized a fact-finding junket for the likes for the likes of Congressman Ed Pastor (D-Arizona), Congresswoman Lois Capps (D-California), Congressman Cal Dooley (D-California) and former secretary of agriculture (under Clinton) Dan Glickman. Here are some of the facts found.

"The fact-finding trip gave us all a broader view of the situation in Cuba. Castro remains a striking and charismatic figure at age seventy-seven. He was hospitable and curious. . . . Cuba has offered to help the U.S. with drug interdiction and has made important breakthroughs in biotechnology research that could benefit Americans. . . . Universal health care and education have been hallmarks of Cuban society." Whoo-boy! I can see Fidel barricading himself in his bunker already.

Indeed, the Maximum Leader was still convalescing from the savage blows delivered by that brute Illinois Republican governor George Ryan in an earlier "fact-finding" mission. Here's how *Chicago Sun-Times* reporter Michael Sneed saw that meeting: "Castro joked as the two men blissfully bantered while the rest of the group gawked and gulped over the dinner table."

President Castro had to lift himself from the mat again after the merciless pummeling dished out by Senator Arlen Specter (R-Pennsylvania) and his dauntless sidekick, lawyer Michael Smerconish. These two went on a "fact-finding" mission a month after Ryan's. "The conversation was spellbinding!" gushed Smerconish. "Castro was vibrant, animated, courteous. Castro's laugh broke up the room. He was fully engaged. He was the opposite of today's sound-bite, blow-dried politicians. No subject was off-limits."

But whoops! One of the "fact-finders" slipped up and broached a touchy matter.

"Torture?" Fidel quickly frowned. Then he quickly smiled. "Is there any proof of torture in Cuba? We don't have much money, but we will give you all that we have if you can prove anyone has been tortured here in the past forty-five years. There are no missing people in Cuba." Everyone laughed and the subject was immediately dropped.

Steven Spielberg visited Havana in fall 2002. He called his meeting with "president" Castro "the most important eight hours of my life." I had to laugh at the AP story about this meeting. It said Spielberg met with Cuban Jews, "who had dwindled from 15,000 before the revolution to 1,300 afterward." *Dwindled*—don't you love that word? So innocuous. Most of that dwindling happened between 1959 and 1962. Think it might have had something to do with Communism?

At about the time Spielberg was enjoying "the most important eight hours" of his life, a peaceful Cuban dissident named Juan Carlos González Leiva had a different experience. "An officer sat on my chest, wrapped my head in my sweater, and started hitting me on the forehead with a blunt instrument, giving me a five-stitch wound." González Leiva is blind, by the way.

So are most fact-finders. The Council on Foreign Relations sponsored a "fact-finding" junket in summer 2002. Its intrepid and indefatigable chairman uncovered this gem: "I was impressed with Cuba's commitment to literacy and health care."

So there you have it. Fidel Castro takes a First World country and turns into a Fourth World basket case and is cheered for his commitment to literacy and health care!

He tortures black political prisoners—and gets the Congressional Black Caucus and NAACP singing his praises!

He drives out the same percentage of Jews from Cuba as Hafez Assad drove out of Syria—and he gets liberal American Jews drooling all over him!

He spends four decades executing and jailing dissident journalists and running a Soviet-style propaganda machine over the airwaves and the presses—and gets fawning interviews, smooches, and lovefests by the Beltway media!

His firing squads pile up thousands yelling "Long Live Christ the King!"—and the National Council of Churches does his bidding in the U.S.!

He takes power in an armed coup, jails and executes every political opponent, bans elections—and is a hero of the United Nations!

For liberals, Castro can do no wrong. He's super Fidel.

CHAPTER FOURTEEN

CASTRO'S TUGBOAT MASSACRE

In the pre-dawn darkness of July 13, 1994, seventy-four desperate Cubans—old and young, male and female—snuck aboard a decrepit but seaworthy tugboat in Havana harbor and set off for the United States and freedom. The tug's name was *13th of March*, a name that will lives in infamy for all Cuban Americans—and for all lovers of freedom and decency.

The wind was howling that ugly night. Outside the harbor, in the darkness, an angry sea awaited. But these desperate people didn't have the luxury of canceling or postponing. Planning the escape had taken months. Castro's pervasive police and assorted snitches hadn't spotted it.

The lumbering craft cleared the harbor. Five-foot waves started buffeted the tug. Mothers, sisters, and aunts hushed the terrified children, some as young as one year old. Turning back was out of the question.

With the *13th of March* a few miles into the turbulent sea, thirty-year-old Maria Garcia felt someone tugging her sleeve. She looked down; it was her ten-year-old son, Juan. "Mami, look!" He pointed behind them toward the shore. "What's those lights?"

"Looks like a boat following us, son," she stuttered while stroking his hair. "Calm down, *mi hijo*. Try to sleep. When you wake up, we'll be with our cousins in a free country. Don't worry."

Little Juan wasn't the only one who saw those lights. Others stood on the tug's stern, pointing and frowning. Soon two more sets of lights appeared. "Mami! There's more!" Juan gasped. "And they're getting closer! Look!" Little Juan kept tugging at his mother.

"Don't worry, son," she stammered again. In fact, Maria suspected the lights belonged to Castro patrol boats coming out to intercept them. And they were closing fast. Soon they had rumbled up to the lumbering tug.

Castro patrol boats they were indeed—fire boats, technically, armed with powerful water cannons. The escapees figured it was back to Cuba and probably jail.

Instead—whack! The closest patrol boat rammed the back of the tug with its steel prow—its passengers were knocked around the deck like ninepins. An accident, right? Rough seas and all.

"Hey, watch it! We have women and children aboard!" Women held up their squalling children to get the point across.

The Castroites thought they made nice targets for their water cannons. The water blast shot into the tug, swept the deck, and mowed the escapees down, slamming some against bulkheads and blowing others off the deck into the five-foot waves.

"*Mi hijo! Mi hijo!*" Maria screamed as the water jet slammed into her, ripping half the clothes from her body and ripping Juan's arm from her grasp. "Juanito! Juanito!" She fumbled frantically around her, still blinded by the torrent. Juan had gone spinning across the deck and now clung desperately to the tug's railing ten feet behind Maria as huge waves lapped his legs. "*Dios mio!*"

These people grew up in Cuba. So unlike the *New York Times*, *The Nation*, CNN, CBS, NBC, ABC, and much of Hollywood, they never mistook Fidel Castro for St. Francis of Assisi. But still—could it be that women and their children were being deliberately targeted?

The escapees grabbed beams, rails, arms, legs, anything to keep from going over. Maria and a crewmate managed to grab Juan and yank the sobbing child aboard. The cannon still swept the deck as men shoved women and children into the tug's hold. Soon the other two patrol boats were alongside.

One of the steel boats turned sharply and rammed the tug from the side. The other rammed it from the front. The one from behind slammed them again. The tug was surrounded. The ramming was no accident. Castro's patrol boats were acting on orders.

"What are you doing?" the enraged men yelled from the battered tug. "*Cobardes!* We have women and children aboard! We'll turn around! Okay?"

The Castroites answered the plea by ramming them again. This time, the blow from the steel prow was followed by a sharp snapping sound from the wooden tug. In seconds the tug started coming apart and started to sink. Muffled yells and cries came from below. The women and children who scrambled into the hold for safety were in a watery tomb. With the boat coming apart, the water rushed in around them. Some were able to grab their children and swim out. But not all.

Soon water filled the hold completely. "I was completely blind!" recalls Maria. "I was completely underwater, fumbling around, grabbing for anything near me, trying to find Juan. I was submerged, so my screams were like those in a nightmare where you scream in terror but nothing comes out.... Soon I grabbed an arm and I felt some arms and legs wrap around my neck and chest from behind me. Just then we popped to the surface. It was little Juan gripping my body from behind!"

"Hold tight, *mi hijo*! Hold tight!" Maria yelled between coughing up sea water. "Don't let go!" Juan was coughing and gagging too, but still gripping his mother tightly, almost choking her.

Maria was in the middle of a maelstrom. Her husband was out there too, somewhere. She was treading water frantically with her last reserves of strength when she felt a strong hand grab her. She focused through the spray and saw about ten people hanging onto an ice chest. A man reached out from the group and pulled her toward them just as a blast from the water cannon hit them again. By now all three tugs had turned on their water cannons.

The Castro boats started circling the sinking tug—faster, faster, gunning the engines to a horrendous clattering roar, and creating a huge whirlpool in the process. "People were screaming all around me," recalls Maria. "A woman on the ice chest had her baby daughter ripped from her arms by the blast and she was screaming, screaming, screaming!"

The hysterical woman let go of the ice chest and went under in search of her child—neither one reappeared from the swirling waters.

The roar from the water cannons, the racket from the boat engines creating the deadly whirlpool—this hellish din muffled most of the screams.

Soon Maria was ripped from the ice chest by another blast from the water cannon. "Juanito hadn't been holding on very tightly any more," she sobbed in testimony. "He'd been coughing real bad, coughing up mouthfuls of sea water. Finally I felt him go limp. Then the blast hit us. I went under again and came up screaming. 'Grab Juan! Grab my boy! *Por favor!*' But everyone was scrambling, everyone was under the blast of the gun. My son! My son!"

This time, ten-year-old Juan never resurfaced. Maria Garcia lost her son, husband, brother, sister, two uncles, and three cousins in the maritime massacre.

In all, forty-three people drowned, eleven of them children. Carlos Anaya was three when he drowned, Yisel Alvarez four, Helen Martinez six months. Fortunately, a Greek freighter bound for Havana happened upon the slaughter and sped in to the rescue. Only then did one of the Castro boats throw out some life preservers on ropes and start hauling people in.

Thirty-one survivors were finally plucked from the seas and hauled back to Cuba, where all were jailed or put under house arrest. But a few later escaped Cuba on rafts and reached Miami. Hence we have Maria Garcia's gut-wrenching testimony. It was presented to the United Nations, the Organization of American States, and Amnesty International, who all filed "complaints," "reports," "protests," whatever.

No government could possible condone, much less directly order such a thing—right? Wrong. One of the gallant water cannon gunners was even personally decorated by Castro. Nothing is done by Castro's coast guard without orders from the top. As always, there was a method to the Maximum Leader's murderous madness. The Clinton team—national security adviser Sandy Berger in particular—came into office hell-bent on "improving relations" with Cuba. Castro knew this. He also knew that Clinton was very touchy about Cuban refugees. In 1980, the Mariel Boatlift criminals (a mere handful of the total exodus, actually) had been shipped to Fort Chafee, Arkansas, under Arkansas governor Bill Clinton's watch. After being told they'd be shipped back to Castroland, the Marielitos went berserk, rioting and burning down half the encampment.

Arkansas voters were aghast. When up for reelection, the man who had accepted the Marielitos, Governor Clinton, was trounced.

Some say the tugboat atrocity was Castro's way of demonstrating to Clinton that he wouldn't let a mass exodus of Cubans happen while Clinton was president. "Bill Clinton is terrified of Castro," said Dick Morris, "He looks over his shoulder for rafters the way Castro is always looking over his shoulder expecting an invasion of Marines."[1]

And indeed, two months after the tugboat massacre, Castro cut an immigration deal with a receptive Clinton administration. What we now call the "wet foot/dry foot" policy came into effect. Make it to shore, you stay, but no longer qualify automatically for political asylum. We intercept you at sea, you go back to Castroland.

To its credit, the U.S. Immigration and Naturalization Service strongly condemned the tugboat massacre. But I can't help thinking that had Ronald Reagan been president, he might have done more than wag his finger at the Communist murderers.

What was the net result of all the protests made about the massacre by the United Nations and other "multilateral" organizations? Well, barely a year and a half later, Castro received an engraved invitation to address the United Nations as a guest of honor.

And did Castro's tugboat massacre put a cork in liberal blatherings about what a helluva guy Castro is? You've got to be joking. Instead, the pet manatee of the Democratic Party, Michael Moore (an "outstanding American," according to Fidel himself), has done what liberals like to do—attack the victims.[2]

"These Cuban exiles," he snorts, "for all their chest-thumping and terrorism, are really just a bunch of wimps. That's right. Wimps! When you don't like the oppressor in your country, you stay there and try to overthrow him. You don't just turn tail and run like these Cubans. Imagine if the American colonists had all run to Canada and then insisted the Canadians had a responsibility to overthrow the British down in the States!...So the Cubans came here expecting us to fight their fight for them. And, like morons, we have."

Moore adds: "These Cubans have not slept a wink since they grabbed their assets and headed to Florida."

"Grabbed their assets," folks. Let that sink in for a second. Does he mean the clothes Cuban refugees wore on their backs? The few crumbs they stuffed in their pockets? Does this imbecile realize that Castro stole all "their assets?" Does this moron know that no one could leave Cuba with anything? Does this obese idiot know that women had their very earrings yanked off their ears by Castroite guards at the airport?

One elderly lady insisted on wearing a small crucifix. The guard demanded she take it off: "You can't take it. That pendant belongs to *la revolución!*"

"The hell it does!" she yelled back in tears. "This crucifix belonged to my son—who you swine murdered at the firing squad! I'll die before I give it to you Communist assassins!"

She was dragged off.

Or perhaps the mothers clinging to their sons and daughters as the Castroite murders fired their water cannons were merely "grabbing their assets" so they could live like piggy Michael Moore.

Such was the "grabbing of assets" as we left Cuba, Mr. Moore. Did someone mention "Stupid White Men?"

CHAPTER FIFTEEN

WHO NEEDS FREEDOM?

Even when innocent Cubans escape to Florida—and freedom—liberals sometimes demand that armed guards send them back to Communist Castroland. They can't believe anyone could prefer Miami to that "happy little island" governed by benign Fidel.

During the Elián González controversy, liberals chanted: "A son belongs with his father. The rule of law should prevail." No Cuban Americans disagreed.

The González family in Miami never wanted a media circus. They only wanted to take care of Elián and wait for his father to immigrate here, *as he originally intended*. Such reunions happen practically every week in Miami. The circus, the using of little Elián "as a political football," was all *Castro's* doing.

The evidence—zealously shunned by the mainstream media—was overwhelming. Mauricio Vincent, a reporter for Madrid newspaper *El Pais*, wrote that he'd visited Elián's home town of Cardenas and talked with Elián's father, Juan Miguel, along with other family members and friends. All confirmed that Juan Miguel longed for his son Elián to flee to the United States.

In phone call after phone call from Elián's Cuban family to his Miami family, the Cubans made themselves very clear: Please take care of Elián. His father's on the way.

Juan Miguel had even applied for a U.S. visa. The U.S. Immigration and Naturalization Service knew this, but it became public only after Judicial Watch uncovered the evidence: an INS document written by INS attorney Rebeca Sanchez-Roig about a conference call with commissioner Doris Meissner. "If coercion could be shown," it read, "then the INS could potentially accept the child's asylum application and advise that there is no prohibition on age to child filing application. As such PA [political asylum] should proceed."

The *Miami Herald* reported that on November 26, 1999, the day after Elián was rescued, Juan Miguel had obtained certified copies of Elián's birth certificate and his marriage certificate to his deceased ex-wife, Elizabeth. These documents are the first order of business for Cubans seeking a visa to the United States. Please notice the date—Juan Miguel did these things *before* Castro intervened in the Elián case, which he did on December 5, 1999. Elián's Miami uncle, Lazaro, said it best: 'I always said I would turn over Elián to his father," he said repeatedly. "But Juan Miguel should come here and claim him. It was not Juan Miguel requesting Elián—it was Fidel."[1]

Why did Castro intervene? People, including little boys, flee from Cuba every week. Why Castro's obsession with getting *this one* back?

Exiled Cuban novelist Guillermo Cabrera Infante explained it best, writing in the *Miami Herald* on April 17, 2000, just days before the raid that would seize Elián from his Miami relatives, "Every year, Santeria, the African-rooted religion popularly practiced in Cuba, publishes a horoscope. The Santeros 'toss the coconut shells' and forecast the future according to whether the shells fall flesh side up or down. The Santeros have tied the future of the Castro regime to the fate of Elián González, who is to them the reincarnation of Elegua, a kind of Christ child. The position of the coconut shells foreshadows ills for the 'tribe' of Cuba and a worse fate for the 'chief,' Fidel Castro.

"As soon as the Santeros learned of Elián's fate (the boy had been rescued at sea, saved from sharks by the appearance of dolphins and after forty-eight hours in the water under a blazing sun did not show the burns and sores typical of those rescued at sea), they declared that he was a divine Elegua and that if he remained in Miami Fidel Castro 'would fall.'"

Now you understand his desperation. So many Cubans nowadays— some say Castro is a Santero too—dabble in Santeria that their priests' prophecy could have seriously shaken Castro's hold on the island.

On January 31, 2000, a Christian evangelical minister from India, the Reverend Kilari Anan Paul, visited Cuba. The reverend was closely following the Elián saga from his native India and was severely miffed by the Cuban exile crackpots and hotheads in Miami. The reverend stood shoulder to shoulder with Castro on this one, completely in favor of the United States returning Elián to Cuba and his father. Toward this noble end, the reverend attempted to meet with Juan Miguel González at his Cardenas home—but found him under house arrest.

Regarding the hapless Juan Miguel, forget the idiotic and smarmy CBS interview conducted by Fidel's chum Dan Rather. Instead, read the last chapter of David Limbaugh's book *Absolute Power: The Legacy of Corruption in the Clinton-Reno Justice Department*. Limbaugh saw through the farce—and I don't just mean the raid President Clinton's attorney general, Janet Reno, ordered against Elián's Miami family. Even many liberals, including Lawrence Tribe and Alan Dershowitz, recognized the raid as a legal atrocity. But Limbaugh documents how the judicial outrages had started *months* before.

A lawyer himself, Limbaugh informs us that several affidavits swore to Juan Miguel's *original wishes* for his son before Castro put the squeeze on him. These were from Juan's first cousins. One even swore that Juan had repeatedly told him how he yearned to escape to the United States, even "rowing over in a washtub" if necessary. More important, on December 1, 1999, the INS asserted that Elián's uncle

Lazaro in Miami was indeed the boy's legal custodian and that Florida's family court was the place to arbitrate further issues.

But then everything changed. On December 5, 1999, Castro began demanding Elián's return, and by January 5 the same INS ruled that state courts had *no authority* in these matters, that neither Elián nor Lazaro on his behalf could apply for political asylum, and that Elián had to return to Cuba by January 14.

The mainstream media sang from Castro's song sheet. But Brit Hume at FOX News asked the pertinent questions, things like: Why is the National Council of Churches involved in this dispute? Are they *really* impartial? Why is Clinton's lawyer Greg Craig pleading Juan Miguel's (read: Castro's) case? And by the way, who's paying him? Can a man who works as a doorman in a hotel in Cuba afford somebody like Craig?[2]

Hume asked the questions other famed investigative reporters wouldn't—and he didn't let up. Just a week after the Janet Reno raid—but before Elián was deported—Hume ran a special report: "Customs officials at Dulles Airport caught those doctors sent from Cuba to be with Elián González with drugs, which they seized. The *Miami Herald* reports the drugs included phenobarbital, a sedative, and Miltown, a tranquilizer."[3] Then came pictures of the calm and smiling Elián in his papa's arms.

That the liberal media is Castrophilic we know. But why did President Clinton trash America's legal standards, reverse a refugee policy dating from the beginning of the Cold War, and become Castro's accomplice in returning Elián to Communism? Some say Castro "had something" on Clinton. Others that Castro threatened him with another Mariel Boatlift. Others say that Clinton wanted, as part of his "legacy," an opening to Cuba. I think these last two were his motivations for the Elián kidnapping.

The mainstream media did its part by portraying Cuban American Miami as far worse than Communist Cuba. On April 2, 2000, Katie Couric of NBC's *Today* show read from her cue cards: "Some suggested over the weekend that it's wrong to expect Elián González to live in a place that tolerates no dissent or freedom of political expression. They were talking about Miami. All eyes on south Florida and its image this morning. Another writer this weekend called it 'an out of control banana republic within America.'"

I've already mentioned Eleanor Clift's gem, but it bears repeating: "To be a poor child in Cuba may be better than to be a poor child in the U.S." Clift saw the stunned look on Bill O'Reilly's face and elaborated a bit. Castro's Cuba, she said "is a place where he [Elián] doesn't have to worry about going to school and being shot at, where drugs are not a big problem, where he has access to free medical care and where the literacy rate I believe is higher than this country's."

Newsweek writers Brook Larmer and John Leland agreed: "Elián might expect a nurturing life in Cuba, sheltered from the crime and social breakdown that would be part of his upbringing in Miami."

While hosting Tipper Gore on his show, CNN's Larry King joined the herd: "Tipper, one of the things that Elián González's father said that I guess would be hard to argue with, that his boy's safer in a school in Havana than in a school in Miami. He would not be shot in a school in Havana."

NBC's Andrea Mitchell, commenting on Castro, found him "old-fashioned, courtly—even paternal." No one said that about the Cuban Americans in Miami, who were routinely portrayed as extremists.

David Limbaugh seemed to be one of the few commentators who actually studied the INS's regulations. The INS's own manual stated: "Asylum officers should not assume that a child cannot have an asylum claim independent of the parents'." The manual offers guidelines for its officers, including examples of asylum claims from six-year-olds. By April 22, 1999, this same INS was kicking down Lazaro's door and wrenching a screaming Elián from the house.

Limbaugh also reminds (or informs) us of an affidavit by Sister Jeanne O'Laughlin. Sister O'Laughlin was president of Barry University and a personal friend of Janet Reno. The good sister was a kindly, intelligent person who originally favored returning Elián to Cuba, for the usual well-meaning (though naïve) reasons: a child belongs with his father.

Well, Sister O'Laughlin, a lifelong Democrat, soon changed her mind as she watched the Castroites at work. Her sworn affidavit mentions Castro's goons scouring her house before Elián met there with his grandmothers, who had been brought from Cuba to meet with him. It mentions the president of the National Council of Churches *confessing* to Sister O'Laughlin that "Castro was dictating negotiations." But it was the abject fear in the eyes of Elián's visiting grandmothers that convinced Sister O'Laughlin.

She confessed to praying and weeping all night after the meeting. This, again, was in her sworn affidavit, ignored by the mainstream media but reported in David Limbaugh's book *Absolute Power*. Limbaugh writes: "After the meeting, Sister O'Laughlin changed her mind. She saw 'fear' in Elián's grandmothers—fear of the Castro regime—and thought it morally wrong to return Elián to Cuba. O'Laughlin was so upset that she decided to go to Capitol Hill at her own expense to lobby Reno to allow Elián to stay in the United States."[4] But who was Janet Reno going to believe, Sister O'Laughlin or Fidel Castro?

As Dan Rather let America know, this whole problem was America's fault. "Today's irony," he said in grave-frown mode on his April 6, 2000, broadcast, "is that to get close to his son, this boy's father had to travel more than a thousand miles to a foreign capital and even then, even now, he must wait for the long-sought reunion. Such are the ways of politics and the law in a free society."[5]

Sure, Castro sinks the boats of fleeing Cubans, jails his subjects who try to escape, and puts Elián's father under house arrest—and it's all America's fault.

With the investigation into *60 Minutes* on President George W. Bush's National Guard service, CBS, Dan Rather, and the *60 Minutes* production team finally got their comeuppance. Couldn't have happened to a nicer bunch. An investigation into the *60 Minutes* show featuring the interview with Juan Miguel on May 2000 might have proven more shocking.

Pedro Porro is a Cuban American who worked for the U.S. Treasury Department in 2000. He was the translator for Juan Miguel during the famous interview with Dan Rather. "I wore an earpiece. Dan's questions would come through, then I'd translate them into Spanish for Juan Miguel," Porro recalls. "Well, when I saw the interview as it appeared on the *60 Minutes* show I didn't know whether to throw up or start crying," he says. "Even during the interview it was obvious that Gregory Craig [former Clinton lawyer and friend then acting as Juan Miguel's (read: *Fidel Castro's*) lawyer] was stage-managing the entire thing. The questions for Juan Miguel were actually fed to Dan Rather by Gregory Craig.

"After a taping session, Craig would call Dan over, give him some more precise instructions, exchange some papers with him. Then Dan would come back on the set and ask those. It was obvious that Dan Rather and Gregory Craig were on very friendly terms.... Craig was acting like a movie director, too. He didn't like the way Juan Miguel's voice was coming across in the English translation. 'Not enough drama,' Craig said. So they went out and got a bona fide dramatic actor to translate and mouth his responses.... It was obvious to me that Juan Miguel was under a lot of stress. You could see it in his face. He never looked at ease. He was never alone, always accompanied by Cuban Interest Section people they called 'bodyguards' or by Gregory Craig himself. My father was a newsman in Cuba. So the whole thing, the elaborate deception of this show, shocked me tremendously when I saw the end product."

NBC's Jim Avila added to the media's deception: "Why did she [Elián's mother] do it? What was she escaping? By all accounts this quiet, serious young woman, who loved to dance the salsa, *was living the good life*.... An extended family destroyed by a mother's decision to start a new life in a new country, a decision that now leaves a little boy estranged from his father and forever separated from her."[6] (Emphasis mine.)

Hey, at least he didn't blame the United States. No, Avila blamed Elián's mother, who gave her life so her son could live in freedom.

CBS's Byron Pitts went back to the more familiar villains. "Six weeks ago this community [Miami Cubans] embraced a boy who had watched his mother die at sea. Tonight there is fear that the embrace has become a choke hold."[7]

ABC's John Quinones seconded Pitts. "It seems like such a contradiction that Cubans, who profess a love of family and respect for the bond between father and son, would be so willing to separate Elián from his father.... It's a community with very little tolerance for those who might disagree."[8]

Bryant Gumbel pointed the finger at the *real* enemy: "Cuban Americans... have been quick to point fingers at Castro for exploiting the little boy. Are their actions any less reprehensible?" He referred to Republican congresswoman Ileana Ros-Lehtinen's support for Elián's staying in the United States as "pretty disgusting."[9]

Time magazine's Tim Padgett relied on the classic stereotype: Those Miami Cubans were "a privileged, imperious elite who set themselves up as a suffering people, as martyred as black slaves and Holocaust Jews, but ever ready to jump on expensive speedboats to reclaim huge family estates the moment the old Communist dictator stops breathing."[10]

Alexander Cockburn published a gem in *New York Press*, writing, "There is a sound case to be made for dropping a tactical nuclear weapon on the Cuban section of Miami. The move would be applauded heartily by most Americans. Alas, Operation Good Riddance would require the sort of political courage sadly lacking in Washington these days." Okay, okay, so the Stalinist Cockburn was joshing. But can you imagine his writing a similar comment about, say, east Los Angeles or Harlem?

The *New York Times*'s incomparable Thomas Friedman was not to be outdone. "I think the American public really got a taste of the degree to which not only Elián had been, in my view, kidnapped by these people [Miami Cubans], but American policy on Cuba has been kidnapped by a very active, vociferous minority." Then this fervent civil libertarian brightened up. "Yup, I gotta confess, that now-famous picture of a U.S. marshal in Miami pointing an automatic weapon toward Donato Dalrymple and ordering him in the name of the U.S. government to turn over Elián González warmed my heart."[11]

Why did Janet Reno's raiders break in with guns, knocking people to the ground? Clinton's people acted on *Castro's* advice. Fidel offered the Clinton administration vital intelligence. His agents in Miami described Lazaro González's home as a veritable armory.[12] Like the liberal media, the Clinton administration trusted Castro's Communist spies more than it trusted ethnic Cuban citizens of the United States. To me, a Justice Department that relies on intelligence from Fidel Castro is a hundred times more dangerous and stupid than its law enforcement officers who might occasionally descend to brutality.

"It is brutal, it is monstrous, it is as mad or bad as anyone can call it." Thus did G. K. Chesterton define Communism in 1919. Chesterton, as usual, was right. Communism started as a monster and grew into a homicidal beast. And President Clinton and Janet Reno handed that beast a helpless child as a toy.

COMING TO AMERICA

When Cubans landed in America's lap by the hundreds of thousands, the potential for trouble was enormous. Cubans landed in the South as excitable, foreign-tongued, octopus-eating strangers. They applied for jobs, worked and sometimes lived right next door, and filled the pews of Catholic churches.

My family landed in New Orleans—deepest, darkest Dixie, red-state America with a vengeance. The city then hosted a huge NASA project that attracted blue-collar workers from surrounding Southern states: Texas, Alabama, and Mississippi.

We know what liberals think about these people. They're the backwoods haters and bigots who gunned down Peter Fonda in the film *Easy Rider* and hatched the plot to assassinate the president in Oliver Stone's ludicrous movie *JFK*. The South, liberals like to think, is a racist place.

My father was a political prisoner in La Cabana's dungeons when we arrived in Louisiana. He listened to the gallant Che's firing squads every dawn, wondering when his turn would come. My mother wondered too. They had two nephews—Bay of Pigs veterans—who were under a death sentence. But my mother didn't have to indulge in despair (and most residents of Little Havana can relate stories ten times as hair-raising and heartbreaking). She was alone in a strange country. She was penniless, friendless, and had three kids to somehow feed, shelter, and school.

A knock on the door in those early days—as we settled into our humble apartment—wasn't exactly comforting. But the knock came from Mrs. Jeffrey, our new next-door neighbor. She had a bleached blonde bouffant and big smile, and she was carrying a basket of fried chicken. Mr. Jeffrey was there too. He offered to help translate a job application my mother had.

The Jeffreys were originally from Texas. They did everything they could to help us. A few days later, she took my mother shopping. The next day she consoled her when my mother broke down crying. Mr. Jeffrey was a World War II and Korea veteran. He knew some Spanish, and I'll never forget him sitting next to my grandfather. He *apologized*, in his heavy Texas twang, for what had happened at the Bay of Pigs—as if it were *his* doing, as if he hadn't done enough for others' freedom already.

The next day, there was another knock on the door. It was our upstairs neighbors, Mr. and Mrs. Simpson. They invited us over—in their hilarious (to us) Southern drawl—to share in that mountain of chicken and burgers they were scorching on the barbeque. The Simpsons hailed from Birmingham, Alabama. To Hollywood and PBS, that's the land of Bull Connor and fire hoses and nothing more. But the next day Mrs. Simpson knocked again and offered to drive us to school (we all spoke Spanish, but we learned English in two months because there was no bilingual education in those days). She'd also turn up holding a shopping bag full of clothes outgrown by the Simpson children. They were for us.

The next day, here came Mrs. Boudreaux from across the street. She was a native Louisianan, perpetually cheerful. She brought a big pot of gumbo and a phone number of a friend who might have a job for Grandad and—*gracias a Dios!*—speaks a little Spanish

Here we were in the very gizzard of the "bigoted" and "hate-filled" South, and our Southern neighbors turned up every day to help us out. Later, when we moved to the suburbs, another family became even more special. Years before, the lady of the house had worked at a local plant riveting the hulls on the famous Higgins boats. Eisenhower called them "the boats that won World War II." One such boat carried her fiancé to shore at Casablanca, another took him to Salerno, and yet another took him to Omaha Beach, where a burst from a German machine gun riddled his legs. Almost forty years later, I watched him limping up the aisle, grimacing slightly with each step. Then he broke into a huge smile while handing me his daughter as a bride.

As one whose family was almost suffocated by their generosity, I'm here to tell you that the arms of Dixie opened damn wide for these foreigners. My family landed in the South, but I've heard compatriots relate similar stories about everywhere in America, literally "from sea to shining sea."

Nobody called the Americans who welcomed us "the greatest generation" back then. But thousands of destitute Cubans knew them (and still remember them) as "*el pueblo que nos abrio los brazos*" (the people who opened their arms to us). We love America, and we look forward to the day when Cuba can enjoy the freedom that we've found from Miami to New Orleans to Los Angeles to New York. *Viva America! Viva Cuba Libre!*

ACKNOWLEDGMENTS

Many people helped me with this book, but let me begin with New York talk-radio legend Barry Farber. "You gotta write that book, Humberto!" (This started almost five years ago.) "America *needs* to hear this stuff!—and they need to hear it in English, and especially in *your* English! Better yet, they *want* to hear this stuff. I hear their excited response when we discuss these things on my radio show. People are *fascinated*. This is all *news*! History may be 'bunk,' as Henry Ford claimed. But Cuba's history under Castro's murderous reign, his threats against our nation—all that isn't really 'history' to most U.S. citizens. They've never heard it before. Our media shuns it all. So it sounds like a late-breaking story!"

It's not like Barry himself is unknowledgeable in these matters. In January 1959, when Castro rolled into Havana atop a tank (which had never fired a shot, by the way) declaring, "I'm a democrat! I'm a humanist! A Christian! I *hate* Communism! I *hate* dictatorships! Cuban people, you have my *solemn* word!" Barry was in Havana as a reporter for NBC radio. He was the first American newsman to interview Che Guevara.

Barry persisted. "Humberto! If *ever* the overused 'untold story' term would fit a book, it's for one *you'd* write about the Cuban revolution—the things we discuss on my show—and now we've got all this Che Guevara stuff, movies, watches, shirts, for heavens sake! Get cracking, will ya?"

Well, here it is. The information and insights in these pages didn't just bubble up in my head spontaneously. Word got out and a throng of friends, family members, and acquaintances—some are bona fide scholars, many more are participants with firsthand roles in the Cuban drama—all rushed in to help me. A deluge of information, anecdotes, recollections, and insights rolled in.

After each session, the source usually had a friend or cousin or in-law with even more of the same, far more than I could ever put in the book. "*Pues claro, chico!* Fulano would be *happy* to help! He knew (Fidel, or Che, or Raul, or Vilma, or Celia, or Cubela, or Camilo, or Batista, or Pedraza, or Masferrer) personally. He was (in the Sierra, or at Moncada, or at the Isle of Pines prison, or at Playa Giron, or in the Escambray, or in the presidential palace, or in Angola)." Then my host looks at his watch. "Ah! Fulano is probably taking his siesta right now, but here's his phone! Give him a call tonight! He'd love to talk!"

Then the *same* process with Fulano. (If it sounds like I'm complaining, please perish the thought. I've rarely learned as much and so enjoyably.)

The thing kept growing. Every bit of this deluge of info surprised me, fascinated me, enraged me, moved me—I simply *had* to put it all down. Though I specialized in Cuba while earning my master's degree in Latin American studies at Tulane University, I had no intention of writing a textbook. Most of the information cascading in was much too juicy to fit a textbook's soporific format.

Anyway, here's a (probably partial) list of my aides in this project. Besides spewing forth a ton of useful information himself, Miguel Uría, who was present at many Castro-Che meetings in the early days, who plunged into the anti-Castro fight from week one, who fought at the

Bay of Pigs, who was a former Castro political prisoner, and who nowadays edits the superb electronic magazine *Guaracabuya, Amigos del Pais*—this *very* busy man also assumed the role of my hunting guide, pointing me here and there to the best sources in the vast and tangled field.

Carlos Bringuier was press spokesman in the early 1960s for the *Directorio Revolucionario Estudiantil*, a group one CIA analyst called "the most militant and deeply motivated of all the Cuban exile organizations seeking to oust Castro." Carlos was also the man who outed Lee Harvey Oswald (and was almost deported back to Castro's Cuba for the impropriety) in August 1963 (observe the date closely). Carlos Bringuier had his own two books, *Red Friday* and *Operacion Judas*, to offer me, then provided ten times as much info and insights in interviews.

What with keeping our taxes low, our nation strong and safe, and our hard-earned tax dollars away from Castro's thieving and bloody paws, you'd think Republican congressmen Lincoln and Mario Diaz-Balart might have enough on their hands. Well, they also found time to help me—but always on *their* time, *not* their constituents' time, please note!

Soon they had me in touch with their father, former Cuban senator Raphael Diaz-Balart. The senior Diaz-Balart, while recounting his relationship with the young Fidel Castro and his grapplings with U.S. State Department and CIA wizards and soothsayers, had me rapt with fascination—and convulsed with mirth. That we could all be as healthy, mentally sharp, and downright exuberant when late septuagenarians as Señor Raphael Diaz-Balart. Indeed, Señor Diaz-Balart contrasts most dramatically in these departments with his former brother-in-law, Fidel Castro.

Both for your sake, dear reader, and mine, I did my damnedest to avoid professional academics for this book. When one appeared, his arms bulging with reams of his highfalutin and always unreadable hooey, his mouth primed to spew forth the usual geyser of idiocies, I ducked into the nearest bushes. I scurried into restrooms and clambered atop a seat in a stall. If he caught me in person at home, I feigned contagious maladies.

So you can imagine my shock when I learned that Victor Triay, Juan Clark, Marta Pelaez, Manuel Márquez-Sterling, and Armando Lago all qualify as professors, yet they talk a normal language, engage a listener, and use examples of everyday situations and everyday people! Even crazier: They laugh! Crazier still, they make their *guest* laugh! Crazier even *still*, their knowledge is vast and penetrating—and avoids the asinine platitudes and stultifying political correctness that defines their profession. Somehow, these Cuban Americans' professional training and daily labors have left their critical and intellectual faculties (and *even* their senses of humor) unatrophied. They all contributed important material to this book.

If someone has written more exhaustively or authoritatively about the Cuban people's armed resistance to Castro-Communism than Enrique Encinosa, I've somehow missed him, as have most Cuban Americans. Enrique's help in this project with his books, films, and insights has been enormous. I owe him big time (and not just for postage).

Enrique Ros is the ultimate source on the anti-Castro fight from Florida and has punched more holes in Camelot's hot air balloon than anyone. Señor Ros's daughter, Republican representative Ileana Ros-Lehtinen, continues the fight for Cuban freedom and American security (don't forget, these are one and the same) from Congress today.

To understand—to *really* get at the bottom of—Castro's recent shenanigans, you simply have to read Dr. Ernesto Betancourt's column in *El Nuevo Herald*. Dr. Betancourt served briefly in Castro's first government. Today he's a researcher for, and the voice of, Radio Martí. Dr. Betancourt made *all* of his research, *all* of his insights, *all* of his well-informed speculations available to me. He was a tremendous help with this project.

Nestor Carbonnel might have enlightened me enough with his superb book, *And the Russians Stayed: The Sovietization of Cuba*. But no, he persisted in helping by answering my every inquiry about the early years of the U.S.-Castro face-off—motives, ploys, personalities, the behind-the-scenes jockeying and skullduggery. Mr. Carbonnel was neck-deep in it himself, and he shared his experiences and insights generously. He was a godsend for this project.

In Stalin's Russia it was GULAG. In Castro's Cuba UMAP stood for the same. Emilio Izquierdo can tell you about them. At age eighteen he was rounded up at Russian machine gun–point and herded into the barbed wire camps. His crime? "Active in Catholic associations" read the Castroite document. Emilio heads the Former UMAP Prisoners Association in Miami today. I was fortunate to have Emilio as a source and inspiration for this project.

Eusebio Peñalver, Angel de Fana, Ernesto Díaz Rodríguez, and Mario Chanes de Armas all served longer in Castro's gulag than Solzhenitsyn suffered in Stalin's. In fact, they were imprisoned three times as long. These men represent the longest-serving political prisoners of the century. They could have easily escaped such lengthy suffering by playing Castro's little game, by agreeing to "rehabilitation" classes, by wearing the uniforms of common prisoners. Castro made the offer often.

Castro got his answer as swiftly and as clearly as the German commander who surrounded Bastogne got his. "It sounds strange, but no man in Cuba is as free as a political prisoner in rebellion," says longtime Castro political prisoner Francisco Chappi. "We were tortured, we were starved. But we lived in total defiance."

"Inside of our souls we were free," says another former political prisoner named Sergio Carrillo, a paratrooper at the Bay of Pigs in 1961 and a Catholic priest in America today. "We *refused* to commit spiritual suicide," Father Carillo stresses.

For a second, let's restrain our rage at the liberal media and Hollywood for studiously ignoring these men and instead praising their jailer Fidel. Today these ex-political prisoners head an organization in Miami called *Plantados Hasta la Libertad en Cuba*. They also helped me with this book, with their recollections for sure, but even more, with the example of their courage and fortitude. Friends, whenever *you* think *you're* having a bad day, you might drop these men a line.

On April 18, 1961, Castro's Soviet-trained and Soviet-led forces were getting such a stomping at the hands of utterly abandoned men they outnumbered forty to one, that at least two sources claim a frantic Fidel Castro actually soiled his pants in panic. The man largely responsible for Castro's malodorous discomfiture that day was a Cuban military man pre-Castro, and a retired U.S. brigadier general today, Erneido Oliva. When his betrayed, decimated, thirst-crazed, and ammo-less men were finally overwhelmed (but not defeated) by Castro's bumblers at the Bay of Pigs, Oliva snarled at his brainless eunuch of an opponent, José Fernandez (a Spaniard, technically), "The only reason *you're* holding a gun on *us* right now, Fernandez, is because we ran out of ammo."

During almost two years in Castro's dungeons, Oliva and his men lived under a daily death sentence. Escaping that sentence would have been easy: simply sign the little confession (Communists *just love* bullshit paperwork!) saying they were "mercenaries of the Yankee imperialists."

Neither Oliva nor any of his men signed the document. His hundreds of men stood solidly with their commander. "We will die with dignity!" snapped Oliva at a furious Fernandez again, and again, and again. To a Castroite such an attitude not only enrages but baffles. It is an honor for me to include General Erneido Oliva's name among those who helped me with this project.

Among the many other Bay of Pigs vets who helped were Alberto "Pilo" Fontova, Fernando Marquet, and Esteban Bovo—part of a list too long to mention. Miami radio star Ninoska Perez-Castellon was also on hand, informing me, directing me, amusing me. Señora Ela Manero saved me many a trip to the library with her painstaking research.

Considering the topic, this could have been a very morose book. I like to think I sidestepped that, and did so with the help of all my invaluable collaborators. So, *amigos* and *amigas: muchisimas gracias!*

And one more thing. On the home stretch of completing this book, with my tongue hanging, with the crowds roaring, with the finish line in sight, I almost lost my life in a hideous accident. On September 11, 2004, as it turned out.

I was thrown from my bicycle and plunged off a tall bridge, bounced off sharp steel girders on the way down, and finally landed face and head first, twenty feet below on jagged boulders. I remained there unconscious and bleeding heavily for half an hour till passersby rushed to the rescue.

The result: fractured skull, subdermal hematoma, smashed eye and orbit, eight-inch gash in the forehead with cracked skull exposed, leg and hip broken in six places, five ribs broken along with arm and hand, and various internal injuries. The first few days in intensive care the speculations ran to survival. We cleared that one. Then came speculations about paralysis, life in a wheelchair (I'm a maniacal outdoorsman, not a happy prospect). We cleared that one. Then came speculations concerning severe brain damage from the horrific trauma to the head (I write and speak for a living, again not a happy prospect).

Well, to end this depressing screed, this past Christmas season, by a process not easily explained by the fine folks who removed prayer from schools and mangers from courthouses, I found myself not just merrily celebrating the holidays along with this book's completion, along with my dad's seventy-eighth birthday, along with my twenty-sixth wedding anniversary, along with my parents' fifty-fifth anniversary, along with my daughter's engagement—but *dancing* at the multifarious and raucous celebrations!

And I'm talking everything from the Hustle and Bump to the Boot-Scootin-Boogie and Cha-Cha-Cha! I was on a crutch and wearing an eyepatch—so, okay, I wasn't exactly John Travolta. But STILL!

So that takes care of the physical recovery, you say. Now how 'bout that brain damage? Well, these rollicking festivities also found me as engaging, witty, erudite, sparkling, talkative, boisterous…Oh hi, honey. (My darling wife often reads over my shoulder, making helpful suggestions.)

"A bit wordy, Humberto. Just write as '*obnoxious* as ever.'"

"Thanks, honey!" You get the point, amigos. Thanks to a chorus of prayers, thanks to a positively suffocating avalanche of moral (and physical) support from my family, and a crowd of—*not* fair-weather, by any means—friends (led by Chris and Cindy Keys, along with the Raymond family) I find myself firmly back in the saddle. And this book is the result.

BIBLIOGRAPHY

SPANISH LANGUAGE SOURCES

Alfonso, Pablo. *Cuba, Castro y los Católicos*. Hispamerican Books, 1985.

Artime, Manuel F. *Traición! Gritan 20,000 Tumbas Cubanas*. Mexico: Editorial Jus, 1960.

Barquín, Ramón M. *El Día Que Fidel Castro Se Apoderó de Cuba: 72 Horas Trágicas para la Libertad en Las Américas*. San Juan: Editorial Rambar, 1978.

Batista, Fulgencio. *Paradojas*. Mexico: Ediciones Botas, 1963.

———. *Piedras y Leyes*. Mexico: Ediciones Botas, 1961.

———. *Respuesta*. Mexico: Manuel León Sánchez S.C.L., 1960.

Benemelis, Juan. *Castro, Subversion y Terrorismo en Africa*. Madrid: Editorial San Martin, 1984.

———. *Las Guerras Secretas de Fidel Castro*. Fundacion Elena Mederos, 2002.

Boza Masvidal, Eduardo. *Voz en el destierro*. Miami, FL: Revista IDEAL, 1997.

Beruvides, Esteban. *Cuba: Anuario Histórico 1960*. 2 vols. Miami: Colonial Press International, 1998.

———. *Cuba: Anuario Histórico 1961*. 2 vols. Miami: Colonial Press International, 1998–2000.

————. *Cuba: Anuario Histórico 1959–63: Indices Onomasticos*. Miami: Colonial Press International, 2000.

————. *Cuba: Anuario Histórico 1962*. Miami: 12th Ave. Graphics, 1995.

————. *Cuba: Anuario Histórico 1963*. Miami: 12th Ave. Graphics, 1995.

————. *Cuba: Anuario Histórico 1964*. 2 vols. Miami: Colonial Press International, 2000.

————. *Cuba: Anuario Histórico 1965*. 2 vols. Miami: Colonial Press International, 2001–02.

————. *Cuba: Anuario Histórico 1990*. Miami: 12th Ave. Graphics, 1994.

————. *Cuba: Anuario Histórico 1991*. Miami: AD Ventures International, 1992.

————. *Cuba: Anuario Histórico 1994 Septiembre–Diciembre*. Miami: Colonial Press International, 2001.

————. *Cuba: Los Crímenes Impunes de Fidel Castro*. Miami: Colonial Press International, 1999.

————. *Cuba: Microbiografía de Fiscales y miembros de los Tribunales Revolucionarios*. Miami: Colonial Press International, 2003.

————. *Cuba y Su Presidio Político*. Miami: 12th Ave. Graphics, 1992.

————. *Cuba y Sus Mártires*. Coral Gables, FL: 12th Ave. Graphics, 1993.

Calatayud, Antonio. *El Testamento de los Desheredados*. Miami: Editorial Ponce, 1981.

Castro, Fidel. *Por el Camino Correcto*. La Habana: Editora Política, 1987.

Castro, Fidel. *Pensamiento Político, Económico y Social de Fidel Castro*. La Habana: Editorial Lex, 1959.

Clark, Juan. *Cuba: Mito y Realidad: Testimonios de un Pueblo*. Miami: Saeta Ediciones, 1992.

Clark, Juan, Angel De Fana, and Amaya Sánchez. *Human Rights in Cuba: An Experiential Perspective*. Coral Gables: Research Institute for Cuba Studies, 1991.

Comisión de Juristas del Colegio de Abogados de la Habana, en el Exilio. *El Caso de Cuba ante el Derecho Internacional*. Miami: AIP, 1967.

II Congreso del Partido Comunista de Cuba. *Informe Central: Presentado por el Compañero Fidel Castro Ruz, Primer Secretario del Comité Central del Partido Comunista de Cuba*. La Habana: Editora Política, 1980.

Conte, Aguero Luis. *Los Dos Rostros de Fidel Castro*. Mexico: Editorial Jus, 1960.

————. *Paredón*! Miami: Colonial Press, 1962.

Crespo Francisco, Julio. *Bandidismo en el Escambray: 1960–1965*. La Habana: Editorial de Ciencias Sociales, 1986.

del Pino, Rafael. *Proa a la Libertad*. Mexico: Editorial Planeta Mexicana, 1991.

Diaz Verson, Salvador. *Canibales del Siglo XX*. Miami: Editoria Libertad, 1962.

————. *Cuando la Razón Se Vuelve Inútil*. Mexico: Ediciones Botas, 1962.

————. *Ya el Mundo Oscurece*. Mexico: Ediciones Botas, 1961.

Encinosa, Enrique. *Cuba en Guerra: Historia de la Oposición Anti-Castrista 1959–1993*. The Endowment for Cuba American Studies, 1994.

————. *Escambray: La Guerra Olvidada*. Miami: Editorial SIBI, 1989.

Fernández, Alina. *Alina: Memorias de la hija rebelde de Fidel Castro*. Barcelona: Plaza / Janés Editores, 1997.

Franqui, Carlos. *Vida, aventuras y Desastres de un Hombre Llamado Castro*. Mexico: Fasciculos Planeta, 1989.

Fuentes, Norberto. *Cazabandido*. Montevideo, Uruguay: Arca Editorial, 1970.

Hollander, Paul. *Los Peregrinos de La Habana*. Madrid: Playor, 1981.

Matos, Huber. *Cómo llegó la noche*. Barcelona: Tusquets Editores, 2002.

Medrano, Humberto. *Sin Patria pero Sin Amo*. Coral Gables: Service Offset Printers, 1963.

Montaner, Carlos Alberto. *Cuba: Un Siglo De Doloroso Aprendizaje*. Brickell Communications Group, 2002.

————. *Fidel Castro y La Revolución Cubana*. Transaction Publishers, 1984.

————. *Informe Secreto Sobre la Revolución Cubana*. Madrid: Ediciones Sedmay, 1976.

————. *Viaje al Corazon de Cuba*. Random House Espanol, 1999.

Ortega, Luis. *Yo Soy El Che!* Mexico: Ediciones Monroy-Padilla, 1970.

Pardo Llada, José. *El "Che" Que Yo Conocí*. Medellín: Editorial Bedoubt S.A., 1973.

Penabaz, Manuel. *La Trampa*. Miami: Zoom Publishing, Inc., 1983.

Portell-Vilá, Herminio. *Nueva Historia de la República de Cuba: 1898–1979*. Santo Domingo: Editora Corripio, 1986.

Posada Carriles, Luis. *Los Caminos del Guerrero*. n.p., 1994.

Rodriguez Cruz, Juan Carlos. *Hombres del Escambray*. La Habana: Editorial Capitan San Luis, 1990.

Ruiz Leovigildo. *Diario De una Traicion, Anurario Politico Cubano*. Editorial Lorie, 1965.

———. *Diario De Una Traicion (CUBA 1959)*. Editorial Lorie, 1965.

Santovenia, Emeterio S. *Cuba y Su Historia*, 4 vols. Miami: Cuba Corporation Inc., 1966.

Suárez Nuñez, José. *El Gran Culpable: Cómo 12 Guerrilleros Aniquilaron a 45.000 Soldados?* Caracas: n.p., 1963.

Suárez, Andres. *CUBA: Castroism and Communism, 1959–1966*. Cambridge, MA, 1967.

Taibo II, Paco Ignacio. *La Batalla del Che*. Mexico: Fasciculos Planeta, S.A., 1989.

Valladares, Armando. *Contra Toda Esperanza*. Barcelona: Plaza/Janés Editores, S.A., 1985.

Vivés, Juan. *Los Amos de Cuba*. Buenos Aires: Emecé Editores, 1982.

All the following source books published by Ediciones Universal, Miami, Florida

Aguirre, Rafael. *Amanecer (Historias del Clandestinaje/ la lucha de la resistencia contra Castro dentro de Cuba)*, 1996.

Arenas, Reinaldo. *Necesidad de Libertad*, 2001.

Asociación Nacional de Educadores Cubano-Americanos y Herencia Cultural Cubana. *Cuba: Exilio y Cultura. Memoria del Congreso del Milenio*, 2002–03.

Betancourt, Ernesto F. *De la Patria de Uno a la Patria de Todos*, 2001.

Bringuier, Carlos. *Operacion Judas*, 1994.

Carrillo, Justo. *A Cuba le Tocó Perder*, 1993.

de Castroverde, Waldo. *Que la Patria se Sienta Orgullosa (Memorias de Una Lucha sin Fin*, 1999.

Córdova, Efrén. *Clase Trabajadora y Movimiento Sindical en Cuba I 1819–1959*, 1995.

Córdova, Efrén, ed. *40 Años de Revolución Cubana: El legado de Castro*, 1999.

Cortina, Néstor Carbonell. *Por la Libertad de Cuba*, 1996.

Dausá, José Enrique. *Luchas y Combates Inconclusos por Cuba: Memorias*, 2001.

Fuentes, Norberto. *La Autobiografia de Fidel Castro*, 2003.

———. *Narcotráfico y Tareas Revolucionarias: El Concepto Cubano*, 2002.

Guerra, Felicia and Tamara Álvarez-Detrell. *Balseros: Historia Oral del éxodo Cubano del '94*, 1997.

Gutiérrez de la Solana, Alberto. *Apuntes Documentados de la Lucha por la Libertad de Cuba*, 1998.

Horowitz, Irving L. *El Comunismo Cubano 1959–1979*, 1980.

Lago, Carmelo Mesa. *Dialéctica de la Revolución Cubana*, 1980.

Leante, César. *Revive Historia: Anatomía del Castrismo*, 2003.

León, Luis Aguilar. *Cuba, Conciencia y Revolución*, 1972.

———. *Reflexiones Sobre Cuba y Su Futuro*, 2001.

Marrero, Levi. *Cuba: Economía y Sociedad*, 1992.

Martín, Américo. *America y Fidel Castro*, 2001.

Montaner, Carlos Alberto. *Cuba Hoy (la lenta muerte del Castrismo)*, 1996.

Oropesa, José Duarte. *Historiologia Cubana*, 2002.

Ros, Enrique. *Años Críticos*, 1996.

———. *Castro y las Guerrillas en Latino America*, 2001.

————. *Cubanos Combatientes: Peleando en Distintos Frentes*, 1998.

————. *Ernesto Che Guevara: Mito y Realidad*, 2002.

————. *De Girón a la Crisis de los Cohetes: la Segunda Derrota*, 1995.

————. *Playa Girón, la Verdadera Historia*, 1994.

————. *LA UMAP: El Gulag Castrista*, 2003.

Ruiz, Leovigildo. *Diario de una Traición, Anuario Político Cubano*.

————. *Diario de una Traición, (Cuba 1960)*.

————. *Diario de una Traición, (Cuba 1961)*.

Soneira, Teresa Fernández. *Con la Estrella y la Cruz—Historia de la Federación de las Juventudes de Acción Católica Cubana*, 2002.

Talleda, Miguel L. *Alpha 66 y su Histórica Tarea*, 1995.

WEBZINE SOURCES IN SPANISH

www.aguadadepasajeros.bravepages.com/

www.camcocuba.org/

www.canf.org/ (Cuban American National Foundation)

www.contactomagazine.com/

www.cubacenter.org/

www.cubafreepress.org/art/cubap990609d.html

www.cubancenter.org/

www.cubanet.org/

www.cuban-exile.com/

www.cubapolidata.com/cafr/news/1998.html

www.diarionoticubainternacional.com/cubamundo

www.elveraz.com/

www.fiu.edu/ (Florida International University)

www.futurodecuba.org/

www.lanuevacuba.com/master.htm

www.latinamericanstudies.org/

www.martinoticias.com/

www.members.aol.com/Guanabacoa

www.neoliberalismo.com/interterr.htm

www.netforcuba.org/

www.nocastro.com/

www.penhacubana.com/

ENGLISH LANGUAGE BOOKS

Abel, Elie. *The Missile Crisis*. New York: Bantam Books.

Anderson, Jon Lee. *Che Guevara: A Revolutionary Life*. New York: Grove Press, 1997.

Arenas, Reinaldo. *Before Night Falls: A Memoir*. New York: Viking, 1993.

Ayers, Bradley Earl. *The War That Never Was: An Insider's Account of CIA Covert Operations Against Cuba*. Indianapolis: The Bobbs-Merrill Company, 1976.

Azicri, Max. *Cuba: Politics, Economics and Society*. London: Pinter Publishers, 1988.

Batista, Fulgencio. *Cuba Betrayed*. New York: Vantage Press, 1962.

———. *The Growth and Decline of the Cuban Republic*. New York: The Devin-Adair Company, 1964.

Beschloss, Michael. *The Crisis Years: Kennedy and Khrushchev, 1960–1963*. New York: HarperCollins, 1992.

Bethel, Paul. *The Losers. The Definitive Report, by an Eyewitness, of the Communist Conquest of Cuba and the Soviet Penetration in Latin America*. New Rochelle, N.Y.: Arlington House, 1969.

Blasier, Cole and Carmelo Meso-Lago, eds. *Cuba in the World*. Pittsburgh: University of Pittsburgh Press, 1979.

Blight, James G. and David A. Welch. *On the Brink: Americans and Soviets Reexamine the Cuban Missile Crisis*. New York: Hill and Wang, 1989.

Blight, James G. and Peter Kornbluh., eds. *Politics of Illusion: The Bay of Pigs Invasion Reexamined*. Boulder, CO: Lynne Rienner Publishers, 1998.

Bonachea, Ramón L. and Marta San Martín. *The Cuban Insurrection: 1952–1959*. New Brunswick, N.J.: Transaction Books, 1974.

Bonachea, Ramon and Nelson P. Valdes. *Cuba in Revolution*. Garden City, N.Y.: Anchor Books, 1972.

Bonsal, Philip W. *Cuba, Castro, and the United States*. Pittsburgh: University of Pittsburgh Press, 1972.

Bourne, Peter G. *Fidel: A Biography of Fidel Castro*. New York: Dodd, Mead & Company, 1986.

Breuer, William B. *Vendetta!: Fidel Castro and the Kennedy Brothers*. Hoboken, NJ: John Wiley & Sons, 1998.

Brigada 2506. *La Sentencia: Brigada de Asalto 2506*. Habana: n.p.

Brown, Charles L. and Armando M. Lago. *The Politics of Psychiatry in Revolutionary Cuba*. New Brunswick, N.J.: Transaction Publishers, 1991.

Brugioni, Dino A. *Eyeball to Eyeball: The Inside Story of the Cuban Missile Crisis*. New York: Random House, 1991.

Calzon, Frank. *Castro's Gulag: The Politics of Terror*. Council for Inter-American Security, 1979.

Cantor, Jay. *The Death of Che Guevara*. New York: Vintage Books, 1983.

Carbonell, Nestor. *And the Russians Stayed: The Sovietization of Cuba*. New York: William Morrow and Co., 1989.

Castro, Fidel. *History Will Absolve Me*. London: Jonathan Cape, 1968.

———. *My Early Years*. New York: Ocean Press, 1998.

Casuso, Teresa. *Cuba and Castro*. New York: Random House, 1961.

Central Intelligence Agency. *The Secret Cuban Missile Crisis Documents*. Washington, D.C.: Brassey's, 1994

Chester, Edmund A. *A Sergeant Named Batista*. New York: Henry Holt and Co., 1954.

CIA Targets Fidel: Secret 1967 CIA Inspector General's Report on Plots to Assassinate Fidel Castro. Melbourne, Australia: Ocean Press, 1996.

Coltman, Leycester. *The Real Fidel Castro*. New Haven: Yale University Press, 2003.

Conde, Yvonne M. *Operation Pedro Pan: The Untold Exodus of 14,048 Cuban Children*. New York: Routledge, 1999.

Daniel, James and John G. Hubbell. *Strike in the West: The Complete Story of the Cuban Crisis*. New York: Holt, Rinehart and Winston, 1963.

Debray, Régis. *Che's Guerrilla War*. Baltimore: Penguin Books, 1975.

———. *Revolution in the Revolution? Armed Struggle and Political Struggle in Latin America*. New York: Grove Press, 1967.

Deutschmann, David, ed. *Che Guevara Reader: Writings on Guerrilla Strategy, Politics & Revolution*. Melbourne: Ocean Press, 1997.

Didion, Joan. *Miami*. New York: Pocket Books, 1987.

Domínguez, Jorge I. *Cuba: Order and Revolution*. Cambridge, MA: Belknap Press, 1978.

———. *To Make A World Safe for Revolution: Cuba's Foreign Policy*. Cambridge: Harvard University Press, 1989.

Dorschner, John and Roberto Fabricio. *The Winds of December: The Cuban Revolution, 1958*. London: Macmillan London Limited, 1980.

Draper, Theodore. *Castroism: Theory and Practice*. New York: Frederick A. Praeger, 1965.

———. *Castro's Revolution: Myths and Realities*. New York: Frederick A. Praeger, 1962.

Dreke, Víctor. *From the Escambray to the Congo*. New York: Pathfinder, 2002.

Dubois, Jules. *Fidel Castro: Rebel, Liberator or Dictator?* Indianapolis: Bobbs-Merrill, 1959.

Dumont, Rene. *Cuba: Socialism and Development*. New York: Grove Press, 1970.

———. *Is Cuba Socialist?* Andre Deutsch, 1974.

Eire, Carlos. *Waiting for Snow in Havana: Confessions of a Cuban Boy*. New York: The Free Press, 2003.

Encinosa, Enrique. *Cuba: The Unfinished Revolution*. Austin: Eakin Press, 1988.

————. *Unvanquished: Cuba's Resistance to Fidel Castro*. Los Angeles: Pureplay Press, 2004.

Escalante, Fabián. *The Secret War: CIA Covert Operations Against Cuba, 1959–62*. Melbourne, Australia: Ocean Press, 1995.

Falcoff, Mark. *The Cuban Revolution and the United States: A History in Documents 1958–1960*. Washington, D.C.: U.S. Cuba Press, 2001.

Fauriol, Georges and Eva Loser. *Cuba: The International Dimension*. New Brunswick, N.J.: Transaction Publishers, 1990.

Fernandez, Alina. *Castro's Daughter: An Exile's Memoir of Cuba*. New York: St. Martin's Griffin, 1998.

Ferrer, Edward B. *Operation Puma: The Air Battle of the Bay of Pigs*. Miami: Trade Litho, 1982.

Fontaine, Roger W. *Terrorism: The Cuban Connection*. New York: Crane Russak & Company, 1988.

Franqui, Carlos. *Diary of the Cuban Revolution*. New York: The Viking Press, 1976.

————. *Family Portrait With Fidel: A Memoir*. New York: Vintage Books, 1985.

Fursenko, Aleksandr and Timothy Naftali. *"One Hell of a Gamble": Khrushchev, Castro, and Kennedy, 1958–1964*. New York: W. W. Norton and Company, 1997.

General Del Pino Speaks: An Insight into Elite Corruption and Military Dissension in Castro's Cuba. Cuban American National Foundation, 1987.

Geyer, Georgie Anne. *Guerrilla Prince: The Untold Story of Fidel Castro*. Boston: Little, Brown & Co., 1991.

Guevara, Ernesto. *The Diary of Che Guevara*. New York: Bantam Books, 1968.

————. *Guerrilla Warfare*. New York: Vintage Books, 1969.

————. *Man & Socialism in Cuba*. Havana: Book Institute, 1967.

————. *Reminiscences of the Cuban Revolutionary War*. New York: Monthly Review Press, 1968

Haig, Alexander M., Jr. *Inner Circles; How America Changed the World*. New York: Warner Books, 1992.

Halperin, Maurice. *The Taming of Fidel Castro*. Berkeley: University of California Press, 1981.

Higgins, Trumbull. *The Perfect Failure: Kennedy, Eisenhower, and the CIA at the Bay of Pigs*. New York: W. W. Norton & Co., 1989.

Hinckle, Warren and William Turner. *The Fish is Red: The Story of the Secret War Against Castro*. New York: Harper & Row, 1981.

Hollander, Paul. *Political Pilgrims; Travels of Western Intellectuals to the Soviet Union, China and Cuba*. New York: Harper Holophon, 1981.

Hunt, Howard, E. *Give Us This Day*. New Rochelle, N.Y.: Arlington House, 1973.

————. *Undercover: Memoirs of an American Secret Agent*. New York: Putnam, 1974.

Infante, Guillermo Cabrera. *Mea Cuba*. Barcelona: Plaza/Janés Editores, 1992.

James, Daniel. *Che Guevara: A Biography*. New York: Stein and Day/Publishers, 1969.

Johnson, Haynes. *The Bay of Pigs: The Leaders' Story of Brigade 2506*. New York: W. W. Norton & Co., 1964.

Kennedy, Robert F. *Thirteen Days: A Memoir of the Cuban Missile Crisis*. New York: W. W. Norton & Co., 1969.

Kornbluh, Peter, ed. *Bay of Pigs Declassified: The Secret CIA Report on the Invasion of Cuba*. New York: The New Press, 1998.

Lazo, Mario. *Dagger in the Heart: American Policy Failures in Cuba*. New York: Funk & Wagnalls, 1968.

Levine, Robert M. *Secret Missions to Cuba: Fidel Castro, Bernardo Benes, and Cuban Miami*. New York: Macmillan, 2001.

Llerena, Mario. *The Unsuspected Revolution: The Birth and Rise of Castroism*. Ithaca, N.Y.: Cornell University Press, 1978.

Llovio-Menéndez, José Luis. *Insider: My Hidden Life as a Revolutionary in Cuba*. New York: Bantam Books, 1988.

Lockwood, Lee. *Castro's Cuba, Cuba's Fidel: An American Journalist's Inside Look at Today's Cuba, in Text and Picture*. New York: Vintage Books, 1969.

López-Fresquet, Rufo. *My Fourteen Months With Castro*. Cleveland: The World Publishing Company, 1966.

Lorenzo, Orestes. *Wings Of the Morning: The Flights of Orestes Lorenzo*. New York: St. Martin's Press, 1994.

Lynch, Grayston L. *Decision for Disaster: Betrayal at the Bay of Pigs*. Washington, D.C.: Brassey's, 1998.

Macaulay, Neill. *A Rebel in Cuba: An American's Memoir*. Chicago: Quadrangle Books, 1970.

Mallin, Jay. *Covering Castro: Rise and Decline of Cuba's Communist Dictator*. Washington D.C.: U.S.-Cuba Institute Press, 1994.

———. *Fortress Cuba: Russia's American Base*. Chicago: Henry Regnery Company, 1965.

Mankiewicz, Frank and Kirby Jones. *With Fidel: A Portrait of Castro and Cuba*. Chicago: Playboy Press, 1975.

Manrara, Luis V. *Betrayal Opened the Door to Russian Missiles in Red Cuba*. Miami: The Truth About Cuba Committee, Inc., 1968.

Márquez-Sterling, Manuel. *Historia de la Isla de Cuba*. New York: Regents Publishing Company, 1975.

Martino, John. *I Was Castro's Prisoner: An American Tells His Story*. New York: Devin-Adair Company, 1963.

Matthews, Herbert L. *The Cuban Story*. New York: George Braziller, 1961.

———. *Fidel Castro*. New York: Simon and Schuster, 1969.

———. *Revolution in Cuba: An Essay in Understanding*. New York: Charles Scribner's Sons, 1975.

Meyer, Karl E. and Tad Szulc. *The Cuban Invasion: The Chronicle of a Disaster*. New York: Frederick A. Praeger, 1962.

Michener, James A. and John Kings. *Six Days in Havana*. Austin: University of Texas Press, 1989.

Miller, Tom. *Trading with the Enemy: A Yankee Travels Through Castro's Cuba*. New York: Atheneum, 1992.

Montaner, Carlos Alberto. *Cuba, Castro and the Caribbean*. New Brunswick, N.J.: Transaction Books, 1985.

Navarro, Antonio. *Tocayo: A Cuban Resistance Leader's True Story*. Westport, CT: Sandown Books, 1981.

Operation Zapata: The "Ultrasensitive" Report and Testimony of the Board of Inquiry on the Bay of Pigs. Frederick, MD: Aletheia Books, 1981.

Oppenheimer, Andres. *Castro's Final Hour: The Secret Story Behind the Coming Downfall of Communist Cuba*. New York: Simon and Schuster, 1992.

Patterson, Thomas G. *Contesting Castro: The United States and the Triumph of the Cuban Revolution*. New York: Oxford University Press, 1994.

Pérez-Stable, Marifeli. *The Cuban Revolution: Origins, Course, and Legacy*. New York: Oxford University Press, 1993.

Persons, Albert C. *Bay of Pigs: A Firsthand Account of the Mission by a U.S. Pilot in Support of the Cuban Invasion Force in 1961*. Jefferson, N.C.: McFarland & Co., 1990.

Phillips, Ruby Hart. *The Cuba Dilemma*. New York: Ivan Obolensky, Inc., 1962.

Quirk, Robert E. *Fidel Castro*. New York: W. W. Norton & Company, 1993.

Ratliff, William. *The Selling of Fidel Castro: The Media and the Cuban Revolution*. New Brunswick, N.J.: Transaction Books, 1987.

Rieff, David. *The Exile: Cuba in the Heart of Miami*. New York: Simon & Schuster, 1993.

Rodriguez, Ana and Glenn Garvin. *Diary of a Survivor: Nineteen Years in a Cuban Women's Prison*. New York: St. Martin's Press, 1995.

Rodriguez, Felix I. and John Weisman. *Shadow Warrior: The CIA Hero of a Hundred Unknown Battles*. New York: Simon & Schuster, 1989.

Russo, Gus. *Live By the Sword; The Secret War Against Castro and the Death of JFK*. Bancroft Press, 1998.

Schlesinger, Arthur. *A Thousand Days*. Houghton Mifflin Company, 1980.

Smith, Earl E. T. *The Fourth Floor: An Account of the Castro Communist Revolution*. New York: Random House, 1962.

Suchlicki, Jaime. *Cuba: From Columbus to Castro*. Washington, D.C.: Pergamon-Brassey's, 1987.

———. *The Cuban Military Under Castro*. Coral Gables: University of Miami Press, 1989.

Sweig, Julia. *Inside the Cuban Revolution: Fidel Castro and the Urban Underground*, 2002.

Szulc, Tad. *Fidel: A Critical Portrait*. New York: William Morrow, 1986.

Taber, Robert. *M-26: The Biography of a Revolution*. New York: Lyle Stuart, 1961.

Thomas, Hugh. *Cuba: The Pursuit of Freedom*. New York: Harper & Row, 1971.

Thompson, Robert Smith. *The Missiles of October*. New York: Simon & Schuster, 1992.

Timerman, Jacobo. *Cuba: A Journey*. New York: Vintage Books, 1992.

Triay, Victor Andres. *Bay of Pigs: An Oral History of Brigade 2506*. Gainesville: University Press of Florida, 2001.

Tully, Andrew. *White Tie and Dagger*. New York: Pocket Books, 1968.

Urrutia, Manuel. *Fidel Castro & Company*. New York: Frederick Praeger.

Weyl, Nathaniel. *Red Star Over Cuba: The Russian Assault on the Western Hemisphere*. New York: The Devin-Adair Company, 1960.

White, Mark J. *The Kennedys and Cuba: The Declassified Documentary History*. Chicago: Ivan R. Dee, 1999.

———. *Missiles in Cuba: Kennedy, Khrushchev, Castro and the 1962 Crisis*. Chicago: Ivan R. Dee, 1997.

Wyden, Peter. *Bay of Pigs: The Untold Story*. New York: Simon & Schuster, 1979.

Young, Allen. *Gays Under the Cuban Revolution*. San Francisco: Grey Fox Press, 1981.

U.S. GOVERNMENT SOURCES

Office of Research & Policy. Radio Martí Program and Voice of America United States Information Agency. Cuba Annual Report: 1990. New Brunswick, N.J., 1991.

U.S. Department of State. *Foreign Relations of the United States, 1958–1960, Volume VI: Cuba.* Washington, D.C.: U.S. Government Printing Office, 1991.

U.S. Department of State. *Foreign Relations of the United States, 1961–1963: American Republics, Vol. XII.* Washington, D.C.: U.S. Government Printing Office, 1996.

U.S. Department of State. *Foreign Relations of the United States, 1961–1963: Kennedy-Khrushchev Exchanges, Volume VI.* Washington, D.C.: U.S. Government Printing Office, 1996.

U.S. House of Representatives, Committee on Foreign Affairs. *U.S. Response to Cuban Government Involvement in Narcotics Trafficking and Review of Worldwide Illicit Narcotics Situation*, February 21 and 23, 1984. Washington, D.C.: U.S. Government Printing Office, 1984.

U.S. House of Representatives, Committee on Foreign Affairs. *Castro-Communist Subversion in the Western Hemisphere*, February, March, 1963. Washington, D.C.: U.S. Government Printing Office, 1963.

U.S. House of Representatives, Committee on Foreign Affairs. *Impact of Cuban-Soviet Ties in the Western Hemisphere*, April 25 and 26, 1979. Washington, D.C.: U.S. Government Printing Office, 1979.

U.S. House of Representatives, Committee on Foreign Affairs. *Cuban Involvement in International Narcotics Trafficking*, July 25 and 27, 1989. Washington, D.C.: U.S. Government Printing Office, 1989.

U.S. House of Representatives, Committee on International Relations. *U.S. Trade Embargo of Cuba*, May–September 1975. Washington, D.C.: U.S. Government Printing Office, 1976.

U.S. House of Representatives, Committee on the Judiciary. *Soviet, East German and Cuban Involvement in Fomenting Terrorism in Southern Africa,* November 1982. Washington, D.C.: U.S. Government Printing Office, 1982.

U.S. House of Representatives, Committee on the Judiciary. *The Role of Cuba in International Terrorism and Subversion,* February 26, March 4, 11, and 12, 1982. Washington, D.C.: U.S. Government Printing Office, 1982.

U.S. House of Representatives, Committee on the Judiciary. *Mariel Cuban Detainees: Events Preceding and Following the November 1987 Riots,* February 4, 1988, Serial No. 97. Washington, D.C.: U.S. Government Printing Office, 1989.

U.S. House of Representatives, Committee on Ways and Means. H.R. 2229, Free Trade With Cuba Act, March 17, 1994. Washington, D.C.: U.S. Government Printing Office, 1994.

U.S. Senate, Committee on the Judiciary. *Cuba as a Base for Subversion in America,* February 8, 1963. Washington, D.C.: U.S. Government Printing Office, 1963.

U.S. Senate, Committee on the Judiciary. *The Tricontinental Conference of African, Asian, and Latin American Peoples, 1966.* Washington, D.C.: U.S. Government Printing Office, 1966.

NOTES

Chapter One: The Terrorist Next Door

1. William B. Breuer, *Vendetta! Fidel Castro and the Kennedy Brothers* (New York: John Wiley & Sons, 1998), 1.
2. Ibid., 2.
3. Herbert Matthews, *New York Times*, February 24, 1957.
4. This quote comes from a letter written by Fidel Castro to Celia Sanchez, quoted in *Fidel Castro on the United States; Selected Statements, 1958–2003*, Hans de Salas-del Valle, ed. This letter is no major secret; to this day it forms a major exhibit in Havana's very own *Museo de la Revolución*.
5. This quote comes from Juanita Castro's testimony to the House Committee on Un-American Activities, June 11, 1965.
6. This quote comes from a secret telegram from then U.S. ambassador to Cuba Philip Bonsal to Secretary of State Christian Herter on June 16, 1960. This telegram was declassified only on December 14, 2002. Exact quote from telegram: "Raul Castro stated the following in confidence to Faure Chaumont, Cuban Ambassador

to USSR, and to Interior Minister Jose Naranjo, as he was planning a trip to USSR to seek a military assistance pact including nuclear weapons. Chaumont told a confidant that Raul said *'my dream is to drop three atom bombs on New York.'"* *Gringos In the Revolution 1956–62*, Paul Wolf, ed.

7. Breuer, 2–3.
8. Andrew Tully, *White Tie and Dagger; How Foreign Embassies Spy On the U.S.* (New York: Pocket, 1968), 76.
9. Dr. Ernesto Betancourt, www.martinoticias.com/Radio Martí News, September 23, 2001.
10. Ibid.
11. *South Florida Sun-Sentinel*, March 21, 2004.
12. Betancourt, www.martinoticias.com/Radio Martí News.
13. Iranian Press Service, May 10, 2001.
14. www.cnn.com, September 18, 2000.
15. Islamic Republic of Iran Broadcasting, January 16, 2005.
16. *Granma International*, Havana, January 17, 2005.
17. From "The Last Revolutionary," Dan Rather's interview of Fidel Castro, CBS News, July 18, 1996.
18. Myles Kantor, "Oliver Stone's Cuban Lovefest," www.frontpagemag.com, May 5, 2004.
19. Marc Morano, "Critics Assail Fidel Castro's 'Sickening' Grip on Hollywood Celebs," www.cnsnews.com, December 17, 2002.
20. Arnold Beichman, "Mona Charen Exposes Menace of Senseless Liberals," *Human Events*, February 17, 2003.
21. "Castro: The Great Survivor," BBC News, October 19, 2000.
22. "Poster Killer," *The Spectator*, January 19, 2005.
23. *Revista Presencia*, La Paz, Bolivia, September 1974.
24. Ronald Bergan, *Francis Ford Coppola, Close Up: The Making of His Movies* (New York: Thunder's Mouth Press, 1998), 53.
25. Sandra Levinson, exclusive interview with Harry Belafonte on Cuba, *Cuba Now*, October 25, 2003.
26. *Granma International*, April 19, 2000.

27. Trevor Armbrister, "Fawning Over Fidel," *Reader's Digest*, May 1996.

28. *Anderson* v. *Republic of Cuba*, No. 01-28628 (Miami-Dade Cir. April 13, 2003)

29. "U.S. Family Wins Judgment Against Cuba in '61 Death," *Atlanta Journal-Constitution*, April 30, 2003.

Chapter Two: The Cuban Führer

1. This quote is from a presidential press conference on July 15, 1959, where President Eisenhower was responding to charges made by Cuban exile Pedro Diaz Lanz that Castro's revolution was Communist.

2. This is from a telegram from U.S. ambassador to Cuba Earl Smith to the State Department's Roy Rubbottom, dated December 29, 1958. It was declassified on December 12, 2002. *Gringos In the Revolution 1956–62*, Paul Wolf, ed.

3. Georgie Ann Geyer, *Guerrilla Prince* (Boston: Little, Brown & Co., 1991), 131.

4. Michael Beschloss, *The Crisis Years; Kennedy & Khrushchev 1960–1963*. (New York: HarperCollins, 1991), 538.

5. Fedor Burlatsky, "Castro Wanted a Nuclear Strike," *New York Times*, October 23, 1992.

6. Guevara biographer Jon Lee Anderson reports that Guevara told Sam Russell, a British correspondent for the socialist newspaper *Daily Worker*, that if the missiles had been under Cuban control, they would have fired them off. *Havana Journal*, October 14, 2004.

7. Arthur Schlesinger, Jr., *A Thousand Days: John F. Kennedy in the White House* (New York: Random House, 1965).

8. *Foreign Affairs*, volume 66, number 1, fall 1987.

9. Stewart Alsop, "In Time of Crisis," *Saturday Evening Post*, November 1962.

10. Quoted in Enrique Ros, *La Segunda Derrota* (Ediciones Universal, 1995).

11. Beschloss, 549.
12. Ibid., 544.
13. Ibid.
14. Ibid. Also appears in Richard Nixon, "Cuba, Castro, and John F. Kennedy," *Reader's Digest*, November 5, 1964.
15. Beschloss, 556.
16. *Washington Post*, January 19, 1969. Quoted also in Ros.
17. Ros, 269.
18. Ibid., 248.
19. Ibid., 282.
20. Peter Schweizer, "Cuban Missile Crisis: Kennedy's Mistakes," *History News Network*, November 4, 2002.
21. Alexander M. Haig, Jr., *Inner Circles: How America Changed the World* (New York: Warner Books, 1992).
22. Paul Bethel, *The Losers: The Definitive Report, by an Eyewitness, of the Communist Conquest of Cuba and the Soviet Penetration in Latin America* (New Rochelle, N.Y.: Arlington House, 1969), 364.
23. Ros.
24. Ibid.
25. Ibid., 199.
26. Ibid., 193.
27. Beschloss, 414.
28. Ros, 258.
29. Andres Perez, *YARA* magazine, Florida International University, 2000.
30. "Bay of Pigs 40 Years After: An International Conference," Havana, Cuba, March 22–24, 2001, National Security Archive.
31. Beschloss, 28.
32. Haynes Johnson, *The Bay of Pigs; The Leader's Story of Brigade 2506* (New York: W. W. Norton & Co., 1964).

Chapter 3: The Cowardly León

1. Paul Bethel, *The Losers: The Definitive Report, by an Eyewitness, of the Communist Conquest of Cuba and the Soviet Penetration in*

Latin America (New Rochelle, N.Y.: Arlington House, 1969), 209.

2. Mario Lazo, *Dagger in the Heart: American Policy Failures in Cuba* (New York: Funk & Wagnalls, 1968), 177.

3. Ibid., 193.

4. Associated Press, January 1, 2001.

5. Lyman B. Kirkpatrick, Jr., *The Real CIA* (New York: Macmillan, 1968).

6. Lazo, 82–3.

7. Spruille Braden quoted in Fulgencio Batista, *Cuba Betrayed* (New York: Vantage Press, 1962).

8. Nestor Carbonell, *And the Russians Stayed: The Sovietization of Cuba* (New York: William Morrow & Co., 1989). The tourist figure also appears in Humberto Fontova, "You Can't Believe Those Crazy Cubans!" www.newsmax.com, April 9, 2003.

9. Carlos Alberto Montaner, *Fidel Castro y La Revolución Cubana* (Piscataway, NJ: Transaction Publishers, 1984).

10. The McLaughlin Group, April 8, 2000. Clift repeated it to a gaping Bill O'Reilly on the *O'Reilly Factor*, May 1, 2000.

11. Christine Klein, "Always a Rerun: The Stars on the Issues," *National Review*, May 16, 2000.

12. "End This Embargo Now: Glover Joins Goodwill Delegation to Cuba's Castro," *Village Voice*, January 18, 1999.

13. Jeff Jacoby, "Castro's Cheerleaders," *Boston Globe*, May 8, 2003.

14. This quote has run dozens of places, including Andrew Breitbart, "Mum's the Word," www.opinionjournal.com, April 11, 2003. Also in Sterling Rome, "Castro's Celebrity Fan Club," www.cnsnews.com, May 1, 2003. I used the quote in my NewsMax article "We Love You Fidel! Oh Yes We Do!" November 18, 2002, and it provoked a response from Spielberg, which led to the following article by NewsMax editor Carl Limbacher, "Spielberg to NewsMax: Cuba Lied About What I Said," May 9, 2003. "Our columnist Humberto Fontova, zinging Castro's American groupies, mentioned a notorious quotation attributed to Spielberg: that

meeting Castro was 'the eight most important hours of [his] life.' Spielberg's people contacted our people to proclaim that the director never made any such statement and that Castro's state-run press concocted the quotation. 'Don't believe everything you read, especially in the Cuban press!' Spielberg's office wrote to us." Which was EXACTLY the point of my NewsMax article all along.

15. Don Feder, "Close Encounters," www.frontpagemag.com, January 13, 2004.

16. Letter from Alice Walker to President Clinton, March 13, 1996. www.cubasolidarity.net.

17. Associated Press, February 16, 2004.

18. "Hijacker Is Glad He's Back in U.S., Rails Against Reds," *Miami Herald*, October 29, 1980.

19. Ibid.

20. "Hijacker Detests Cuba," *Washington Post*, April 26, 1977.

21. Ibid.

22. Carlos Alberto Montaner, *Viaje al Corazon de Cuba*, (New York: Random House Español, 1999).

23. Eduardo Ferrer, *Operacion Puma: La Batalla Aerea de Bahia de Cochinos* (International Aviation Consultants, 1976).

24. *New York Times*, July 16, 1959.

25. Smith, Earl E. T. *The Fourth Floor: An Account of the Castro Communist Revolution* (New York: Random House, 1962).

26. Nathaniel Weyl, *Red Star Over Cuba: The Russian Assault on the Western Hemisphere* (New York: Devin-Adair Company, 1960).

Chapter 4: The Dope Trafficker Next Door

1. "Cuba and Cocaine," *Frontline*, PBS, February 5, 1991.

2. "Mexico Told U.S. Nothing of Probe Into Drug Czar," *Los Angeles Times*, February 22, 1997.

3. Marc Frank, "Former U.S. Drug Tsar Meets Castro in Cuba," Reuters, March 3, 1997.

4. Dr. Ernesto Betancourt, www.martinoticias.com/Radio Martí News, September 23, 2001.

5. "Castro Drug Probe Collapses in Heap of Dead Ends, Lies," *Miami Herald*, November 24, 1996.

Chapter 5: Rock Against Freedom!

1. "The Experts' Opinion," www.cubatravelusa.com, December 1, 2002.

2. Alberto Bustamante, "Notas y Estadisticas Sobre Los Grupos Étnicos En Cuba," *Revista Herencia*, volume 10, 2004. Herencia Cultural Cubana, Miami, Florida.

3. Christopher Ruddy, "Powell and Castro," www.newsmax.com, May 14, 2001.

4. "Nelson Mandela Addresses Canadian Parliament," CBC News, June 18, 1990.

5. "Senator George McGovern Addresses Police Foundation, Urges Normalization with Cuba," *Marco Island Sun Times*, February 5, 2004.

6. Ibid.

7. Ibid.

8. Ibid

9. David Corn, "A Cuban Frost," *Jewish World Review*, April 9, 1999.

10. Humberto Fontova, "Cuba Is Way Too Cool!" www.newsmax.com, May 18, 2004.

11. Interview with Emilio Izquierdo, Jr., president of Ex Confinados Politicos de la UMAP.

12. Fontova, "Cuba is Way Too Cool!"

Chapter 6: Castro's Murder, Incorporated

1. From the documentary *Los Vi Partir* by Enrique Encinosa, 2002.

2. Ibid.

3. "Sundance Goes To Havana," www.cbsnews.com, January 26, 2004.

Chapter 7: Fidel's Sidekick: The Motorcycle Diarist Che Guevara

1. Lewis Carroll, *Alice in Wonderland* (New York: Signet, 2000), 83.
2. Humberto Fontova, "Che Guevara: Assassin and Bumbler," www.newsmax.com, February 23, 2004.
3. Víctor Llano, "El Carnicerito de La Cabaña," *Libertad Digital*, November 22, 2004.
4. Antonio Navarro, *Tocayo: A Cuban Resistance Leader's True Story* (Westport, CT: Sandown Books, 1981).
5. Guillermo Cabrera Infante, *Mea Cuba* (Barcelona: Plaza/Janés Editores, 1992).
6. Enrique Ros, *Cubanos Combatientes; Peleando en Distintos Frentes* (Ediciones Universal, 1998).
7. Ibid.
8. BBC correspondent Mark Doyle, November 25, 2004.
9. Paul Bethel, *The Losers: The Definitive Report, by an Eyewitness, of the Communist Conquest of Cuba and the Soviet Penetration in Latin America* (New Rochelle, N.Y.: Arlington House, 1969), 51.
10. Ibid., 40.
11. Ibid., 51.
12. Mario Lazo, *Dagger in the Heart; American Policy Failures in Cuba* (New York: Funk & Wagnalls, 1968), 243.
13. Llano, "El Carnicerito de La Cabaña."
14. Ernesto "Che" Guevara, *Man and Socialism in Cuba* (Havana: Guairas, Book Institute, 1967).

Chapter 8: Cuba Before Castro

1. Jesus Hernandez Cuellar, "Crónica del Presidio Político en Cuba," *Contacto* magazine, December 1998.
2. Jules Dubois, *Fidel Castro: Rebel, Liberator or Dictator?* (Indianapolis: Bobbs-Merrill Company, 1959), 2.
3. Andres Suarez, *Cuba: Castroism and Communism, 1959–1966* (Boston: MIT Press, 1967).

4. Trevor Armbrister, "Fawning over Fidel," *Reader's Digest*, May 1996.

5. Armando Valladares, *Against All Hope* (San Francisco: Encounter Books, 2000).

6. Alberto Bustamante, "Notas y Estadisticas Sobre Los Grupos Étnicos En Cuba," *Revista Herencia*, volume 10, 2004. Herencia Cultural Cubana, Miami, Florida.

7. Mario Lazo, *Dagger in the Heart; American Policy Failures in Cuba* (New York: Funk & Wagnalls, 1968), 137.

8. Ibid.

9. Agustin Blazquez and Jaums Sutton, "Three Little Blacks," www.newsmax.com, May 23, 2003.

10. Aleksandr Fursenko and Timothy Naftali, *One Hell of a Gamble: Khrushchev, Castro, and Kennedy 1958–1964* (New York: W. W. Norton & Co., 1997).

11. Bill Press, "Mr. Carter Goes to Cuba," www.cnn.com, May 14, 2002.

Chapter 9: Stupid Liberals in the CIA

1. Georgie Ann Geyer, *Guerrilla Prince* (Boston: Little, Brown & Co., 1991), 240.

2. Rufo López-Fresquet, *My Fourteen Months With Castro* (Cleveland: World Publishing Company, 1966).

3. Tim Weiner, "Bay of Pigs Enemies Finally Sit Down Together," *New York Times*, March 23, 2001.

4. Geyer, 190.

5. Juan Antonio Rubio Padilla, "La Opinion Publica," April 27, 1961. Found at www.autentico.org.

6. Gus Russo, *Live by the Sword: The Secret War Against Castro and the Death of JFK* (Baltimore: Bancroft Press, 1998), 15.

7. John H. Davis, *The Kennedys: Dynasty and Disaster* (New York: McGraw-Hill, 1984).

8.   Russo, 242–44.

9.   Ibid., 248.

10. Speech by Castro at the Brazilian embassy in Havana. Interestingly, Cubela had met Fitzgerald's man in Brazil the day before. Carlos Bringuier, *Red Friday* (Chicago: Chas Hallberg & Co., 1969), 110.

11. Russo, 377.

12. Alexander M. Haig, Jr., *Inner Circles; How America Changed the World* (New York: Warner Books, 1992), 116.

13. Russo, 344.

14. Raphael Diaz-Balart, "La Amnistia," *La Rosa Blanca.*

15. Nathaniel Weyl, *Red Star Over Cuba: The Russian Assault on the Western Hemisphere* (New York: Devin-Adair Company, 1960), 104.

16. Ibid.

17. Geyer, 126.

18. Howard E. Hunt, *Give Us This Day* (New Rochelle, N.Y.: Arlington House, 1973).

19. Ibid.

20. Weyl, 104.

21. Enrique Encinosa, *Unvanquished: Cuba's Resistance to Fidel Castro* (Los Angeles: Pureplay Press, 2004), 19.

22. Peter Kornbluh, ed. *Bay of Pigs Declassified: The Secret CIA Report on the Invasion of Cuba* (New York: New Press, 1998).

23. Tad Szulc, *Fidel: A Critical Portrait* (New York: William Morrow & Co., 1986).

24. Testimony of Arthur Gardner, "Communist Threat to The United States through the Caribbean," U.S. Senate Subcommittee, August 27, 1960.

25. Earl E. T. Smith, *The Fourth Floor: An Account of the Castro Communist Revolution* (New York: Random House, 1962), 30–52.

Chapter 10: "We Fought with the Fury of Cornered Beasts"

1.   Paul Bethel, *The Losers: The Definitive Report, by an Eyewitness, of the Communist Conquest of Cuba and the Soviet Penetration in*

Latin America (New Rochelle, N.Y.: Arlington House, 1969), 372.

2. Enrique Encinosa, *Cuba en Guerra* (Miami: Endowment for Cuban American Studies, 1994), 59.

3. Ibid.

4. Enrique Encinosa, *Al Filo Del Machete*, 2002.

5. Michael Moore, *Downsize This!* (New York: HarperCollins, 1997), 193.

6. Mona Charen, "Oliver Stone Gets the Axe," www.townhall.com, April 18, 2003.

7. Ronald Bergan, *Francis Ford Coppola Close Up: The Making of His Movies*. (New York: Thunder's Mouth Press, 1998), 53.

8. Encinosa, *Cuba en Guerra*, 59.

9. Ibid., 128.

10. Ibid., 180.

11. Ibid., 127.

12. Grayston L. Lynch, *Decision for Disaster: Betrayal at the Bay of Pigs* (Washington, D.C.: Brassey's, 1998).

13. Humberto Fontova, "Cuban Mothers," www.newsmax.com, January 15, 2004.

14. Murder tally comes from *The Black Book of Communism; Crimes, Terror, Repression* (Cambridge: Harvard University Press, 1999).

15. "Hollywood Liberals' Fantasy World," www.worldnetdaily.com, April 17, 2004.

16. "Castro Visit Triumphant," *Harvard Law Record*, April 30, 1959.

17. Ibid.

Chapter 11: Operation Cuban Freedom—NOT!

1. Victor Andres Triay, *Bay of Pigs: An Oral History of Brigade 2506* (Gainesville, FL: University Press of Florida, 2001).

2. Peter Wyden, *Bay of Pigs: The Untold Story* (New York: Simon & Schuster, 1979), 202.

3. Edward B. Ferrer, *Operation Puma: The Air Battle of the Bay of Pigs* (Miami: Trade Litho, 1982), 210.

4. Ibid., 213.

5. Wyden, 240.

6. Ibid., 298.

7. Jesus Hernandez Cuellas, "Chronicle of an Unforgettable Agony: Cuba's Political Prisons," *Contacto* magazine, September 1996.

8. Martin Arostegui, "Castro Weaponizes West Nile Virus," *Insight* magazine, September 16, 2002.

9. Haynes Johnson, *The Bay of Pigs: The Leader's Story of Brigade 2506.* (New York: W. W. Norton & Co., 1964), 345.

10. Humberto Fontova, "Mr. Wonderful and the Bay of Pigs," www.newsmax.com, April 14, 2004.

11. Gus Russo, *Live by the Sword: The Secret War Against Castro and the Death of JFK* (Baltimore: Bancroft Press, 1998), 8.

12. Ibid., 9.

13. Ibid.

14. Ibid.

15. Stephen Ambrose, *Eisenhower: Soldier and President* (New York: Simon & Schuster, 1984), 539.

16. Ibid., 533.

17. Ibid., 499.

18. Néstor Carbonell Cortina, "Bahia de Cochinos: Lo Que No Dijo el Informe del Inspector de la CIA," www.autentico.org. Carbonell quotes Eisenhower from *Foreign Policy*, U.S. volume VI, 1057–60.

19. Ambrose, 554.

20. Ibid.

21. Michael Beschloss, *The Crisis Years; Kennedy & Khrushchev 1960–1963.* (New York: HarperCollins, 1991), 124.

22. Proverbs 16:18.

23. Gus Russo, *Live by the Sword: The Secret War Against Castro and the Death of JFK* (Baltimore: Bancroft Press, 1998), 170.

24. Brigadier General Rafael del Pino, www.cubapolidata.com, April 25, 2002.

Chapter 12: Fidel as Business Partner

1. Xinhua News Agency, 2004.
2. Testimony of former American POW on Vietnam "Cuba Program," Office of International Information Programs, U.S. Department of State.
3. Juan Tamayo, "Torturers' Aim Was Total Surrender, Savage Beatings Bent Captives to Will of Man Dubbed 'Fidel'," *Miami Herald*, August 22, 1999.
4. Paul Bethel, *The Losers: The Definitive Report, by an Eyewitness, of the Communist Conquest of Cuba and the Soviet Penetration in Latin America* (New Rochelle, N.Y.: Arlington House, 1969), 192.
5. George Talbot, "Cuba Conference Opens Amid Controversy," *Mobile Register*, October 13, 2003.
6. G. Fernández, Ediciones Periodísticas, March 12, 2001.
7. Interview with Armando Lago, author of *Cuba: The Human Cost of Social Revolution* and *The Politics of Psychiatry in Revolutionary Cuba* (Piscataway, NJ: Transaction Publishers, 1991).
8. Interview of David Kay by George Stephanopoulos, ABC News, October 5, 2003.
9. Hans de Salas-del Valle, ed. *Fidel Castro on the United States: Selected Statements, 1958–2003* (Washington, D.C.: Center For a Free Cuba, 2003).
10. Ibid.

Chapter 13: Fidel's Useful Idiots

1. Cabrera mentions the incident in his book *Mea Cuba* (Barcelona: Plaza/Janés Editores, 1992).
2. José D. Cabús, *Castro ante la Historia* (Mexico City: Editores Mexicanos Unidos, 1963), 24. See also Servando González, *The Secret Fidel Castro: Deconstructing the Symbol* (Oakland, CA: InteliBooks, 2002.)

3. Interview with Ernesto Betancourt, who is friends with Huber Matos. The incident is also mentioned in Matos's book *Como Llego La Noche* (Barcelona: Tusquets, 2002).

4. Paul Hollander, *Political Pilgrims: Travels of Western Intellectuals to the Soviet Union, China, and Cuba* (New York: Harper Holophon, 1981). Mona Charen uses the shorter version, which I used and cited in Chapter Two.

5. Ibid.

6. Ibid.

7. Rafael del Pino, *Proa a la Libertad* (Mexico City: Editorial Planeta Mexicana, 1991).

8. Randall Robinson, "Why Black Cuba Is Suffering," *Essence*, July 1999.

9. Congressman Adam Clayton Powell, William A. Wieland, Robert A. Stevenson, Memorandum of a conversation, Washington, D.C., March 12, 1959. Found at www.latinamericanstudies.org.

Chapter 14: Castro's Tugboat Massacre

1. Enrique Encinosa, *Unvanquished: Cuba's Resistance to Fidel Castro* (Los Angeles: Pureplay Press, 2004), 192.

2. Speech made by Fidel Castro, at the ceremony for the fifty-first anniversary of the attack on the Moncada, Ernesto Che Guevara Square, Santa Clara, Cuba, July 26, 2004. (Quoted at www.havana-journal.com, August 10, 2004.

Chapter 15: Who Needs Freedom?

1. Enrique Encinosa, *Unvanquished: Cuba's Resistance to Fidel Castro* (Los Angeles: Pureplay Press, 2004), 192.

2. Tim Graham, "Back to the 'Peaceable' Paradise: Media Soldiers for the Seizure of Elián," Media Research Center Special Report, May 23, 2000.

3. Cyber Alert, "Drugs for Elián?" Media Research Center, May 3, 2000.

4. David Limbaugh, *Absolute Power: The Legacy of Corruption in the Clinton-Reno Justice Department* (Washington, D.C.: Regnery, 2001), 315.

5. Graham, "Back to the 'Peaceable' Paradise: Media Soldiers for the Seizure of Elián."

6. Ibid.

7. Ibid.

8. Ibid.

9. Ibid.

10. Ibid.

11. Ibid.

12. Interview with Enrique Encinosa.

INDEX

Vincent, Mauricio, 165
Vives, Juan, 144–45
Vohden, Ray, 141–42

W
Walker, Alice, 40, 41
Wallace, Mike, 12
Walters, Barbara, 12
Walters, Vernon, 144
Wannall, Raymond, 1, 2, 4–5
Warren Commission, 96
Washington Post, 20, 46, 146
Waters, Maxine, 41, 152
Weather Underground, 144
West Germany, 37
Wiecha, Robert, 93, 104
Wieland, William, 48
Wild Geese, 73
Wilhelm, Charles, 8–9
Williams, Enrique Ruiz, 133
Wolfe, Tom, 90
World War II, x, 1, 11, 15, 56, 70, 148–49
Wyden, Peter, 126

Y
Yale University, 119
Year of the Rat (Timperlake and Triplett), 53
Yo Soy El Che! (Ortega), 70

Z
Zuckerman, Mort, 12